What people are saying about

DELIGHT!

In *Delight!*, Justin Rossow widens our lens for understanding grace as he explores the delight God has in us and the delight God gives to us. **The impact will have ripples into every area of your spiritual walk.** *Delight!* brings both lightness and depth to the Scriptures and to our relationships with our Great God.

Heidi Goehmann

author of *Altogether Beautiful: A Study of the Song of Songs* and *He Calls Me Loved: A Study of Isaiah*

Have we lost our sense of delight? Today delight seems to be reduced to each person's version of personal happiness. Or delight is simply missed altogether because we are too busy and anxious to notice it. In a deeply reflective and devotional way, **Rossow puts delight back on the agenda of the theology of the Christian life**. Taking us on a biblical journey of discovery around God's vision of delight for us, he invites us to receive this gift, revel in it, and, yes, delight in it!

Leopoldo A. Sánchez M

author of *Sculptor Spirit: Models of Sanctification from Spirit Christology* and *Teología de la Santificación: La Espiritualidad del Cristiano*

I have spent a great deal of my life believing in my head that Jesus loved me, yet living practically as if I were always on the verge of being in big trouble. This book offers **a refreshing, biblical vision of how to live a life captivated and covered by the love of God**. Even more astonishing is the discovery of a God who is full of delight.

Jamie Wiechman

co-founder of Breathe Life Ministries – www.breathelifetoday.org

Three years ago, a prayer warrior sent me a private message from afar: *hephzibah*. "My delight is in her." Every time I read this message my heart is full. I draw closer to the Living God. I understand more deeply our Creator's nature and call. And yet, I've never heard another person in the church talk about delight. Not until Justin Rossow's book arrived unexpectedly—like manna, like grace—in my inbox. **Oh, the life-giving words on every single page!** I truly believe that if a few thousand churches were to read this as a study it might change the face of American Christianity today. I hope yours is one of them.

Heather Choate Davis
songwriter for *Life in the Key of God* and author of
Happy Are Those: Ancient Wisdom for Modern Life

"Jesus loves me, this I know…" Except I didn't know; not really. *Delight!* showed me in a new way that God doesn't just tolerate you or grudgingly let you in because you believe: God wants to be in relationship with you. Did you know you can make God *laugh*? Make the Spirit *happy*? **In this book I learned that saying yes to relationship with God doesn't just save you, it makes Jesus smile with delight**. Rejoicing. In heaven. About you. About me. This is good news.

Conrad Gempf
author of *Mealtime Habits of the Messiah*
and *Jesus Asked: What He Wanted to Know*

Every once in awhile a book comes along that changes the narrative. With **a fresh, hope-filled perspective** and life-giving personality Justin Rossow unveils an invitation that is really hard to refuse. Come along with Jesus for the adventure of a lifetime! Delight, not duty. Ahhhhh. So refreshing!

Jeff Meyer
author of *Fear Not, Dream Big, & Execute* and founder of *The Dream Accelerator*

With playfulness and scriptural acumen, Justin reminds us that God throws parties—the best ones—and we're all invited. This is no Pollyanna book, though: it's a **dazzling, tenacious, and robust call to live in a delight** that is far stronger than fear. Reading *Delight!* will breathe new life into your adventure of following Jesus.

Steve Wiechman
co-founder of Breathe Life Ministries – www.breathelifetoday.org

"The LORD makes firm
the steps of the one
who delights in him"

Psalm 37:23, NIV

DELIGHT!

Discipleship as the adventure of loving and being loved

JUSTIN ROSSOW

Delight! – Discipleship As The
Adventure Of Loving And Being Loved

NEXT STEP PRESS ▶
We help you take a next step.

Table Of Contents

Acknowledgments

I am grateful to countless fellow travelers who helped me get to the point of longing for, researching, living out, and writing *Delight!*

I can trace the origins of this project to my family, to a mom and dad and sister and all kinds of aunts and uncles and cousins and grandparents who wanted to follow Jesus and who knew what it meant to be confused or uncertain and still to take a step of faith.

My parents invited us kids into the discerning process when it came to following Jesus as a family; modeling that openness to my own children has been a joy and a blessing.

Many congregations have heard bits and pieces of this book over the years, from Trinity, Clinton Township to Salem, Affton; from Peace in Hurst to St. Luke, Ann Abor, and many other congregations or gatherings where I have been invited to preach or teach. I am thankful for their open hearts and open ears.

Some dear friends faithfully read and responded to draft chapters as I wrote, including Steve and Jamie and my beautiful wife, Miriam. Her love and support and encouragement and delight made writing this book possible.

Conrad Gempf interacted in depth with the material and saved me from some of my worst blunders and contributed to some of my favorite paragraphs. This book owes much to his insight and humor.

My stalwart British friend, Brett Jordan, did a very admirable job with the cover and internal layout while putting up with my effusive American style. (Don't tell Brett, but I think he's *awesome!!*) Ellen Davis, the queen of hyphens and ellipses, again blessed me with her proofreading prowess.

My thanks to all of these wonderful people are wrapped up and surrounded in my thanks to the One who delights in me, and invites me into an eternal relationship of mutual delight. Come quickly, Lord.

JJ and *SDG*,

Justin Rossow
1 September, 2020

INTRODUCTION

An Image of Mutual Delight

Over the last couple of years, an image of mutual delight has repeatedly captivated my heart and mind. You know the mutual delight I am talking about, or something like it. You might experience it during a moment of peace in the company of dear friends. You would recognize it in the eyes of two lovers as they first discover they're in love. But I think you can see this image of mutual delight most clearly in that moment when a darling child rushes into their parent's arms.

In my imagination, the child is older than an infant, but still small enough to be picked up easily. The parent could be a mom or a dad, or even a grandparent, cousin, or friend. The important thing is the moment when the little girl or boy runs into a trusted embrace, and mom or dad lifts them up and twirls them around, and brings that darling child, still dangling in the air, face to face.

And I don't know if mom made a funny noise, or dad tickled a little as part of the hug, but the delight of the moment makes the child giggle. That giggle makes mom laugh. That laugh makes the little boy squeal. And so these two go, on and on, for longer than you would think reasonable, simply enjoying each other…

You know what that's like. Mutual delight: that experience of loving and being loved; of shared joy, joy in another person's joy, that image of a mom or dad beaming into the face of a smiling child until both are rolling in the grass laughing—that image **of mutual delight has changed how I view my relationship with God.**

Of course, following Jesus can be hard. Of course, following

Jesus can be confusing, and difficult, and it can end badly (ask any of his original 12; only one got to die peacefully of old age…). Of course the call to follow this Jesus is a call to pick up your cross, to lose your life, to bear a new and different kind of yoke.

But this same Jesus also promised that losing your life was the only way to find it; that by joining in his death *already now*, you join in his resurrection life, *already now*; that his yoke is easy and his burden is light.

Following Jesus is not supposed to be a weight to carry that drains the fun out of life. Following Jesus means being so full of new life that you can experience joy even in the midst of difficulty.

And that joy, **the joy of knowing Jesus, flows directly from Jesus' joy of knowing you.**

Time and time again, the Scriptures paint for us a picture of a God who absolutely delights in people, a God who not only loves them and saves them, but enjoys them and wants to spend quality time with them. The God Jesus knows and reveals as Father is the God of relationship, who delights in specific individuals and throws parties in heaven because of what you just did this last week.

Of course, following Jesus means coming to grips with your failures, with your sin, with your shame. Of course discipleship entails repentance, and molding, and refining. Of course dying to your sinful self daily isn't a lot of fun. An old, traditional confession of sins starts, "I, a poor, miserable sinner…" *Repentance* is an essential part of discipleship.

Another old, traditional confession also expresses to God the reason I want to be forgiven: "…that I may *delight* in your will and walk in your ways…" Right next to repentance, ***delight* is an equally essential part of discipleship**. You cannot be a consistent, faithful follower the way Jesus intends without the key ingredient of delight.

Now, watch it! To say you *have* to have delight can become just as much a burden as saying you *have* to repent, when in both cases Jesus intends for you to receive these habits of following as a gift, not a burden. The Holy Spirit works *repentance* in you as a gift, to lead you into a deeper and more intimate relationship with God in Jesus Christ. But what I really want to get at in the rest of this book is this: **The Holy Spirit works *delight* in you as a gift**, to lead you into a deeper and more intimate relationship with God in Jesus Christ.

Now that I can see both repentance *and* delight as gifts, it seems strange to look back at my experience of church and church people. Almost all of the church people I have ever known would point to the need for repentance in the life of a believer; but few and far between were the individuals who knew one of the secrets of the Kingdom: **delight is an essential part of your faith journey**.

Of course, you might not use the word "delight" very much; you might prefer a different vocabulary word. But whatever you call it, I mean that moment when the little boy runs laughing into his mother's arms and she picks him up and brings him close and each can't get enough of the other's joy. I call that loving and being loved "mutual delight." Jesus invites you into that kind of mutual delight in his relationship with you.

Maybe that invitation feels more like challenge to you, way up here at the very beginning of a book on discipleship as delight. Or maybe it makes your heart beat a little faster and awakens a longing deep in your soul. Or maybe you have no idea how to think about mutual delight with God. All of those reactions are valid.

Although I never heard "discipleship" described by anyone as "the adventure of loving and being loved," I'm not trying to roll out a new doctrine. I am convinced that the Scriptures themselves invite us to see our relationship with God, perhaps even *primarily*, as **an interaction of mutual delight**.

Whether you are confused, excited, or skeptical about that claim, I invite you to take this journey with me. I want to show you what I have seen in Scripture and share with you what the Holy Spirit has been shaping in me, and perhaps, will shape in you, too. There is such a freedom in loving and being loved, in living not under the burden of religious practice but in the confidence of God's delight, that I can hardly tell you how much a difference delight has made in my own, personal life!

But I am getting ahead of myself.

Here's a brief road map for those of you who like to know where a book is headed. Everybody else, feel free to skip to Chapter 1. (Or, hey—skip to whatever chapter you like! I put this book together in this order with purpose, but you can practice your freedom and delight by reading any of this in any order you choose!)

Section 1: The Architecture of Delight is an overview, an orientation to the landscape of words and ideas related to delight. A biblical understanding of delight is not limited to a single vocabulary word or even a specific experience. We should expect that the God who shaped us to be body-and-soul-together kind of creatures would bring **delight to the whole person**, not just the heart or mind or sensations in isolation. In five short chapters, Section 1 sets up the playground equipment we will be exploring in the rest of the book. These chapters will be especially fun for word nerds! Other kinds of readers may choose to jump ahead and come back to individual chapters in Section 1 later on; just know that I'll refer back to bits and pieces of the discussion in these first chapters in the other sections of the book.

Section 2: God Delights in You grounds our discussion of delight in ways the Bible has for expressing God's heart for us. In Chapters 6–8 we'll look more in depth at three prominent themes that explore God's delight. The Almighty calls us Treasured Possession, rejoices over us with singing, and invites us to own the statement of faith, "I am my Beloved's and my Beloved is mine." Each new image for God's delight helps us expand and deepen our view of who we are and what God really thinks about us.

God's delight in us leads to our delight in God (which, of course, God absolutely delights in!). So **Section 3: Your Adventure of Delight** is devoted to how God shapes delight in us and we express that delight in our lives. We will look at how **God's Will Directs Your Adventure**, how **God's Work Shapes Your Adventure**, and how **God's Word Propels Your Adventure** in chapters 9–11. We'll see how different God's Will, Work, and Word seem to us when we view them through the lens of delight.

Finally, in Chapter 12, I'll share some concluding thoughts about **Living With Delight**. A posture of delight and an attitude of adventure make you dependent on Jesus and vulnerable to the work of the Spirit in scary and wonderful ways. Following Jesus is the most difficult and most delightful thing you will ever do.

The ultimate goal of this entire journey of delight is to relieve the burden of being a Christian with the joy of being a follower. To follow Jesus is to have confidence in God's delight and to have freedom to try and to fail. Following Jesus means you are caught up in a love story beyond your wildest dreams. To follow Jesus is to put your foot on a path of adventure, marked by challenges and difficulties and sorrow and failure, but **marked most fundamentally by mutual delight**.

As we read Scripture and think and pray and discern together, I hope you will also come to see discipleship as the adventure of loving and being loved.

SECTION 1

The Architecture of Delight

Reading Plan

Day 1
Setting the Stage
&
Chapter 1: Joyful Delight

Day 2
Chapter 2: Thoughtful Delight

Day 3
Chapter 3: Playful Delight

Day 4
Chapter 4: Delicious Delight

Day 5
Chapter 5: Desirable Delight

Day 6
Group Discussion

Setting the Stage

God delights in the people God created, redeemed, and continues to sustain; and God loves it when those people feel the same way about their Creator, Redeemer, and Sustainer. **That mutual delight is one of the central themes of Scripture**, a theme that can get drowned out by other ways of telling the story. So how do we get at a biblical understanding of delight?

The introduction already gave us one way to try and get a handle on our relationship with God through the lens of delight, a kind of definition by image: "that moment when a little boy runs laughing into his mother's arms and she picks him up and brings him close and they each can't get enough of the other's joy." Whatever vocabulary word you would use to describe that scene, that's what I mean by "delight."

You could probably come up with a group of synonyms or a word cloud of related vocabulary that gets at the mutual delight of loving and being loved. You could put delight in the center and then surround it with words like rejoice, joy, exult, enjoy, or jump for joy; you might even include words like pleasing, pleasurable, delightful, desirable, enjoyable, or fun. Your word cloud might look a little different than mine, but I bet we would find significant overlap.

The Scriptures work a bit like that, as well. Getting a handle on a biblical concept of delight is not as simple as doing a word search in your favorite translation. It's not even as simple as doing a word search in Hebrew followed by a word search in Greek. The vast library of books and genres we call the Bible, written across widely divergent times, languages, and cultures by very different personalities in very unique styles—**the Bible has its own "word cloud" when it comes to the concept of delight**.

I want to spend some time with that word cloud in these opening chapters. If you are a real vocabulary geek (I love that about you), you will find enough Greek and Hebrew in this section to geek out about (though you may wish I had been more thorough or more nuanced in some places). If you are not the English major type (I love that about you), you will find enough big picture concepts to make these short chapters worthwhile (though you may wish I had been a little less thorough or less nuanced in some places…).

Regardless of your personal preference for the material, I want you to see that the biblical "word cloud" for delight (at least as far as we will explore it, which is both *way too far* and *not nearly far enough*)—**the biblical "word cloud" for delight is slightly different from our own**. Words like "pleasure" or "desire" don't necessarily fit easily into my concept of "delight." Or at least, they carry connotations that feel very unreligious. And my idea of delight seems to be primarily focused on my emotions, though I do have room for "enjoying" experiences that are mental or physical.

In contrast, the biblical concept of delight seems to be much more focused on the whole person: **body, soul, mind, will, and emotions all wrapped up together in one**. I guess that shouldn't surprise me. I remember learning at a young age Luther's explanation to the first section of the Apostles' Creed: "I believe that God has made me and all creatures; that he has given me my body and soul; my eyes, ears, and all my members; my reason and all my senses, and still preserves them." I think "delight" in the Bible is an "eyes, ears, and all my members, my reason and all my senses" kind of concept. And that gets me really excited.

So we're going to look at some Hebrew and some Greek in what follows, but mostly as a way of tracking and describing how, **in God's economy, the whole person is the domain of delight**.

Again, these first chapters have a different character than the rest of the book, and if you want to skip ahead and maybe use this section as a reference later, that's OK with me. Getting at how the concept of delight gets built out across Scripture will help us explore mutual delight in our relationship with God.

But the most important thing is simply this: *God loves you and delights in you in a visceral, emotional, intellectual, and playful way. And God invites you to experience your relationship with the Father, Son, and Holy Spirit, already now, in ways that are visceral, emotional, intellectual, and playful, all at the same time.*

CHAPTER 1

Joyful Delight

Things That Make You Go "Woohoo!!"

The biblical concept of delight doesn't involve *merely* the emotions; biblical delight involves the *whole person*. But just because delight involves the whole person doesn't mean emotions aren't important. Your emotions are a very important part of your whole person! So, as you might expect, joy is right at the center of the Bible's word cloud for delight.

One of my favorite Bible verses for delight comes from Zephaniah 3:17. Here's the way one common translation, the New International Version (or NIV), puts it:

> The LORD your God is with you,
>   the Mighty Warrior who saves.
> He will **take great delight** [*sus*] in you;
>   in his love he will no longer rebuke you,
>   but will **rejoice** over you with singing.
>
> *Zephaniah 3:17*, NIV

I love that image! (In fact, I love it so much, it will show up again in Chapter 7.) God's delight in you is so overwhelming, that this Mighty Warrior finds himself singing for joy! His is a multifaceted emotional response that gets expressed in very physical ways. The vocabulary of delight in this single verse is rich and complex (and gets rather complicated).

The primary word translated here as "delight" is the Hebrew "*sus*." (You pronounce it like "*Dr. Seuss.*") "Sus" often (if not always) gets translated as "delight."

שׂוּשׂ (Sus) – exult, rejoice, take delight in, make mirth, be glad

But notice that we are dealing with "great delight" in this context. We're actually getting a Hebraic "buy one, get one free" deal, where you double down on vocabulary words to express the strength of the concept. In the original formulation, the Mighty Warrior is "delighting with great delight" which, I suppose, is about the same thing as "taking great delight" in something. Look at how another translation, the English Standard Version (or ESV) translates the same verse:

> The LORD your God is in your midst,
>> a mighty one who will save;
> he will **rejoice** [*sus*] over you with **gladness** [*simchah*];
>> he will quiet you by his love;
>> he will **exult** [*gil*] over you with loud singing.
>
> *Zephaniah 3:17,* ESV

"Take great delight in you" (NIV) has become "rejoice over you with gladness" (ESV). They are functionally equivalent, and looking at these two different translations together helps get at why we don't want to define the biblical concept of delight too narrowly.

There's a lot going on here! The ESV, while losing the word "delight," picks up on the fact that there are actually two different vocabulary words for delight being used in this "buy one, get one free" construction: **rejoice** (sus/take delight—*Dr. Seuss*) **with gladness** (*simchah*, joy/delight—like "sim card" but with a good German *Ach!* at the end, just backwards: *chah!*).

שִׂמְחָה (Simchah): joy, gladness, mirth, delight

That 2-for-1 deal is one reason I think this type of delight is especially connected to the emotion of joy: delighting/rejoicing is happening in express connection to gladness/joy. **We're talking about an emotional experience of delight.**

In fact, the emotion is so strong, it is **accompanied by a physical response.** Here we have another Hebraism: when two actions are parallel in Hebrew poetry, they are usually either antonyms or synonyms: the text is either helping you understand the topic by giving its exact opposite (antonym) or its dynamic equivalent (synonym). It's as if the Hebrew poets made the *meanings* of the words rhyme rather than the sound of the words.

In Zephaniah 3:17, we have the phrase "take great delight in you" in a parallel construction with "rejoice/exult over you with loud singing." Those two ideas are either in stark contrast to each other or the author is emphasizing their similarities; their meanings "rhyme."

Here it seems obvious to me that "delight" is supposed to be understood as a rough equivalent of "exulting with loud singing." While this second "rejoice/exult" vocabulary word rarely gets translated directly as "delight" in English, it does fit in the broader word cloud of delight as it relates to the concept of joy. This joy in particular is **a jump-up-and-spin-around brand of joy.**

(The Hebrew word *gil* [sounds like *feel*] can actually be used for any strong emotion that makes you jump up and spin around—fear, for example—but here it is clearly a positive emotional experience.)

> גִּיל (Gil): rejoice, tremble, exult, spin around because of violent emotion

The variety of delight expressed in Zephaniah 3:17 is a joyful delight, an emotional response so strong that even a Mighty Warrior has to jump up, spin around, and start singing!

That's what God thinks of you!

When you show up for worship, Jesus is like: "Woohoo! My friends are here! Dad! We get to spend time with some of my favorite people in the world! High five!" When you make the effort in your busy day to read Scripture, the Holy Spirit is all: "Woohoo! I get to spend time with someone I love! Isn't this awesome?!" When you confess your sins, when you share your doubts in prayer, when you bring your burdens and your anxieties and your fears to your Heavenly Father, that Mighty Warrior sets aside his heavy helmet, still hot from combat, and picks you up in his muscular embrace, and with a voice capable of calling angel armies to battle, quiets you with his love, and takes great delight in you, and croons a love song over you that begins with the joyful refrain: "Woohoo! My darling, beloved, delightful child is in my arms again!!"

Your Father gets all emotional thinking of you.

You make Jesus jump for joy.

The Spirit's delight in you is perhaps best expressed in song.

And the Scriptures, taken as a whole, seem to think that **God intends the feeling to be mutual.**

In the epic love song to the Word of God we know as Psalm 119, our sus/joyful delight word shows up not in reference to how *God feels* about spending time with you, but to describe how *you* might feel as you get to spend time with God. The Psalmist sings,

> In the way of your testimonies I **delight** [*sus*]
> as much as in all riches.
>
> *Psalm 119:14*, ESV

In other words, knowing God's way is like winning the lottery! Or at least, like the feeling you get when you win the lottery; or the feeling you get when you are offered the job you really wanted, or when you have your bid accepted on the house of your dreams, or when your crush says yes to a date—and **you jump up and spin around in joy, and you start singing and laughing!**

The Psalmist says, "Knowing *your* way, God—your testimonies, commands, blessings, promises—when I know from your Word what you are up to in my life, it's like striking it rich! I *sus* in your way as much as I would in all riches!"

Net worth of the world's richest person: $154 billion.

Knowing Jesus: priceless.

And the immense value of that relationship is supposed to bring us joy! Real "Woohoo!!" jump up in the air and spin around, hug total strangers and laugh through your tears while you do a little jig and start singing at the top of your voice kind of *joy*.

"In the way of your testimonies I *delight* as much as in all riches."

When was the last time you imagined *knowing God's way* as

something that would make you *jump for joy*? When did you last approach Scripture as if it might make you start dancing? How often do your emotions spill over into song as you get to know and follow Jesus just a little more closely?

You know, I sometimes think Christians have gotten a bit of a bum rap. By and large, I think others see us as the kind of people who don't have any fun, or at least, people who don't want anyone else to have any fun. We end up being characterized as those who always follow rules intended to take the joy out of living, the people who dare not smile too loudly in church, who never relax, never joke, never join in the fun.

And while there may be some good reasons not to join into the so-called "fun" the world around us is having, I think we do the Gospel a disservice when we present ourselves as serious people who are mostly about serious things and want everyone to stop doing anything that might end up leading to an emotional experience of joy.

Jesus had a reputation for hanging out with sinners, and was accused of eating and drinking a little too much, and partying a little too hearty for the religious folks. (I'm not saying Jesus ever did drink too much; I'm just saying, he was at *those kind of parties* often enough that the label of glutton and drunkard was thrown around, even if in hyperbole…)

I think faith in that Jesus should make you smile more often. I think you are supposed to break into a spiritual jig on occasion. **I think Jesus intends for you to experience more Woohoo! in your discipleship walk**.

Don't get me wrong. I'm not saying following Jesus is supposed to be sunshine and daisies all the time. But even when the road is difficult or dark, I think **Jesus intends you to receive the gift of Joyful Delight in your relationship with him**.

One reason I say this is because of what Jesus himself says at a pretty dark and difficult part of the story. Jesus and his closest followers are in that Upper Room on the night he was betrayed. It's Maundy Thursday evening, the part of the story that leads directly to struggle and arrest in the Garden, trial and torture under Pilate and Herod, and the terrible agony of crucifixion.

Jesus gets up from the table and, because he knows where he is from and where he is going, he wraps a towel around his waist and shows his closest friends the full extent of his love by personally and humbly washing each of their feet. He teaches on service and love, and vine and branches.

Then Jesus says something that I think should change our preconceived notions of what it means to follow him. Of course, Jesus gives the command to love and serve in line with his own love and service. That's why we call it *Maundy* (Command) Thursday. But *the reason he gives the command in the first place* is a real doozy.

"I have told you these things," Jesus says—and he is talking about his command to love one another—"I have told you these things, *so that **my joy** may be in you, and **your joy** may be complete.*"

Did you hear that?? Joy!

The New Testament Greek word the Bible uses for joy in this scene is *chara* (like "caress," but with a "–rah;" Ka-RAH!) and means joy or delight. This joy word is directly related to the New Testament word for grace: charis (like "caress," but with an "–iss;" Ka-RISS!). We're talking about real joy!

χαρά (Chara): joy, delight, gladness (as a result of grace)

On that Maundy Thursday night in the Upper Room, Judas is getting ready to go and meet up with the soldiers he will bring to Jesus' private place of prayer. Jesus is about to enter into a prayerful wrestling with the Father that will leave him so distressed he sweats blood. Next on the agenda is beating and mocking and abandonment and death. **And Jesus wants to share his *joy*.**

If we hadn't already been using "Maundy Thursday" and "Good Friday" for so long, we could have opted for "Chara Thursday" and "Charis Friday." Because the reason for the service and the self-denial and the love of neighbor; the reason for the Garden and the Cross and the Empty Tomb; the ultimate goal of lives lived out in the gracious Kingdom of the crucified and risen Son is quite simply *joy*.

Joyful delight is not about trying to turn your frown upside down. Joyful delight is not a way of whitewashing tombs so that the awful reality of this sinful world seems to stink a little less.

Joyful delight is a powerful, emotional response to God's action in Jesus even in the midst of the difficult and painful and confusing and hard. Joyful delight means jumping for joy even when you can't get up out of your wheelchair.

"I have told you these things so that my joy may be in you, and your joy may be complete."

Jesus sees you and jumps for joy, spins around, shouts "Woohoo!" and sings his happy song. Jesus invites you to imagine what it would be like to experience life with him in that same kind of joyful delight.

What about Jesus has brought you joy this week? You might want to tell him that.

You might even want to sing him your happy song.

I know he'd love it!

CHAPTER 2

Thoughtful Delight

Things That Make You Go "Wow!!"

The broad concept of biblical delight addresses your emotions, but it doesn't stop there. Another very particular way the Bible has for talking about delight has to do with your mind as well as your heart. This kind of thoughtful delight comes from figuring something out, seeing how it works, and then rejoicing in how it all fits together. When you use your reason to understand something so well it makes you go, "Wow!" you are experiencing this thoughtful delight.

Do you know any engineers? I think I might have one living in my house. My son is only eight, but he has been interested in how things work since before he could talk. He loves to figure out how something comes apart, and how it goes back together, how to build it or fix it. He is excited to share his designs and what he imagines he could one day build. A screwdriver may be one of his favorite toys. He will push me out of the way to get a closer look at something that's broken, and at eight, has a better chance of repairing it than I do.

Caleb loves to figure a thing out so he can see how it works; and **he gives his approval when it works the way it is supposed to**. My son knows Thoughtful Delight.

If you, like me, aren't much of an engineer, perhaps you have experienced Thoughtful Delight as you filled in the final words of a really challenging crossword puzzle, or when you solved the fictional murder mystery before the main character provides the great reveal, or when you put together a special meal that balanced just so, or when you finessed the queen of hearts at trick three to bring home a small slam. When you see the big picture, and how all the pieces fit, and they fit together so well it

makes you go, "Wow!" you are beginning to get a sense of what
Thoughtful Delight is all about.

In the Hebrew of Isaiah 42, God draws our attention to the
special Servant of Yahweh:

> Behold my servant, whom I uphold,
>> my chosen, in whom my soul **delights** [*ratsah*];
> I have put my Spirit upon him;
>> he will bring forth justice to the nations.
>
> *Isaiah 42:1*, ESV

The Hebrew word ratsah, pronounced "rah-TSAH" (rah, rah,
ree; kick 'em in the -tsah!), comes with the connotation of
understanding and acceptance. God can *ratsah* your offerings:
when they are done the right way, with the right heart, God
delights in them and *accepts* them. Parents can also *ratsah* their
children; that is, approve of them, accept them, understand
them, and delight in them. Proverbs 3:12 is a good example:
"The LORD disciplines those he loves, as a father the son he
delights in." That *delight* word is *ratsah*.

רָצָה (Ratsah): approve, accept be pleased with, delight in

In the Bible, Jesus is the ultimate Servant of the LORD, the Son
in whom the Father delights. So when Matthew tells us about
this Jesus, Matthew says the preaching and healing ministry of
Jesus is intended to fulfill Isaiah 42. Matthew quotes the Old
Testament Hebrew in New Testament Greek:

> Here is my servant whom I have chosen,
>> the one I love, in whom I **delight** [*eudokéō*];
> I will put my Spirit on him,
>> and he will proclaim justice to the nations.
>
> *Matthew 12:18*, NIV

Matthew's Greek word gives us another gloss on this idea of
thoughtful delight: *eudokéō* comes from the prefix *eu-* (*oi!*),

which means *good*, and the verb *dokéō* (*dough-KEH-oh*), which is to *think*; literally, **to think well of something or someone**. It probably won't surprise you to learn that God the Father puts it exactly this way both at Jesus' baptism and at his transfiguration. In both cases, the voice from the cloud says, "This is my beloved Son, with whom I am *well pleased* [*eudokéō*]."

> εὐδοκέω (Eudokéō): be pleased with, think well of, approve, delight in

God accepts, approves of, is pleased with, delights in, thinks well of this Jesus, the Chosen Servant and Beloved Son on whom God has placed the Spirit, so that Jesus can proclaim God's righteousness to the nations. This particular brand of delight is something the Father has for the Son in the unity of the Spirit. But it doesn't stop there.

Because Jesus stood in the place of repentant sinners as he stepped into the Jordan River to be baptized, repentant sinners now stand in the place of Jesus as they enter the waters of baptism. Being baptized into Christ means being baptized into his death and resurrection. Being baptized into Christ means Jesus bears the verdict your sins deserve and takes that death penalty to the cross. Being baptized into Jesus means you now stand beneath the cloud and receive the verdict that first and foremost belongs to Jesus: "beloved daughter, beloved son, in whom I delight—with whom I am well pleased."

As a baptized follower of Jesus, you live out your life in the present, fallen world not under the weight of your sin and shame, but under a **Verdict of Delight**. God accepts you. God approves of you. God is pleased with, delights in, thinks well of *you*. That's your new status, your new identity, the new state of affairs brought about by the life, baptism, death, resurrection, ascension, and promised return of the Chosen Servant and Beloved Son.

As a chosen servant and beloved child, you have received the Holy Spirit, just like Jesus did. And, just like Jesus did, you will be led into the wilderness to be tested by the devil. You will proclaim God's righteous acts to the nations in the power of the

Spirit, just like Jesus did. At times, you will be filled with joy in the Spirit, just as Jesus was. The same Spirit who dwelt with Jesus now dwells with you, to shape you more and more every day to be like the Chosen Servant and Beloved Son into whom you have been baptized.

In Jesus, God now says of you: "Behold my servant, whom I uphold, my chosen, in whom my soul **delights**." Wow!!

God's delight doesn't mean life will be easy for you, any more than being God's Beloved meant that life would be easy for Jesus. But that Verdict of Delight changes the way you experience even the hard stuff.

Knowing that you bear the same Spirit who accompanied Jesus in the wilderness, trusting that the same Spirit who shaped Jesus' ministry is actively shaping your discipleship walk, believing that the same Father whom Jesus trusted even on the cross has claimed you as beloved child—all of that changes how you experience challenge and failure and heartache and loss.

The apostle Paul—who was quite a joyful fellow considering everything he went through—the apostle Paul was led to write:

> For the sake of Christ, then, I *eudokéō* weaknesses,
>   insults, hardships, persecutions, and calamities.
> For when I am weak, then I am strong.
>
> *2 Corinthians 12:10*

Different translations try to capture the thrust of *eudokéō* in different ways.

- The ESV translates, "I am *content* with…"
- The NIV has, "I *deligh*t in…"
- The King James Version even says, "I *take pleasure* in weaknesses, in insults, in calamities, in persecutions and difficulties…"

But Paul doesn't mean the weaknesses and insults and hardships are somehow fun; rather, Paul can take a certain Thoughtful Delight (eudokéō) in how God's strength is at work, even in the midst of our weakness and failure.

Paul sees God present and active even in the midst of challenge, and failure, and heartache, and loss. And it makes Paul say, "Wow!!"

So you and I are not supposed to pretend to be happy when we are grieving. We aren't supposed to put on clown's make up so we can go to church where everyone who is a *real* Christian is bubbling over all the time. We don't ignore or minimize how hard life is, how weak we are, or how often we fail.

And knowing that the Spirit is still shaping us to be like Jesus, even in our failures; knowing that our brokenness is held in nail-scarred hands; knowing that God's power is made complete in our weakness, we can look unflinchingly at the difficult, and challenging, and broken things in our own lives and see how it all works—see how **God is still present and active**—and then approve, and accept, and somehow *think well* of even the weakest and most vulnerable areas of our lives.

We do not delight in weakness or difficulty or pain as such; rather, we approve and accept and delight in God's power active in the midst of our weakness, in our difficulty, even in our pain.

Following Jesus isn't easy. But God's power is fulfilled in my weakness. I can delight in that.

CHAPTER 3

Playful Delight

Things That Make You Go "Whee!!"

One of the words in Hebrew that can sometimes be translated as *delight* is a word for sport or play. You see the playfulness of that delight word in the context of Isaiah's vision of the coming of the Shoot from the stump of Jesse, on whom the Spirit of the Lord will rest. Do you remember the scene?

As Isaiah looks forward to God's promises becoming a reality, he describes a time of complete peace and harmony. You know some of the descriptions the prophet uses in Isaiah 11; verse 6 is perhaps most familiar:

> The wolf will live with the lamb,
>   the leopard will lie down with the goat,
> the calf and the lion and the yearling together;
>   and a little child will lead them.
>
> *Isaiah 11:6*, NIV

One of the details of that peaceable kingdom has to do with an infant or toddler *playing* by the cobra's den. The mountain of God has so much peace and harmony going on that even the playful toddler who is having fun sticking her hand in and out of the snake pit (!) won't come to any harm:

> The infant will **play** [*sha'a'*] near the cobra's den, and
>   the young child will put its hand into the viper's nest.
>
> *Isaiah 11:8*, NIV

That *play* word describes the kind of delight you get from *just having fun*. Coasting down a big hill on a bike, swinging on a tire swing, taking a running leap off the dock, grabbing the front seat on a roller coaster: anything that makes you go, "Whee!!" and then bust out laughing is probably a good approximation of the Hebrew word *sha'a*. (It's even fun to say: shah-AH!)

שָׁעַע (Sha'a'): sport, take delight in, play

That playful delight shows up repeatedly in Psalm 119:

> I will **delight** [*sha'a'*] in your statutes;
>   I will not forget your word ...
>
> I find **delight** [*sha'a'*] in your commandments,
>   which I love ...
>
> Let your mercy come to me, that I may live;
>   for your law is my **delight** [*sha'a'*] ...
>
> If your law had not been my **delight** [*sha'a'*],
>   I would have perished in my affliction.
>
> *Psalm 119:16, 47, 77, 92*, ESV

Psalm 119 seems to think we should take Playful Delight in God's Word. That play/sport/delight vocabulary word can be translated as "meditating" on God's Word, but not meditating as in just thinking about it intellectually, but playing with it; exploring it.

Reading Scripture is supposed to be *fun*. Living out your life of discipleship is supposed to be fun. You're supposed to have a sense of *joyful curiosity* in your walk with Jesus: "I wonder how this is going to work out..."

A sense of play, of lightheartedness, of exploration, of discovery all belong to the discipleship walk. God's Word is intended to be a delight to me: it's like playing a game; it's like enjoying a sport I love. Playful Delight makes you go, "Whee!! This is awesome!"

Have you ever experienced Playful Delight during a Bible study, or a sermon, or reading a commentary, or sitting at home with your Bible, or having a conversation with a friend? You see something you've never seen before, and you go, "Wow, that's amazing! This is so much fun! I love this stuff!"

That's what it's supposed to be like. That's one of the ways we're supposed to experience following Jesus. (Of course, Playful Delight is not the only way we experience it. Of course, following Jesus can be hard. But **following Jesus should also be just plain fun!**)

When I think of sport and play, and what it means for a parent to delight in a child and for a child to delight in their parent, I think of the dynamics of young children's sports. If a child plays a sport thinking that what they do on the field or in the pool or on the balance beam is **something that's going to affect their relationship** with their mom or their dad, if they think they *have to be* the best, or score *enough* goals—if they know that when they only score one goal, their dad is going to say, "Well, you could have scored *two*…" or if they swim a lap in 30 seconds, they know mom is going to say, "Yeah, but it could have been 29…" —if they go out onto the field thinking that what they do in the game they *have to do* in order to earn the delight of their parents, how do you think they are going to experience that sport, that play?

I think playing sports like that has to be a burden. I think **pressure to perform** like that turns you into a bad teammate. If I know my mom is not going to be proud of me unless I score at least three goals, then you better pass the ball to *me, me, me!* Playing in order to earn delight makes kids selfish and self-centered and bad teammates on the field.

I also think playing sports like that robs children of their joy. *Sport* is no longer *play* **if I'm performing in order to win favor**.

But what if that child takes the field, dives into the pool, takes the court **knowing full well that their mom or their dad absolutely delights in them**? What if they heard before they took the field, "I'm proud of you! Go get 'em!" What if, when they trip over the soccer ball because they missed it and have to come off the field because their knee is scraped up—what if they meet a parent on the sideline who smiles, and laughs with them, and kisses their knee, and says, "Now get back out there and try again, you goof! And kick *the ball* this time!"

What if that young child **intrinsically knows that they are loved**, that their parents delight in them, that their parents are proud of them and that nothing that happens on the field could change that? What if that young child knows from experience that their parents are there to rejoice with them when they do well, and to commiserate with them when they fail, but that fundamentally—*fundamentally*—they are loved?

That knowledge, that confidence brings all kinds of freedom. With that confidence, you can go out and try. You don't have to be afraid! You can explore and experiment and discover and try something new—and even fail!—and it's going be OK.

I want you to know that when you put down this book, when you go out and try to follow Jesus in your workplace or in your home, when you go out and try to live a life of love or forgiveness, when you go out and try to let Jesus shape your response, **there is nothing you have to do to earn your Father's favor**. There is nothing you have to do to make Jesus like you just a little bit better.

Jesus is not proud of you because of what you do out there in the real world. **Jesus already loves you deeply and intimately**. He already rejoices over you and takes delight in you.

When we go out into God's world with God's Word on our lips, I think there are times when God just laughs at us: "Oh, you idiots! Come here, my beloved... now try and kick *the ball* next time!"

I think there are times God laughs *at* us, quite honestly; and of course there are times when God laughs *with* us. And yes, there will be times when Jesus *weeps* with us, too. But the Bible's fundamental message is that God delights in you apart from what you have to do to earn it.

You do not play for God's delight; you play *from* God's delight. God's delight frees you up to experience your life, even your failures, in a way that lets you go, "Whee!! What a ride!"

CHAPTER 4

Delicious Delight

Things That Make You Go "Yum!!"

What are some of your most favorite things to eat? I'm not just talking comfort food here: I mean the bite that, when you put it in your mouth, makes you go, "Mmmm. Oh, man. Yum!! Is that *good*! Oh, wow... does anyone have a napkin?" That mouthwatering, delicious, flavorful, scrummy kind of wonderful—do you know what I mean?

My great-grandmother made a coffee cake with large, plump raisins and a white icing that wasn't too sweet, with just the right amount of spice so that when you put it in your mouth, the sharp spice and the juicy raisins and the touch of icing combined with the moist cake to melt in your mouth and make you go, "Yummmmm..."

A bar and grill down the street from us has coriander-crusted Ahi tuna on their menu: they take sushi grade tuna and dust it with ground coriander and then sear it at high heat so the coriander forms a thin crust but the center of the tuna is still bright pink and juicy and then they drizzle it with a magic honey, butter, and citrus sauce that just drips off your fork. One bite and you start guarding your plate from people who like to share food at restaurants...

My mom and dad started a family tradition two years before I was born that has continued on to the third (and one day, fourth) generations: New Year's Day morning we always celebrate with a steak and eggs brunch. Of course, the steak must be charcoal grilled. And of course, most years that means shoveling snow to get to the grill (or find the grill!) and maybe even chipping ice out of the bottom. But when those steaks come in steaming out of the cold, and the meat is red and juicy all the way through, salted to perfection, and you get that bite of summer in the dead of the long, cold winter, it makes the New Year seem full of possibility!

If you take the fish you just caught—and I have done this with walleye and crappie in Michigan, with sand bass and striper in Texas, and with snapper, grouper, and mackerel in Florida—if you take fresh fish you caught that day and sauté it in butter, olive oil, lemon juice, and Chef Paul Prudhomme's Blackened Redfish Magic™ until it starts to fall apart but while it is still firm, and then spoon that beautiful, flaky fish into fresh, warm corn tortillas and cover it with a slaw made up of shredded cabbage, lemon juice, mayonnaise, salt and pepper, and fresh chopped white onion and then squeeze a slice of lime of the top, you will think you have just died and gone to heaven.

I could mention the amaretto Italian ice cream I found in a café in Northern Germany; or *real* Lübecker Marzipan covered in dark chocolate and eaten in the city of Lübeck; or the glass of Rhine wine I drank one golden afternoon on a ferry ride *down the Rhine*; or the red wine I shared with my wife at a small winery up in the mountains of Colorado, when the owner invited us back to pour and cork our own bottle to take home; or the butter horn recipe passed down from my wife's grandmother to my daughter that draws delighted oohs and ahhs from the crowd every Christmas; but perhaps the most wonderful taste explosion I ever had came from a cookbook sold by the University Musical Society in Ann Arbor, Michigan one season when I was the Associate Conductor of their Choral Union and my wife sang alto.

First, you skin and core a fresh pineapple and cut it into thick rings. Then you grind whole peppercorns in a mortar and pestle; not too finely, mind you! You want big chunks of peppercorn that you now press gently but firmly into the flesh of the pineapple. Spray the fruit lightly with olive oil on both sides and then sear on a very hot charcoal grill; it won't take long, but make sure you get the crosshatch grill marks on both sides! Placing each grilled pineapple ring onto an individual dessert plate, scoop a large helping of quality vanilla bean ice cream into the center.

Then drizzle the whole thing with the reduction of almost equal parts orange juice, triple sec, tequila, and honey that you have had simmering on a back burner for the last half hour. When you take that first bite of the warm, juicy pineapple and get the sharp bite of the peppercorn, the cold, creamy vanilla, wedded to the sweet but tangy drizzle, your mouth throws a party in your honor with streamers, balloons, confetti, and a Big Band it rented for the evening. Just talking about it makes me, mmm... I think I need a napkin...

The witness of Scripture seems to think God's Word is like that. We get the delight concept (if not the vocabulary word) in Psalm 119:

> How sweet are your words to my taste,
>   sweeter than honey to my mouth!
>
> *Psalm 119:103*, NIV

And when the text says, "honey," I'm pretty sure there is a variant reading, or Medieval gloss, or Patristic allegory that translates that word as "the reduction of almost equal parts orange juice, triple sec, tequila, and honey that you have had simmering on a back burner for the last half hour, drizzled over a scoop of vanilla ice cream cradled in a grilled pineapple ring pressed with cracked peppercorn." Or something like that...

God's Word, when we chew on it and ponder it and meditate on it, brings with it a special variety of delight: Delicious Delight. **Receiving and internalizing God's Word is like eating food that not only sustains and nourishes, but food that delights!** (We'll get into that more in Chapter 11: God's Word Propels Your Adventure.)

As Jesus feeds and nourishes and delights you with the Word, he also feeds and nourishes and delights you with his very self. Delicious delight is not just an image of savoring God's Word, it's an image of *savoring the very presence of the Almighty God.*

Psalm 34:8 (NIV) says, "**Taste** and see *that the* LORD *is* good; blessed is the one who takes refuge in him." And Psalm 37 gets us back to the vocabulary of delight:

> **Delight** [*anog*] yourself *in the* LORD,
> and he will give you the desires of your heart.
>
> *Psalm 37:4*, ESV

So it's not just God's words that are a delicious delight, but
the Divine Person—God's presence, God's personality, God's
delight in us—and we are invited to taste, and savor, and relish,
and enjoy *God*. In fact, to delight yourself in the Lord is to
receive from God the desires of your heart.

In this case, the Hebrew word for "desire" has to do with
a request or petition; I am asking for this because I want it.
(We will meet the "desire" word that has to do with delight
momentarily...)

The delight verb in Psalm 37 (*anog* ["analog" with a silent
"al"]) comes from a noun (ōneg [rhymes with "no leg"]) that refers
to something delectable, dainty, tender, and therefore delicious.

עֹנֶג (Ōneg): daintiness, tender or delectable,
an exquisite delight

Approaching God like that—treating the very presence of the
Almighty as something delectable and delicious—results in the
granting of your requests and petitions, the fulfillment of the
desires of your heart.

In other words, if you let your taste buds become enthralled
with the flavor of the presence of the Great I AM, then *what you
long for most* will begin to shift toward *what God has been wanting
to give you all along*. Your desire will shift to what Jesus is giving
you, as Jesus gives you himself.

I don't see this as some hyper-religious sleight of hand that
transforms "the thing you really wanted all along" into the thing
you are "supposed to" want if you are a "real Christian." This isn't
the über-cheesy "evangelism technique" of leaving something
that looks like money on the restaurant table, but is really just a
note that says, "Here's a tip: Jesus loves you!" We're not talking
bait and switch here.

As you come to savor God and **God's presence as its own**

delight, rather than as a means to some other desired delight, your prayer life will actually change. The things you *want* and therefore the things you *ask for* will begin to shift.

I'm not saying Jesus *won't* give you the specific blessing you have been praying for; just that, the more you experience *Jesus himself* as the thing that gives you pleasure—that fulfills your hunger, that gives you delight—the more likely it is that the specific blessing you had set your heart on begins to pale in comparison with the true delight of your relationship with Jesus, both now and in the life of the world to come.

I remember praying for a sports car when I was 10. I mean, we're supposed to bring before God the desires of our hearts, right? I guess that sort of childish prayer treats God like a great vending machine in the sky: if I can figure out how to put in the right amount of change, I can get something yummy to drop down here where I can pick it up.

But you don't have any *relationship* with a vending machine outside of that *transaction*; why would you? I began to learn more about prayer when I learned to savor a relationship with God instead of trying to figure out the right transaction to get what I really wanted all along. Once you have developed a palate for the presence of Jesus, a Lamborghini just doesn't taste the same.

At least, that's what I think Psalm 37:4 is getting at: "**Delight** [*analog*] yourself in the LORD, and he will give you the desires of your heart." I *don't* think that means, "If you will just go through the right religious motions, God will give you what you want."

Instead, I think it means, "If you stop just going through the religious motions and learn to take delight in the Person and Presence of God, the desires of your heart will begin to migrate toward the desires of *God's* heart." And when the desires of your heart align with the desires of God's heart, I think we might be back to *mutual delight*, loving and being loved, mom smiling into the face of her son until her joy and his joy overflow in love and laughter.

Perhaps it's a matter of focus: as long as you are focused on yourself, you will never get the thing that delights you most, because you will never find complete delight in anything.

As you begin to take your eyes off of yourself and what *you* want, as you begin to focus on God and what *God* wants to give, you begin to take delight in all kinds of things you hadn't even noticed before.

Enjoying Jesus means enjoying everything else in your life in a new way. I think God actually promises something very similar. The contrast in Isaiah 53 is between taking delight in *your own* words or wants or ways and taking delight in *God's* words and *God's* gifts and *God's* ways; indeed, taking pleasure in God's Person and work.

The Hebrew word for "pleasure" or "desire" in Isaiah 53 is not the "petition or request" word we met in Psalm 37 (*analog*). This "pleasure" is a delight word (*chephets* [the *che-* is pronounced Kay: *KAY-fets*]) and has to do with something that you *desire* because it brings you pleasure or *delight*.

חֵפֶץ (Chephets): delight, pleasure, desire, longing

In a kind of word play, that pleasurable, Desirable Delight (*chephets* [*KAY-fets*]) is contrasted with a Delicious Delight (*ōneg* [rhymes with "no leg"]) in Isaiah 53:13-14.

Both words mean *delight*; what's at stake is where you find your delight. Are your eyes focused inward, on yourself? Or have you begun to take delight in the things God wants to give?

> If you turn back your foot from the Sabbath,
>   from doing your **pleasure** [*chephets*] on my holy day,
>   and call the Sabbath a **delight** [*ōneg*]
>   and the holy day of the LORD honorable;
> if you honor it, not going your own ways,
>   or seeking your own **pleasure** [*chephets*],
>   or talking idly [speaking your own words];
> then you shall take **delight** [*anog*] in the LORD,
>   and I will make you ride on the heights of the earth;
> I will *feed you* with the heritage of Jacob your father,
>   for the mouth of the LORD has spoken.

Isaiah 53:13-14, ESV

Notice what comes first: if you take a delicious, savory delight in the word/command/promise of Sabbath rest in God's presence, then you will develop a palate for enjoying the delicious, savory delight of God's Person; indeed, you will be fed by God's own hand (Or mouth? Is this a *baby bird* image??) with the promise Yahweh first gave to Abraham, Isaac, and Jacob.

Learning to delight in the Sabbath is the culinary prerequisite to learning to delight in God for God's own sake.

Hmmm...

What if I came to worship as if it were a joy, expecting to delight in God's words, and commands, and promises?

What if I approached Scripture as if it were a delight, sweeter than honey on the tongue, so delicious I can't get enough?

What if I took an attitude of delight to my prayer life and, instead of prayer being the last leftovers of whatever time remains at the end of a full day, those moments became for me chocolate chip cookies still warm out of the oven, or the lobster bisque they serve at the upscale restaurant under the shadow of the St. Louis arch, or the crust that would form on grandma's vanilla ice cream when she poured Vernors over it on a hot, summer afternoon at the farm?

What if I took a delicious delight in the things God commands, the things Jesus intends to bring me closer to him? Do you think I would begin to take more delight in God's Person and Presence?

God thinks so.

In fact, God promised: "Call the Sabbath a **delight** [*ōneg*]... then you shall take **delight** [*anog*] in the LORD... and I will feed you..."

Or again, hear the gracious invitation in Isaiah:

> Come, all you who are thirsty, come to the waters;
>> and you who have no money, come, buy and eat!
> Come, buy wine and milk without money and without cost.
> Why spend money on what is not bread,
>> and your labor on what does not satisfy?
> Listen, listen to me, and eat what is good,
>> and your soul will delight [*anog*] in the richest of fare.

Isaiah 55:1-2, NIV

That reminds of something Jesus once said:

> Very truly I tell you, you are looking for me,
>   not because you saw the signs I performed
>   but because you ate the loaves and had your fill.
> Do not work for food that spoils,
>   but for food that endures to eternal life,
>   which the Son of Man will give you.
> For on him God the Father has placed
>   his seal of approval.
>
> *John 6:26–27,* NIV

Remember that Lamborghini I was praying for when I was 10? I wonder if that isn't included in the category of "food that spoils..." I wonder what else I hunger and thirst for that might seem to taste as good as cotton candy to a 10-year-old, but leaves me with a sugar headache and a sick stomach...

But the conversation isn't finished:

> Jesus said to them, "Very truly I tell you,
>   it is not Moses who has given you the bread from
>   heaven, but it is my Father who gives you the true
>   bread from heaven.
> For the bread of God is the bread that comes down
>   from heaven and gives life to the world."
>
> "Sir," they said, "always give us this bread."
>
> Then Jesus declared, "I am the bread of life.
>   Whoever comes to me will never go hungry,
>   and whoever believes in me will never be thirsty."
>
> *John 6:32–35,* NIV

Jesus says he is the heavenly bread or food that gives life, even eternal life, to the whole world.

And if you immediately jumped to Holy Communion when you read those words, my problem is not with your Sacramental theology. (Actually, the doctrine of Real Presence—that Jesus is somehow physically but mysteriously present in, with, and under the bread and the wine—makes more sense of the biblical witness to me than any other way of understanding the Lord's Supper.)

My problem with drawing a straight line from John 6 to Communion is first, that it narrows the scope of the text drastically; and second, that the dry, bland, almost cardboard wafer and the mass-produced sip of grape product you likely experience on a regular basis is a two-dimensional, black and white tintype compared to the 4K, HD, surround-sound experience I think Jesus has in mind.

This Jesus is, after all, the guy who (in John 2) keeps the party going by turning the jugs of water set aside for the ritual cleansing of your hands into the most *delicious* wine the steward of the wedding reception had ever tasted. It's like Jesus took the premise that, if I just go through all the religious motions, God will give me what I want, and turned it on its head: stop just going through the religious motions, and learn to take delight in God *for God's own sake*, and the desires of your heart will begin to migrate toward the desires of God's heart.

Although it would be a practical impossibility, for reasons of finance as well as of personal preference, I could wish that the bread you had at Communion was by far and away the best bite of food you had all week; that the richest, most delicious, most full-bodied wine you ever tasted was while kneeling at the rail.

Because when Jesus gives you himself—in the promise of the Lord's Supper on Sunday or in his Word of promise during the week—when Jesus gives you himself, he is not asking you (for your own good) to choke down some health food shake with unidentifiable chunks of nutrients that tastes even worse than it smells.

Rather, Jesus is inviting you to experience and to explore the delicate balance and delightful bouquet of a wine fit for the banquet table of heaven. Jesus is inviting you to enjoy and relish the most succulent morsel you have ever had the pleasure of savoring. When Jesus commands you to treat his word of promise and his command to rest in his presence as something delicious,

Jesus knows full well that, having drunk from that vintage and tasted that eternal food, you will find a new definition of delight.

Following Jesus isn't supposed to be a bland and heavy burden; following Jesus is a Delicious Delight!

Jesus gives you himself. Mmmmmmm. Yum!

What the crowds said in confusion, we pray in faith: "Sir, always give us this bread!"

CHAPTER 5

Desirable Delight

Things That Make You Go "Yes, Please!!"

In the last chapter we met a pleasurable, Desirable Delight (*chephets* [*che-* pronounced Kay]) that Isaiah contrasted with the Delicious Delight of knowing and following God. What was *wrong* with the *chephets* in Isaiah 58 was the *focus* of the pleasure or desire, not the simple act of desiring something pleasurable.

In fact, *chephets* is one of the delight words the Bible uses to describe the mutual delight we share in our relationship with God! God *desires* you because you bring God *pleasure*; and God invites you to find that same *Desirable Delight* in who God is, for you.

I suspect using words like "pleasure" and "desire" to talk about our relationship with God might seem a bit weird to you; it seems a bit weird to me, too. But I think it seems weird to us, at least in part, because of the direction our language has taken. Words like "pleasure" and "desire" have started to lose a neutral meaning; as if the words "pleasure" and "desire" actually mean "*guilty* pleasure" and "*sinful* desire" all by themselves.

This narrowing of a general meaning happens in the natural development of a language over time, and it has happened in the domain of delight before. The fancy word "concupiscence," for example, literally refers to *any* strong desire or longing in the original Latin, whether that desire is for something good, bad, or indifferent. But as far back as I can find, "concupiscence" as a Latin theological term means only evil, sinful, fallen, fleshly desire—the functional equivalent of original sin.

Closer to home, we regularly use words like "lust" and "covet" almost exclusively to mean something sinful and negative. I mean, I guess someone could still have a "*lust* for life" and I wouldn't think they were evil; and I can "*covet* your prayers" without being deviant. But really, those are the only two positive examples I can think of!

If anything involves "lust," or "coveting," or even "pleasure" or "desire," we naturally know it is probably sexual, and certainly nothing holy or good. To add marketing insult to semantic injury, you can find the reverse is also true: all kinds of products are advertised in terms that *should* be sinful, but are used in ads provocatively to mean "pleasurable." From fragrances with names like *Obsession* or *Lush Lust*, to images of sexy models sensually eating hamburgers, to Las Vegas travel packages being promoted as visiting "Sin City," mass marketing tells us that *sinful* means *desire*, and *guilty* means *pleasure*.

But biblically speaking, *sin* is very rarely as *pleasurable* as marketing makes out. What's more, *pleasure* and *desire* are not necessarily *sinful!* God made human beings to be body and soul together; and although your body and soul are both fallen, your body and soul were both created to be good. When Adam and Eve were in the Garden, it was even very good. God intended it that way.

Your desires and your pleasures aren't *inherently evil*; your desires and pleasures are just *fallen*, because you are a sinful human being (just like me). Your desires and pleasures aren't evil because they are *fleshly* desires (as opposed to desires of your *soul*); they are evil because your flesh and soul are corrupted by sin. Before sin entered the world, there was no such thing as a "*guilty* pleasure" or a "*sinful* desire." In the Garden, there was only *good* pleasure and *holy* desire!

In fact, in the Garden, even "coveting" wasn't the sinful thing we know today! God intentionally made all the trees of the garden to bear fruit that was worthy of being "coveted"—fruit that was pleasurable, and delightful, and inspired strong desire. The same Hebrew word in the Ten Commandments ("Thou shalt not *covet*...") is used in Genesis to describe the trees God placed in the Garden; pre-Fall, "covet" was another Desirable Delight vocabulary word!

In our language and experience, there is no such thing as

coveting without *sin*, because we only know coveting as desiring something that is not good or holy for us to desire; that's why a statistically large percentage of the Ten Commandments are devoted to different kinds of sinful coveting.

Take a closer look at what's *sinful* about coveting. The sin is not the strong, pleasurable desire *by itself*; strong desire is sinful when the *object* of that desire is not intended by God *for you*. Adam and Eve's sin was *not* finding the Tree of the Knowledge of Good and Evil *delightful*—God made it that way! Just as God made all the other delightful and desirable and pleasurable trees!! (Genesis 3:6 says Eve found the fruit of that one Tree to be *pleasurably desirable*, but Genesis 2:9 uses *the very same delight vocabulary word* for how God made all the trees in the Garden!)

Adam and Eve's sin was placing their desire and delight on something God had set a limit around, a command God intended as a blessing. Go ahead: desire and long for the delight of your *spouse*; just keep your heart and hands off of *other people!* And know that when God commands you not to covet, or lust after, or desire, or find pleasurable delight in the person whose delight is intended to be found in someone else, **God designs that limit to be a blessing** to everyone involved!

The sin is not in the act of desire; the sin is in a *misplaced object* of the desire, a desire that then becomes self-centered and self-serving. Desire and pleasure do not automatically become sinful *when they are physical*; desire and pleasure—both physical and spiritual—become sinful *when they are fallen*.

You and I know only sinful pleasure and desire not because we are *physical* human beings, but because we are part of a *fallen* humanity. The New Creation knows both pleasure and desire without the shackles of sin. And even now, ahead of time, we are invited to imagine and experience what it means to know a God who finds *pleasurable delight* in us, and for us to return the sentiment.

I know; it just seems weird to talk about God that way. When we talk about desire or pleasure we can easily get the wrong impression, but the Scriptures are pretty clear that there is a right sort of desire and a right sort of pleasure.

The Bible can talk about God taking *pleasure* in and *desiring* us; Scripture can even get a little bit racy at times. We're talking Song of Solomon stuff; places in Scripture where Yahweh is the bridegroom and Israel is the bride, or Jesus is the bridegroom and the Church is the bride (we'll talk more details in a later chapter). God says some things about you that will heat up a room as you read your Bible.

This Desirable Delight works in both directions, from God toward us and from us back toward God. Some passages in Paul (Romans 7, for example) talk about the New Person, the New Resurrection Humanity that is already being formed in us by faith. And according to that New Person, Paul looks at God's Word, and God's will, and God's ways and gets kind of hot and bothered. Paul says some things about our relationship with God that are PG-13 at least! But Paul's desire and pleasure are the exact opposite of the self-centered, sinful desires of lust or coveting; Paul is expressing a God-centered desire the way God intended, and it reflects God's Paul-centered desire and joy! This sanctified desire is **an expression of mutual delight,** of loving and being loved.

Of *course* we aren't supposed to push that image too far. *Of course* we shouldn't impose our own, sinful passions and desires and pleasures onto what God feels about us or what we are invited to feel toward God.

But if we are going to talk about discipleship as delight, you need to know that **even the most intimate, personal, loving, and intense experience you can know as a human being** is taken up and baptized and used by God to talk about the intimate, personal, loving, and intense relationship God has with you in Jesus.

Again in Isaiah, after words of judgment and desolation, come words of promise and hope for the future. Listen to how relational, how intimate this description is:

> You shall no more be termed Forsaken,
>> and your land shall no more be termed Desolate,
> but you shall be called

My **Delight** [*chephets*] Is in Her,
and your land Married;
for the LORD **delights** [*chephets*] in you,
and your land shall be married.

Isaiah 62:4, ESV

The promised restoration of the relationship between God and God's people is accompanied with the promise of love and delight, a desirable, almost sensual delight; a pleasurable delight known specifically in the intimacy of marriage. The intimacy, the disclosure, the knowing and being known entailed in such an image is almost breathtaking. God intends to know you—and be known by you—in intimate ways that bring delight.

God's people respond with a similar Desirable Delight. They respond to God's invitation with a, "Yes, please!" (The word *please* is related to *pleasure*, but I can't discern any hint of a negative connotation. So if it helps you feel better about this chapter, just translate "pleasure" and "desire" into a resounding, "Yes, please!!")

This desirable delight isn't a sinful pleasure, it's a *good* pleasure. In fact, that's one way to translate the Hebrew word *chephets*: Good Pleasure. You sometimes hear it put that way: God's will is called God's "good pleasure."

God's will is the thing God wants done; but God wants it done because it brings such delight. When the Hebrew of the Old Testament got translated into Greek, the language of the New Testament, the Hebrew word for Desirable Delight (*chephets*) often came across as the Greek word for "will" or "good pleasure" (*thélēma*, pronounced THELL-aye-ma).

θέλημα (Thélēma): good pleasure, will, delight

Desirable Delight means that **God's will** and **God's pleasure** are intimately linked—for God, as well as for us!

Let's look at two specific verses from two different Psalms and set the original Hebrew and the Greek translation of the delight vocabulary word together:

[Blessed is the person]
　　whose **delight** [*chephets/thélēma*]
　　is in the law of the LORD,
　　and who meditates on his law day and night.

Psalm 1:2, NIV

Direct me in the path of your commands,
　　for there I find **delight** [*chephets/thélēma*].

Psalm 119:35, NIV

If it seems a little odd to be saying, "Yes, please!" to God's *law* and to the path of his *commands*, consider two things. First, words like "law" and "command" are something like "desire" or "pleasure" in that they only have a negative connotation *after* the Fall. Before the Fall (and after the Resurrection) we respond to God's law with delight!

Only sin makes God's commands and God's law a burden; only sin allows the law to awaken in us sinners a desire for something that is not given to us to desire.

In fact, already now, according to the New Person being shaped in us by the Spirit, we begin to find a desirable, pleasurable delight in God's law (that's Romans 7 again); God's *Good Pleasure* or "God's will" expressed in God's law becomes our *Good Pleasure*, too. Even though sin still clings to us, the renewed part of who we are, the New Person says, "Yes, please!" to the will, ways, and law of God, given to us by God as a blessing and a delight.

Of course, as long as sin endures (which won't be always), our present response will constantly be imperfect; even as we affirm and delight in God's law, we will always also turn away from God's commands in disgust and run from God's law in fear. But it wasn't supposed to be that way; and it isn't always going to be that way; and even now, it doesn't have to always, *only* be that way.

Sometimes, along with the sinful inclination to run and hide from God's law, we also have an experience of delight: a New Person, New Creation delight in God's law and God's ways and God's commands. According to the New Person I already am, and am still becoming, and won't be in full until the life of the world to come, I take delight in knowing God's heart and receiving the commands that God gives in order to bless. God's "will" is synonymous with God's *Good Pleasure*. God's law and God's commands are delightful of and by themselves; only my sin makes them seem otherwise to me.

The second thing to remember is that sometimes in the Bible—and Psalm 1 and 119 are good examples—sometimes words like "law" or the "path of God's commands" are intended to be a lot broader and more comprehensive than we typically think. I usually oppose "Law" with "Gospel," but in the broadest sense, the word "law" can mean **everything that God has revealed about God's own nature and action in the story of Scripture**. That certainly entails commandments and restrictions (as well as wrath against sin, and punishments, and consequences), but the "everything God has revealed about God's own nature and action in the story" also includes God's heart of grace and forgiveness, God's care for the outsider and orphan, God's desire to dwell with people, God's action on our behalf, God's promise of rescue, deliverance, renewal, and restoration.

"The path of God's commands" includes *behavior* (doing what we should, as well as not doing what we shouldn't) and *faith* (trusting God to come through on the promises God has made). In its broadest sense, the term "law" can include both Law and Gospel, commands and promises, behavior and faith, wrath and grace.

So in the context of Psalm 1 and Psalm 119, I think we are supposed to be imagining the broadest and most complete sense of God's "law" and of God's "commands." **I delight in the whole story God is telling and how that story catches me up in the grand narrative of God's grace!**

But even when we are able to catch a glimpse of that grace-filled story, even when can see how God's commands and promises work together for our joy—even then, we have to admit that, according to our sinful nature, **both God's commands and God's promises are abhorrent to us as sinners.**

At the same time, according to the new life that is ours in Jesus already now, ahead of time, God's commands and God's promises, both Law and Gospel, the way the Spirit tells the story and the role we are invited to play in it—**God's commands and God's promises become a *Desirable Delight*** that makes our hearts beat a little quicker, gets us excited and interested and engaged, and makes us go, "*Yes, please!* Give me more of that!"

I suppose that dynamic of **God's good intention and our mixed response** is true of every variety of delight we have looked at in this section. Jesus intends for us to experience mutual delight with him in joyful, thoughtful, playful, delicious, and desirable ways. And the sin that still clings to each of us taints our present experience of each and every one of those expressions of delight.

That mixed response is not what God intended. And it's not always going to be that way. While we wait for that final restoration, God invites us to **experience a foretaste of the delight to come**. Even now, ahead of time, Jesus invites you to know Joyful Delight, Thoughtful Delight, Playful Delight, Delicious Delight, and even Desirable Delight in your relationship with him.

That delight comes naturally to our New Nature; but that Old, Sinful Nature still distorts every experience of delight in our present, fallen reality. As you try to live out this invitation to experience delight in your relationship with Jesus, you should expect your own heart and mind to rebel against that freedom and that intimacy and that delight.

As soon as savoring God's Word becomes a joy, expect daily Bible study to suddenly become a chore.

As soon as accepting the invitation to be honest and frequent in prayer makes a real difference in your relationship with God, expect a regular routine of prayer to feel empty and hollow.

Having run, without thought or effort, toward the loving arms of your smiling Father, expect the journey to suddenly feel like an uphill climb with a heavy pack.

Your sinful heart will play tricks on you.

Your sinful heart hates forgiveness and intimacy and restoration.

Your sinful heart hears both God's commands and God's promises and wants you to believe that they are heavy weights you can't possibly carry.

Your own sinful heart is much more comfortable with burden than delight, because *burden* is a sinful heart's native language, home country, and natural state.

But don't despair! It won't always be like this!

And it doesn't have to be *only* like this, even now!

Already now, by the power of the Spirit and in the resurrection life you share with Jesus even ahead of the Resurrection, God wants you to know **not burden, but delight**.

Following Jesus isn't supposed to weigh you down; it's supposed to make you dance.

Following Jesus isn't supposed to limit your fun; it's supposed to open you up to freedom you have never known before.

Following Jesus isn't a burden to carry, even when you carry your cross; to follow Jesus is certainly to know suffering and trouble and dying to self and struggling with doubt, but fundamentally—fundamentally!—**following Jesus is about delight**.

First and foremost, discipleship is about Jesus' *delight* in you. You make Jesus laugh, you make him sing, you make him go, "Woohoo!" and "Wow!" and "Whee!" and "Yum!" and "Yes, please!"

And then, as a sort of rebound, in a response of delight that only increases his delight, you get to turn around and go, "Woohoo!" and "Wow!" and "Whee!" and "Yum!" and "Yes, please!" to Jesus, too.

Jesus delights in you; and Jesus loves it when you feel the same about him. That's what following Jesus is all about.

This first section took a cursory look at a biblical "word cloud" for the concept of delight. The delight God intends and expresses is a "whole person" kind of delight. Loving the Lord your God with all of your heart, soul, mind, and strength involves your emotions, your thoughts, your sense of play, your physical senses, and your desires. And God loves you in that same vast and complex "whole person" kind of way.

We could have done a lot less (or a lot more!) with biblical vocabulary words, but looking at the conceptual architecture of delight in the Scriptures gives us tools to explore this mutual delight more in depth. In the rest of this book, we will take a closer look at loving and being loved. In Section 2 we'll explore some of the ways God expresses divine delight in us; and then in Section 3 we'll look for how we are invited to experience and express our delight in God.

From this point on, you will find discussion questions at the end of each chapter. Find one or two people to go through this book with you, or introduce this book to a group that already meets regularly. You will get more out of this journey if you have fellow travelers on the way.

Even if you don't process this book specifically in a group, ask some of the discussion questions to people you run into during the course of your week: friends, family, coworkers, or acquaintances. Getting to know the people around you a little better brings its own type of delight!

That conversation will also help you process God's Word in your life, even when the talk is not overtly religious. Trust that Jesus is up to something in your life; you will hear echoes of Jesus' activity on the lips of people Jesus places around you. We follow Jesus better when we follow him together.

GROUP DISCUSSION FOR SECTION 1

The Architecture of Delight

Pick one or two of the following questions to help you get to know a friend, family member, or small group better.

1. What does delight mean to you?

   What kinds of things do you find delightful?

   What other words capture that moment of joyful pleasure?

2. Find an example of some everyday experience—like eating a good brownie or catching a big fish—that expresses each of these unique delight words.

   a. Joyful Delight (*Woohoo!*)

   b. Thoughtful Delight (*Wow!*)

   c. Playful Delight (*Whee!*)

   d. Delicious Delight (*Yum!*)

   e. Desirable Delight (*Yes, Please!*)

3. Which experiences were easy to think of? Which were hard to come up with? Why do you think that is?

Go a little deeper with someone you trust to point you back to Jesus. You don't have to reflect on all of the following, but spend some time on the ones that catch your spiritual attention.

1. Talk about how you delight in God in each of the five ways, above.

2. Talk about how God delights in you in each of the five ways, above.

3. Identify one or two ways that Jesus is inviting you to experience a little more delight in your faith walk right now.

4. How will you keep a lookout for delight this week?

A Prayer For Delight

Heavenly Father,
you delight in me more than I could ever
imagine! Thank you! Thank you for loving me,
and choosing me, and taking delight in who I
am—in the unique person you made me to be.
Increase my joyful curiosity as I look for what
you are doing in me and through me.

Give me a sense of excitement as I read your
Word and spend time with you in prayer. Cause
me to delight in your presence as you take
delight in spending time with me.

Send the Spirit of Jesus to dwell in me: in my
emotions, my mind, my soul, my senses, and
my will. Father, enable me more and more to
delight in your will and walk in your ways
to the glory of your holy name.

Amen.

SECTION 2

God Delights in You

CHAPTER 6

Treasured Possession

Reading Plan

Day 1
Faithfulness to Complex Truth
&
Recognizing the Tension

Day 2
Salvation in Two Acts

Day 3
What We Miss (Part 1)

Day 4
Salvation in Three Acts

Day 5
What We Miss (Part 2)
&
A Tension With a Shelf Life

Day 6
Group Discussion

Faithfulness To Complex Truth

I once got to be part of a vision process. The congregation I was serving wanted to describe who we were trying to be as a community, and where we believed Jesus was taking us next. The whole conversation around vision was an awesome experience!

One of my favorite "core values" that came out of that discovery process was "Faithfulness to Complex Truth." I still love that! Faithfulness to Complex Truth was not new to that congregation; just a new way of expressing a value already held by a majority of the people, most of the time. Naming that value didn't make us 100% Faithful to Complex Truth 24/7/365, but we tried. And when we failed, we had something to help us see how and why we failed. When we had to make a decision as leaders or as a congregation, Faithfulness to Complex Truth helped inform that decision.

I vividly remember an early back and forth on the vision leadership team around that core value. One woman on the team strongly opposed the formulation, "Faithfulness to Complex Truth."

"Truth isn't complex," she would say. "Truth is simple. 'Jesus loves me, this I know.' Why do you want to make things so complicated all the time...?"

So we didn't adopt that value right away; we tabled that discussion until our next monthly meeting. During the course of that month, and in many of the months that followed, things got rather complex for my friend. Her story is not mine to share, except to say that she was actively trying to see where Jesus was inviting her to take a next step, and then move forward in faith. When you pay attention to what Jesus is doing and try to respond, life can be adventurous, but seldom *simple*.

Add to that intentional attitude of following the fact that she was a mother of teenagers, a part of a large and connected family, and a friend to sinners (and pastors) who mess up and hurt other people and fail in big ways and small, and you can imagine that living out Dependence on Jesus (another of our core values, the One Value to Rule Them All) got complicated pretty quickly.

She came back to our next vision meeting and said, "OK; OK! Truth is kind of complex! I mean, I know Jesus loves me, but man! Living that out is really confusing sometimes! Knowing what to do, or what to say, or how to feel is hard! It would be a lot easier if we didn't hold that core value, but I am on board. Let's add Faithfulness to Complex Truth to the list. And can I get a little help with that?"

Of course, her statement that "truth is simple" isn't wrong; the truth is simple enough to be put into a children's song. But it can also be so complex that adults can't figure it out by themselves. Both are true at the same time…

Which sort of proves the point: *sometimes seemingly contradictory things are true at the same time*. In fact, the truth is probably best served by holding both sides of that tension. Truth is simple, and truth is complex; and depending on the experience you are looking at or the context you are in, either of those seemingly opposite statements might help you see your life in a different light.

Sometimes that happens with the Bible. Sometimes Scripture presents us with two sides of the same truth, two seemingly contradictory realities. Wisdom Literature does this all the time. The wisdom lies not just in the wise sayings—take Proverbs 26:4-5, for example: "Answer not a fool according to his folly, lest you be like him yourself. Answer a fool according to his folly, lest he be wise in his own eyes." (ESV)—wisdom is found not just in the sayings, but in **knowing which wisdom saying applies to the situation** you find yourself in. Are we supposed to answer a fool? Or not? Wisdom says, yes! And knowing when you should and when you shouldn't is what shows you are wise.

So our job isn't to resolve the tension between two biblical perspectives or find their least common denominator; our job is to hold on to both sides of any truly biblical tension and seek to be, well, you guessed it: *faithful to complex truth*…

Delight is a theme that runs throughout the Bible, from cover to cover; delight is one important and central way of telling the story of salvation; but it isn't the only way. I am concerned that **other central ways of telling the story can all too easily**

displace delight (if they haven't already). I'm concerned that in our churches and schools and small groups and family devotions we all too easily let go of the delight side of the tension and let other important, and true, and central ways of talking about Jesus dominate delight.

So, I want to talk to you about the immense value Jesus places on you as an individual when he calls you his "treasured possession." But that important and central truth of Scripture could easily get drowned out by other important and central truths of Scripture.

In order to help you hear delight clearly, I want to point out one of the faithful tensions in our biblical faith. My hope is that, by holding on to that tension in Scripture—**by being faithful to complex truth—you will also get a better handle on delight**.

Recognizing The Tension

Growing up Lutheran, I got pretty used to a both/and mentality pretty early on. Many of the theological or Scriptural tensions we need to maintain were obvious: Law *and* Gospel, Sinner *and* Saint, Pepperoni *and* Mushroom... but it wasn't until fairly recently that I even recognized **the tension related to delight,** a tension I was first taught way back in confirmation class without really being aware of it.

In Luther's explanation to the First Article of the Apostles' Creed ("I believe in God the Father Almighty, maker of heaven and earth.") I was taught that God's creative act is both free and personal. God created and still sustains *me*, personally. God does this "purely out of divine, fatherly goodness and mercy, **without any merit or worthiness in me...**"

Then, in his explanation to the Second Article of the Apostles' Creed ("And in Jesus Christ, his only Son, our Lord, who..."), Luther says that Jesus "**redeemed** me, **purchased** and won me from sin, death, and the power of the devil, not with gold or silver, but with his holy, precious blood and his innocent suffering and death, that I may **be his own...**"

Do you see the tension I missed back in confirmation? I mean, which is it? Should I see myself as having *no value or worthiness*? Or am I *so precious* that Jesus would be willing to buy me back at the exorbitant price of his own suffering and death?

If it were just Luther, or just a couple of explanations to help parents help their kids know and follow Jesus, then I could mark up the inconsistency to the strength of Wittenberg's beer. (Sorry; Lutheran joke. Wittenberg is where Luther spent most of his adult life and ministry. And they did have beer. And Luther did drink it.)

But noticing that apparent contradiction in catechism class helps me see that same apparent contradiction in other places, too. Take Isaiah, for example (he seemed to come up quite a bit in our opening exploration of the architecture of delight). On the one hand, Isaiah can write in no uncertain terms:

> All of us have become like one who is unclean,
>   and **all our righteous acts are like filthy rags**;
> we all shrivel up like a leaf,
>   and like the wind our sins sweep us away.
>
> *Isaiah 64:6,* NIV

But on the other hand, listen to these words of God in Isaiah:

> But now, this is what the LORD says—
>   he who created you, Jacob,
>   he who formed you, Israel:
> "Do not fear, for I have **redeemed** you;
>   I have summoned you by name; you are mine...
>
> For I am the LORD your God,
>   the Holy One of Israel, your Savior;
> I give Egypt for your **ransom**,
>   Cush and Seba in your stead.
> Since you are **precious** and honored in my sight,
>   and because I love you,
> I will give people in **exchange** for you,
>   nations in exchange for your life."
>
> *Isaiah 43:1, 3-4,* NIV

Do you see the tension? I mean, which is it? Are we so worthless that *even our best is disgusting*? Or are we so precious that God would *buy us back* at *any* price?

Of course, Isaiah was written over a long and varied ministry of the prophet and covers so many topics and time periods that you could reasonably wonder if it was all written by the same guy. But Isaiah isn't the only place we find a tension between our worthlessness and our immense value. Check out these two seemingly contradictory perspectives from the book of Psalms. In one Psalm of David we get:

> For you created my inmost being;
>> you knit me together in my mother's womb.
> I praise you because
>> **I am fearfully and wonderfully made**;
> your works are **wonderful**,
>> I know that full well.
>
> *Psalm 139:13-14*, NIV

In another Psalm of David we get almost the exact opposite:

> Surely I was **sinful** at birth,
>> **sinful** from the time my mother conceived me.
>
> *Psalm 51:5*. NIV

Holding onto these different perspectives on what human beings are like even from the womb is not as simple as noting the difference between a Psalm of praise and a Psalm of confession. This tension between our *worth* and our *worthlessness* is too prevalent for that. Consider Jesus, who opens his Sermon on the Mount with one way of talking and ends the same sermon with a very different image for our value.

Jesus begins his Sermon on the Mount in Matthew chapter 5 by saying, "Blessed are the **poor in spirit** [the spiritually bankrupt—the people who know they have nothing of worth to offer God in spiritual matters], for the kingdom of heaven is theirs [the only way it can be: as a gift]" (*Matthew 5:3*, NIV).

And then, two chapters later, in Matthew 7:9–11, as Jesus is bringing the same Sermon on the Mount to a close, he says: "Which of you, if **your son** asks for bread, will give him a stone? Or if he asks for a fish, will give him a snake? If you, then, though you are evil, know how to give good gifts to **your children**, how much more will **your Father** in heaven give good gifts to those **who ask** him!"

So which is it, Jesus?! Do I come to God *spiritually bankrupt*, with the empty hands of a *beggar*? Or do I come to God with *childlike faith*, with the empty hands of a darling child?

Which is it, David?! Am I so infected with original sin that I was corrupt even before I was born? Or am I unique and wonderful because I was handmade by God?

It seems like there must be something wrong with my faith, if I have to believe such contradictory things. But Faithfulness to Complex Truth means **sometimes I actually have to hold on to both sides of the tension** between seemingly contradictory realities if I am going to follow Jesus the way he intends.

In this case, if we only hold on to the delight side of this tension, we risk losing a fundamental truth of our faith: salvation is by grace alone, for Christ's sake alone, without any contribution or worthiness in me. That is a truth we cannot let go.

But the danger on the other side is just as great. If we only hold on to the stinking sinner side of this tension, we can get *forgiveness* right at the expense of *delight*. We can affirm our *sinfulness* and miss our *value*. We can learn to accept God's *grace* and never experience his *love*.

I am convinced that **we need to hold onto the Triune God's delight in us, and our delight in the Triune God, just as firmly as we hold onto salvation by grace alone for Christ's sake alone.** (That's a really difficult thing for a Lutheran to say, but I am pretty sure I believe it!) To release that tension on either side is to risk losing the promise of the Gospel that Jesus intends for you today; that Jesus intends for you to take into your week; a complex truth Jesus intends for you to hold onto, tightly, with both hands, until Jesus himself resolves that tension in the resurrection of the dead and the life of the world to come.

Salvation In Two Acts

The first way of talking about what God was up to in Jesus tells the Story of Salvation as if it were a Drama in Two Acts. The curtain opens on the state of fallen humanity, a humanity turned inward on itself and turned away from God. Here is where all of the "no merit or worthiness in me" stuff comes in.

This way of telling the story deals with the reality of original sin: we, according to our sinful, fallen condition, are spiritually bankrupt. We are spiritually blind, dead, and enemies of God; by nature objects of wrath. Even our most righteous acts are like filthy rags. If it were up to us to do anything on our own to earn God's favor, even something small like accepting or not rejecting the promise, then we would be lost.

And that's what makes salvation by grace alone for Christ's sake alone so sweet! Having no good thing in me, that is, in my sinful nature, I must rely on an outside force to work my salvation for me, on my behalf. I cannot deal with my sin problem on my own, and therefore Jesus must deal with my sin for me. I cannot try hard enough or be good enough or even believe strong enough to merit forgiveness, so apart from my work and effort, Jesus merits forgiveness for me.

The central movement of this drama is from Wrath to Delight; on our own, in our sin, we have earned God's judgment and wrath (Act 1). On the cross, Jesus takes the judgment and wrath we have deserved and gives us in exchange the delight and righteousness that belong to him. His sacrifice as our substitute means we are saved apart from our own merits or works and declared righteous because of what Jesus did when we believe it was done for us. Now, because of Jesus, God actually delights in us! (Act 2).

This way of telling the story portrays Jesus' death as a **"sacrifice of atonement,"** that is, a substitution that allows the sacrificial animal to carry away the sinner's sin (all the way to its death), and the sinner to receive the unblemished status of the sacrificial animal.

When John the Baptist says of Jesus, "Behold, the Lamb of

God, *who takes away the sin of the world!*" we should probably expect Jesus to receive the death sentence deserved by the world, and expect the world to be declared not guilty as a result. Poor, miserable sinners receive the Verdict of Delight because the One in Whom God Delights took their Verdict of Guilt and made it his own, carrying it to the cross.

This Drama of Salvation in Two Acts highlights several key aspects of the story. It accounts for original sin, lets us be real sinners and receive real forgiveness, makes the cross of Jesus central to the story, and clearly shows our dependence on Jesus and the depth of God's unmerited grace. I can stand before the Judgment Seat with confidence, knowing that I am sprinkled by the blood of Jesus, covered over by a robe of righteousness, so that when God looks at me, he sees Jesus.

If you think about it, *sprinkling something with blood* seems like an odd way to make it "clean." But that sacrificial blood is a sign that this person has had their sins removed. They are "clean" as in "forgiven," and marked as one who no longer has to fear the holy presence of a holy God.

Do you remember how "Passover" got its name? As part of the worst and final plague, the blood of the Passover lamb was placed on the door of any Hebrew house in Egypt, and when the Angel of Death saw the blood of the lamb, he "passed over" that house. The firstborn in all of Egypt, from the lowest slave up to Pharaoh himself—and even the cattle!—died that night. But the blood of the lamb stood as a sign that death, the natural outcome of sin, had been taken away by a substitute. The Passover lamb was not a Sacrifice of Atonement, but the same principle applies: the sacrifice dies in the place of the sinner and the sinner, marked by the blood of the sacrifice, goes on living.

You have been marked by the blood of Christ, the Lamb of God. You can hide yourself in Christ, hide yourself behind Christ, and know that the Angel of Death passes over. In the place of what your sins have deserved, you receive instead the status that only Jesus deserves. If your guilty conscience or your fear of judgment is keeping you up at night, you can run to Jesus and rely on his sacrifice and trust that, while there is **nothing**

you could ever do to help earn your salvation, there is also **nothing you _have_ to do.**

God delights in you for the sake of Christ.

What We Miss (Part 1)

As important and comforting as that way of speaking the Gospel is, if this Drama of Salvation in Two Acts is the _only_ way we have of telling the story, we can inadvertently draw some pretty natural conclusions that just don't fit with the rest of the biblical witness. If we only know how to talk about what God does "without any merit or worthiness in me," we can leave some pretty gaping holes. It's a small step from "no worthiness" to feeling completely worthless.

I know a pastor who chooses not to use the old confession in the front of the hymnal that starts, "I, a poor miserable sinner…" It's not that this pastor thinks he has earned some credit before God; it's just that after years and years of only ever being characterized as a poor, miserable sinner—after growing up in a family where the primary mode of expressing your faith was as a poor, miserable sinner—after pastoring congregations where people went out of their way to seem more poor and more miserable than the next person, **my friend can't use those true words anymore without the wrong implications springing up in his heart and mind.**

If you think following Jesus is defined by an attitude of being poor and miserable, and that attitude shapes not just your confession of sins, but your hymns of praise, and your prayer life, and your church potluck, and how you interact with people at work, and the way you treat your family, then your experience of following Jesus will be poor and miserable. Anything not poor and miserable won't be seen as following Jesus at all…

I know a woman who grew up in the Church and has been part of Christian ministry her entire life who struggles with her own self-image and her own self-worth. She has been told she is worthless so many times over the years that she has started to believe it. Even when she receives a promise of love or delight from her heavenly Father, she knows it only comes for the sake of Christ, and not for her own sake. She knows, because she has been repeatedly taught, that even her most righteous acts are like filthy rags, so it seems natural and obvious to her that she should only ever be disgusted with whatever she does. She knows to her bones that she is a wretched sinner, not because of any particularly heinous acts, but because she has heard over and over and over again that she cannot earn God's favor, that she cannot merit salvation. Whenever she checks her own price tag, she sees that on her own she is ugly, worthless, God's enemy, an object of wrath. And she finds herself telling herself she is *ugly*, *worthless*, and *an object of wrath* again and again in dark and lonely moments, sometimes most days in any given week.

The Church that meant to teach this woman not to *rely* on her own value ended up teaching her she has *no value at all*. The Church that meant to give my pastor friend a *tool* to help unburden his conscience before God instead handed a *cudgel* to the people around him who only had one rule of faith: poor, miserable sinner.

If the only way you know the story of salvation is as a drama with two acts, you can lose the immense value of the individual. You can lose the everyday delight Jesus intends as a mark of discipleship.

You can even misplace the importance of creation, and devalue any hope for the New Creation. I mean, look where the Drama of Salvation in Two Acts begins the story. *The curtain opens on the state of fallen humanity, a humanity turned inward on itself and turned away from God.* Theologically, that's a fine place to start the story. It's certainly descriptive of our current experience. And it aligns with places like Psalm 51: "Surely I was sinful at birth, sinful from the time my mother conceived me."

But that's not where the Story of Scripture starts. **Fallen by nature is not the natural state of human beings**. Original sin wasn't original. Genesis opens with God's creation and then God's verdict on creation—including humanity: "And it was very good."

Because we are born into a fallen humanity, we are by nature sinful and unclean. Because we are born into God's good creation, we are also fearfully and wonderfully made. **The Fall complicates, but does not negate, God's verdict of Very Good**.

Sometimes when we talk about being covered over with Christ's righteousness or hiding behind Jesus, it's easy to get the impression that we are all rather nondescript blobs of shapeless yuck. Even our righteous acts are filthy rags. We are universally sinful, and so universally *the same*.

The Good News that those nondescript blobs of shapeless yuck are covered over with the righteousness of Jesus can fall kind of flat if we only talk about individuals as shapeless yuck. "Everybody is the same in their sin," seems like a theologically sound way of putting it. But if you remove "sin" from that sentence, you are left with "everybody is the same." That is not so theologically sound! Many Christians I know want to remove sin (which is good) and then, as an unintended consequence, act as if everybody is the same (not so good).

You were not mass-produced by God to be the same as everybody else! You are delightfully unique, hand-knit by God to be one of a kind. Yes, being covered over by Christ means dying to yourself, losing your life; the old is gone. But belonging to Christ also means the New has come! As the Holy Spirit shapes you to look more and more like Jesus, you don't end up looking more and more like everybody else. **You look more and more *unique* the more you look like Christ**.

That's the theology of the Body: each and every one of us members has a unique role, a unique function, a unique part to play in the community of faith. If everyone were an eye, where would the sense of taste be? If we are all only nondescript blobs of shapeless yuck, even covered with Christ, where would the Body be?

But even worse than amalgamating God's unique human creations into a generic fallen humanity is the tendency for the Drama of Salvation in Two Acts to miss not just how the story starts, but *how it ends*. In this way of telling the story, Act 2 is complete when the forgiveness won by Jesus as a sacrifice in our place is delivered to sinners; when their sin is taken away, and they receive the verdict of not guilty that belongs to Christ. Once that Great Exchange has taken place, there is nothing more to add to the drama.

That moment of salvation, that moment when your sins are replaced by the righteousness of Christ, could be any number of different moments in your personal story. Depending on your theological persuasion, you could see it as the moment when you accepted Jesus as your personal Savior, or when you were baptized, or when you received the Holy Spirit, or when you received the Lord's Supper, or when you committed your life to following him. (We tend to be such zero-sum people, as if being saved at your baptism meant you couldn't also be saved at a moment of personal conviction, or vice versa! I think all of these moments and more can, should, and do count as moments of salvation in God's way of dealing with people, and the more moments of salvation, the better!)

But however you characterize that moment of salvation, it is a moment here in time, a present reality, that leaves you with a promise of more to come but sews up most of the loose ends ahead of the final curtain. I am saved and forgiven, and when I die I get to go to heaven. Sounds good, right? I suppose I do have to be somewhat careful that I don't mess it up in the meantime, and there is that pesky thing about discipling the nations, but by and large the most important thing in the story *has already happened for me.*

The Drama of Salvation in Two Acts starts after the fall into sin and ends in the present, with forgiveness being delivered to real sinners in real time. And that's great! Except that **the hope of the Bible from cover to cover is not just that sinners will be forgiven, but that this fallen creation will be restored**.

Biblical hope is never focused on dying and going to heaven (though being with Jesus is good); instead, the Bible points to something better, to a time when this fallen order is replaced with God's renewed creation, when God dwells in communion with human beings who don't need repentance or forgiveness any longer; when God's will is done on earth as it is in heaven; when we know fully, even as we are fully known; when we experience God not merely as a reflection in a dull mirror, but face to face.

The hope of the Bible is nothing short of taking this whole, fallen mess and not only restoring it, but transforming it to be something even more glorious than it was when God declared it *very good*. That's the full hope of the Scriptures: the Resurrection of the Dead and the Life of the World to Come. That's the future of human beings who, body and soul, belong to Jesus: a body and soul together, with Jesus, in New Creation glory.

That's the way the story ends.

And it's so much better than just dying and going to heaven.

I have a friend who likes to say, "Heaven's great, but it's not the End of the World." I like that. A lot.

So on the one hand, the Drama of Salvation in Two Acts gets some really important stuff right in clear ways. If the death of Jesus on the cross is a Sacrifice of Atonement, then salvation happens **outside of me**, for the sake of Christ. If I am covered over with his righteousness, I never have to be good enough or pure enough or try hard enough to earn God's favor; I simply rely on Christ. I come, empty and broken, and trust that God places everything Jesus earned into the empty hands of this crouching beggar. Salvation is **by grace, through faith, for Christ's sake**.

On the other hand, that way of telling the story only covers the time after the Fall and before the Resurrection of the Dead, *an important but relatively short chapter in the history of eternity*. If you only ever tell the story this way, you can lose **the immense value of unique individuals**. You can lose a **sense of joy** in following Jesus. You can even deemphasize **the inherent goodness of God's creation** and lose sight of the promise that we are **designed to be more** than forgiven sinners.

The answer to these potential deficiencies is not to ban this way of talking or discard this lens through which we can view the work of Jesus for us. Instead, we want to hold on to this one unique and valuable way of talking about who we are while we also grasp in firm hands another, complementary (and somewhat contradictory) way of telling the story.

We need the Drama of Salvation in Two Acts; but we also

need to learn how to tell the story of Scripture as the Drama of Salvation in Three Acts. We need to know the movement from Wrath to Delight; but we also desperately need to own, down to our DNA, the movement from Delight, to Longing, to Even More Delight.

You are a poor, miserable sinner.

But you are also so much more.

Salvation In Three Acts

A second, thoroughly biblical, central, and comprehensive way of telling the story of Scripture is as a Drama of Salvation in Three Acts. Instead of the curtain opening on the present state of the fallen creation, this way of telling the story goes all the way back to the beginning.

In Act 1, God *delights* in creation, and Adam and Eve in the Garden of Eden delight in God right back. (In fact, some scholars suggest the word "Eden" comes from another Hebrew vocabulary word for delight: Luxurious Delight!) God made these people; God loves these people; these people belong to God.

Then something drastic happens. These people who delight and belong to God come under the influence, lordship, and ownership of a foreign power. Like the coin or the sheep or the Prodigal Son, God's people become lost. They wander from the place they belong. Sin has made them captive to a foreign enemy.

In Act 2 of the Drama of Salvation in Three Acts, God's people are **not the enemy** (unlike Act 1 in the Drama of Salvation in Two Acts, where sinful humans are God's enemies). God's people are not God's enemies; rather, they are under the authority and ownership of the enemy. **God's people still *delight* God; but they no longer *belong* to God**. Now humanity belongs to sin, death, and devil. The divine desire and longing for God's own treasured possession is so great, God vows to find a way to buy them back.

The cross is again the key turning point in the story. The suffering and death of Jesus is **the ransom** that buys God's people back, that brings them home, that reestablishes their relationship with the God who made them and to whom they belong.

That's Act 3: God's treasured possession is restored to its rightful place and the Delight that had turned to Longing in Act 2 has given way to Even More Delight in Act 3. God's people are again *God's people*; they belong to God forever, and nothing can snatch them out of God's powerful and loving hand.

If the first way of telling the story aligns with a Sacrifice of Atonement, this second way embodies the dynamics of **a Sacrifice of Redemption**. (The Old Testament contains a wide variety of sacrifices—from fellowship offerings, to thank offerings, to wave offerings—many of which overlap in meaning, and many of which don't. We aren't going to do an OT Deep Dive at this point; still, the shape of the sacrificial system in general, even if the practice fell short of the design, can give us an insight into what's on in God's mind and heart.)

The Sacrifice of Redemption again harkens back to the very first Passover. God's people have come under foreign ownership—they are slaves in Egypt—and God is going to win them back. The God of Israel engages the gods of Egypt head on. In the last and fiercest battle of this war for ownership of God's people, the God who claims to be the Author of Life and Death takes on the head of the Egyptian pantheon, who also claims to rule over life and death. The last plague, the death of the firstborn, will determine which God can actually put their money where their mouth is. At the command of Yahweh, the Angel of Death visits all the firstborn in Egypt.

By divine mandate, the firstborn of Israel should have died that night, too; but in an act of divine mercy, the blood of the Passover lamb turns Death away. From that point on, Yahweh claims ownership of the firstborn in Israel (even of the cattle). By rights, they should have died; God has the authority to give life and to take it. And those God spares are now property of the Most High.

To commemorate that victory over Egypt and the sparing of the firstborn, God gives a command for future generations: any firstborn must be **bought back, redeemed, bought at a price**. The Law sets the price of redemption at the life of a lamb (just like at that first Passover); or, if the family can't afford it, they could bring two small pigeons. But the firstborn (even of the cattle) belongs to Yahweh, and **you have to buy back your firstborn into your family**.

That's what Mary and Joseph were doing in the Temple when they met Simeon and Anna. Do you remember the scene? Mary and Joseph brought two pigeons, along with the infant Jesus, to buy their firstborn back into their family. They had to *redeem* their son, a son who belonged to their family, but still had to be *bought back* at a price. (Yes; before Jesus redeemed anyone, he himself was redeemed by Mary and Joseph!)

A Sacrifice of Redemption is **the price you pay to buy something that used to be yours back, so it is yours again, and yours permanently**. Your firstborn son was never an enemy; but he didn't belong to you for a time. Once you had paid the redemption price, he was yours again the way he was supposed to be all along. The movement is **from Delight, to Longing, to Even More Delight**.

John the Baptist said of Jesus, "Behold, the Lamb of God who takes away the sin of the world!" That's the Sacrifice of Atonement, the Drama of Salvation in Two Acts, where you go from being God's enemy to being God's beloved child because of the cross.

Jesus said of himself, "The Son of Man has come not to be served but to serve, and to give his life as **a ransom** for many." That's the Sacrifice of Redemption, the Drama of Salvation in Three Acts, where you go from being God's treasured possession, to being God's treasured possession *under the ownership of an enemy*, to being God's treasured possession *back home where you belong*, because of the cross.

The movement goes from (1) Mine; to (2) Mine, but Lost to Me; to (3) Mine, Restored with Rejoicing. You can see all three stages of that progression in some of the parables you probably know well, parables like the Lost Sheep, the Lost Coin, or even the Lost (Prodigal) Son in Luke 15. The sheep, the coin, and the son all three (1) *begin where they belong*, (2) end up *missing* in a way that causes *searching and longing*, and (3) are *restored* to their proper place with such *joy* that parties and banquets are in order.

Two of my favorite parables of Jesus emphasize the transition from Act 2: Longing to Act 3: Even More Delight. These pithy stories come in a couple of brief verses in Matthew 13, right in the middle of a bunch of other, longer and more famous parables. In verse 44, Jesus says the kingdom of heaven is like this situation: some guy finds a treasure buried in a field, and in his *joy*—that's one of our Delight vocabulary words from Section 1: this is Emotional Delight that makes you jump up, spin around, shout "Woohoo!" and start singing your happy song—in his *joy* he jumps up, spins around, shouts "Woohoo!" and *sells everything he has* so he can afford to buy that field.

In the next verse, Jesus tells a similar parable. The kingdom of heaven is like this situation: a professional pearl dealer, who has a lifetime's worth of experience and a lifetime's worth of inventory, finally finds that once-in-a-lifetime pearl. Sometimes it's called the Pearl of Great Value, sometimes the Pearl of Great Price (price and value are intimately related). At the bargain basement price of *every single pearl in his possession*, along with his house and his retirement plan and his brand new camel caravan and his cottage by the sea, that merchant makes the purchase of a lifetime and walks away with a pearl that made all those long years of searching worthwhile.

The value validated the price. In fact, the value exceeded the expense, so that this unbelievably high price—everything you own—was *greeted with joy* and *paid in full, with delight.*

Those two verses in Matthew 13 helped me see that I had been reading Hebrews 12 wrong all my life. Hebrews 12 speaks of Jesus, the "author and perfecter of our faith," the one who first put pen to paper to tell our story, and the one who himself is responsible for how this drama will unfold.

> For the **joy** [*chara*] set before him
>   he endured the cross,
>   scorning its shame,
> and sat down at the right hand
>   of the throne of God.
>
> *Hebrews 12:2*, NIV

I guess I always imagined that the *joy* (there's that Emotional Delight word again)—that the joy set before Jesus was something like receiving the applause of heaven, the praise of saints and angels, and having the honor of sitting at the right hand of God.

Then it occurred to me: *before* the Incarnation, *before* the cross, Jesus *already had* the applause of heaven, the praise of saints and angels. Jesus was already seated at the right hand of God, and had to leave that place of honor in order to endure the cross, and then take back his rightful place.

None of those could be the motivating joy for Jesus, *since they were his already.*

So what was it? What was the joy set before Jesus?

What could possibly make Jesus jump up and spin around and shout, "Woohoo!" and *endure the cross*?

What could possibly make Jesus scorn the shame of public humiliation and torture as if it were a bargain-basement price?

What was the joy set before Jesus?

I think it was: you.

The thing that Jesus now has that he didn't have before the cross and open tomb, is you.

The treasure buried in a field that was worth giving away everything, is you.

The single motivating factor for Christmas and Good Friday and Easter, is you.

You.

You.

You!

Your value validated the price. In fact, your value exceeded the expense, so that this unbelievably high price—everything Jesus owned, even his own life—was greeted with joy and paid in full, with delight.

Jesus looked at the possibility of having you as his own forever, and then he looked at the cross, and in his *joy* he said, "Yes! Worth it! What a bargain!"

For your sake, Jesus said, "Yes! They can deny me and betray me; they can spit on me and mock me; they can put a crown of thorns on my head, and drive nails through my hands, and hang me up to die! I would gladly pay that bargain basement price if it means an eternity with Carla, an eternity with James, an eternity with Connor, with Ida, with Carrie..."

With *you!*

If you ever have cause to doubt your own value, if you ever wonder what your small existence is worth, if you ever find yourself in a dark and lonely place where your inner voice tells you again and again, and sometimes most days in any given week, that you are ugly, or stupid, or worthless—*check your price tag.*

Because your price tag reads: "The Very Life of the Son of God."

And Jesus read that price tag, and considered eternity with you and eternity without you, and then *with tears of joy* sold everything he had so he could afford to buy *you.*

You made all those long years of searching worth it.

You were the joy set before Jesus that led him to endure the cross and even scorn its shame.

You.

You were worth it.

What We Miss (Part 2)

As important and comforting as that way of speaking the Gospel is, if this Drama of Salvation in Three Acts is the *only* way we have of telling the story, we can inadvertently draw some pretty natural conclusions that just don't fit with the rest of the biblical witness. If I come to you and say, "I am so sorry. I sinned, and I know I sinned. I stepped on your toes, and I am ashamed; I need you to forgive me. Please." And the only thing you know how to say to me is, "God really values you..."

I mean, that's *nice*... but my problem isn't that I don't feel valuable; my problem is that I am a stinking sinner, and I know it, and I have experienced it in my own life. I have a *sin problem*; I have this burden of guilt I am carrying, and if all you can tell me is, "God loves you and God delights in you," I'm going to know, in my heart, that it's just not true, according to my fallen, sinful nature.

God's answer to sin is forgiveness. God's answer for a guilty conscience is the promise: "You are forgiven, for the sake of Jesus." What the person carrying a burden of guilt needs to hear is that Jesus died on the cross and took the burden of their sins away, that what they did was awful, but that it will not be held against them, and our relationship is not damaged beyond repair. That's what I need to hear; that's what you need to hear.

So if the only truth you have is delight, you might not be able to deal with real sin, or you might even downplay your own sinfulness; after all, you are a delight to God! How bad could you really be?

As soon as delight stops being what *Jesus* tells *you* he feels about *you* and becomes what *you* tell *Jesus* he *should* feel about you, you have begun to think pretty highly of yourself.

I think the danger of that self-importance is one reason why, growing up, I always heard such a clear presentation that on your own, you can never please God; on your own, you have no value; on your own, even on your best day, you are blind, dead, and an enemy of God. As soon as I start focusing on how delightful I am, I can lose sight of my own sinfulness. Even worse, **I can lose my dependence on Jesus**. God already loves me; what do I need Jesus for?

If the reality of God's delight in you, this unique, handmade, treasured possession and beloved child—if the reality of God's delight in you overshadows your desperate need for Jesus, you've let go of one of the most central teachings of Scripture.

If all I have is delight, I can't deal with sin, or even take sin seriously. And I am in danger of not needing Jesus, since I am so "delightful" all on my own.

So on the one hand, if all you have is "poor, miserable sinner," you can miss that this creation, even though fallen, is still a good gift intended by God to delight; but on the other hand, if all you have is delight, you can miss that this creation, even though it was originally Very Good, is still fallen.

Focusing *only* on delight can mean ignoring pain and suffering in your life or in the world around you. Focusing *only* on delight can mean discounting injustice or whitewashing grief.

If I have no way of dealing with sin or brokenness, then I better pretend not to see sin or brokenness around me and hope that it goes away quietly. While *only* having *atonement* language can cause you to stop looking for your future rescue, *only* having *redemption* language can cause you to pretend that your future rescue is already complete; that this is as good as it gets; that the Very Good creation is already restored, or at least mostly restored—or maybe, if you turn your head and squint, looks like it might be just about restored.

If the only way you know how to tell the story is a Drama of Salvation in Three Acts, where you go from Delight, to Longing, to Even More Delight, you can end up sticking your head in the sand and ignoring the sin and brokenness and dysfunction and pain and suffering in your life and in the life of the world around you.

So you have to have both.

You have to hold onto Atonement and Redemption at the same time. You need to know the depth of your depravity without losing sight of the value Jesus himself places on you.

Faithfulness to Complex Truth means holding firmly to both sides of the truth at the same time, even when they seem to be pulling in opposite directions.

A Tension With A Shelf Life

In this brief time between the Fall and the Resurrection of the Flesh, we must hold onto our *unworthiness* as tightly as we do to our *immeasurable value*; as long as this broken, sinful world still exists, *repentance* and *delight* will both define the life of a disciple.

This tension is not a defect in our faith; this tension is absolutely essential for holding onto God's promises in the midst of our current reality. Sometimes, in our lives this side of eternity, seemingly contradictory things are true at the same time.

Even your most righteous acts are like **filthy rags** *and* you are **precious and honored** in God's sight.

You are so **infected with original sin** that you were corrupt even before you were born *and* you were **unique and wonderful** even before you were born because you are handmade by God.

You can only approach the throne of grace with the **empty hands of a beggar** *and* you are invited to come to your daddy with the **empty hands of a darling child**.

God loves you **only for the sake of Christ** *and* God loves you **for your own sake**; you delight God only **because of who Jesus is** *and* you delight God **because of who you are**, because of who God created you to be.

The reality of this broken and sinful world combined with the reality of God's love for us in Jesus means that we will have to hold onto this tension as long as this fallen world endures.

Which won't be always. You won't always live in a broken and fallen world. You won't always be both sinner and saint at the same time. You won't always need repentance, or forgiveness, or hope, or even faith. This essential tension in your faith has a very specific shelf life.

The Day is coming when you will no longer need *hope*, because your hope will come true. The Day is coming when you will no longer need *faith*, because your faith will be sight. The Day is coming when you no will longer need *repentance* or even *forgiveness*, because sin will be done with forever.

The Day is coming when the lost treasured possessions will be brought home at last and forever, and God's enemies will never take possession of them again. The Day is coming, soon, when Jesus himself will resolve the tension between our unworthiness and our immense value, in the resurrection of the dead and the life of the world to come.

And then, finally, **there will be nothing left but delight**: God's delight in you, Treasured Possession, and your delight in God, forever and ever. And the amazing thing is, Jesus looks and longs for that day even more than we do.

I can't wait!

GROUP DISCUSSION FOR CHAPTER 6

Treasured Possession

Pick one or two of the following questions to help you get to know a friend, family member, or small group better.

1. Think about some significant purchases in your life.

   Why were they significant? How did you decide to pay that price? What was the result?

2. What does healthy self-esteem look like?

3. What was your home church growing up, or the first congregation you started going to?

4. Do you think you heard more about God's wrath or about God's delight in that faith community?

   Has that had any lasting effect on your faith walk?

   In what ways?

**Go a little deeper with someone you trust to point you back
to Jesus. You don't have to reflect on all of the following, but
spend some time on the ones that catch your spiritual attention.**

1. "I'm pretty awesome!" or "I'm a failure!" Which feels more
   natural for you to say? Where does that natural tendency
   come from?

2. What challenges and blessings do you experience in
   connection to your own self-image? Can you sense any
   invitation from Jesus in those challenges and blessings?

3. Which of the following ways of stating the Gospel do you
   need to hear this week?
   a. At the cross, Jesus took your status as blind, dead, and
      an enemy of God, whose most righteous acts are filthy
      with sin, and gave you instead his status as beloved heir,
      chosen, valued, righteous, and holy. You delight God
      because of who Jesus is.
   b. You are a treasured possession, and although you came
      under the ownership of sin, death, and devil, Jesus valued
      you so highly that he willingly paid the price of the cross
      in order to buy you back and make you his again. You
      delight God because of who you are—the unique person
      God created you to be.

4. Discuss a. and b. above, and why you need either or both
   this week. End your discussion by actually speaking
   the Good News of Jesus to the specific people in your
   conversation.

You are dearly and individually loved!

A Prayer For Delight

Jesus, you are my Sacrifice of Atonement: your blood, shed on the cross, covers my sin, cleanses my guilt, and makes me holy in God's sight. Thank you so much!

Jesus, you are my Sacrifice of Redemption: your death on the cross paid the ultimate price to bring me back into God's family, where I belong. Thank you so much!

Holy Spirit, deepen my understanding of your love, and help me see myself like you do: as a valuable, beautiful, delightful, and unique person worth redeeming.

Heavenly Father, show me more and more how I can live in confidence that you love me for my own sake, and how I can live in gratitude that you love me only for the sake of Christ.

Cause me to delight in your will and walk in your ways, to the glory of your holy name.

Amen.

CHAPTER 7

He Will Rejoice Over You With Singing

Reading Plan

Day 1
Songs of Belonging

Day 2
Intimate Delight Expressed in Song

Day 3
A Mother's Tender Delight

Day 4
The Song of the Mighty Warrior

Day 5
The Joy of Being Rescued

Day 6
Eternal Songs of Eternal Belonging
&
Group Discussion

Songs Of Belonging

I remember, when I was a little kid—I mean little!—how my grandpa would cross his legs at his knee, set me down on his foot (as if it were a saddle), and hold both of my hands for balance (as if I were holding reins). Then grandpa would bounce his leg on his knee and give me quite a horsey ride.

I can still vividly picture that green tweed recliner, forbidden to anyone but grandpa, which sat in the corner right next to the stone fireplace at the farm. I can still remember the spider plant on the windowsill, the beams of golden light from the lamp tree in the corner, and the mild smell of dog hair (from the faithful pet whose master's attention I was usurping) mixed with a faint whiff of old man and Aqua Velva.

But what I remember most is the Song. I never found out if he made it up, or if he had received it passed down from previous generations of grandpas, but whenever I "rode the horsey," I was sure to hear my grandfather's warm baritone: "Bumb-idy, bumb-idy, bumb-idy boo; bumb-idy bumpty-boo... Bumb-idy, bumb-idy, bumb-idy boo; bumb-idy bumpty-/boum-boum!"

Each syllable was accentuated with a movement of grandpa's foot that sent me bouncing up and down. The final, "boum-boum!" came with a kick so large I would have fallen off without his coarse hands holding me tight. It brought a squeal of delight every time. And my giggles would crack grandpa up, until I was laughing at his laughter, and he was laughing at mine.

I don't know where the Song came from or why it was so important, but I do know what it meant to me. Grandma was always the one who would wrap her arms around you and squeeze you tight and put her face right up next to yours for all kinds of hugs and snuggles and kisses. But *grandpa*, the farmer and Lutheran pastor, usually expressed his love with a sidelong glance and a warm, if somewhat stiff, pat on the back.

In later years, when I understood the jokes, and could follow the theological conversations, and got in on the sharp wit and keen sense of self-effacing humor, grandpa's affection was much more real and tangible for me. But as a youngster, that Song was the deepest and warmest and most personal expression of love and pride and delight that I knew from my grandpa.

Years later, a much older man still took his great-granddaughter Naomi, my first-born, and crossed his legs, and held her with frail hands, and bounced her up and down until she squealed with glee, all the while singing, "Bumb-idy, bumb-idy, bumb-idy boo; bumb-idy bumpty-/boum-boum!"

I will always have that memory of grandpa, bouncing me on his knee and singing—of grandpa, bouncing my daughter on his knee and singing. All of us grandkids share that experience. To know that Song, and to receive that Song, to have that Song sung over you means you have a place in our family: you are loved; you are special; you belong.

Sometimes songs are like that: they let you know you belong to the family.

My family has adopted and modified a unique birthday song that first came from my Aunt Nancy's family. After you sing, "Happy Birthday," (with an extra "God's blessings to you!" verse more often than not), you must move immediately into a rendition of, "Come, children, and join in our festival song..." It's quite a lovely tune and a wonderful addition to our family tradition. Except...

Except that, when it came into our family, we added a family twist. Now, when it comes to the very last verse, and you all sing, "Happy birthday to *you!* Happy birthday to *you!* Happy birthday, dear *Nancy*; happy birthday to *you!*" everyone inserts tickling for emphasis.

"Happy birthday to *you!* <tickle> Happy birthday to *you!* <tickle> Happy birthday, dear *Nancy*; <tickle, tickle, poke> happy birthday to *you!* <tickle, tickle, poke, poke, poke, squeeze, tickle, poke>"

It can get a little rowdy, and at least one of my children suffers from PTBDTP (Post-Traumatic Birthday Tickle Phobia), but living through full-contact birthday songs is part of what it means to belong to our family.

In my family, you always tickle the ones you love...

Do you have something like that?

Do you have a family rite of passage, a story or a joke or a song, something that lets you know you belong to a unique group of loved individuals who all belong to each other? What are some of the ways you connected with your parents or your grandparents, with your kids or your grandkids?

Was there a special song for bed, a special book you always read, or a prayer you always said together? Not every family memory is a pleasant one, and not every family habit is healthy, in my family or in yours; still, you can catch glimpses of relationship and caring, even in this present, fallen experience, that identify your family or circle of friends as *people who belong to each other.*

I remember...

I vividly remember a song my mother used to sing to me when I was small—like, "in the crib" small. She must have sung it when I was older, too, because I remember it; but I continue to associate that song with some of my earliest memories. Even though it has been years since I heard her sing it, the haunting melody still sends tingles down my spine:

Hush-a-bye,
don't you cry;
go to sleep my little baby.

When you wake,
you will find
all the pretty little horses:
dapples and grays, pintos and bays,
all the pretty little horses.

Our first child, Naomi, was born quite a bit early, and when she finally came home from the hospital, she was still soooo small: just a little gecko of a baby! You could cup her whole fragile body between your palm and your forearm. She wasn't quite big enough to actually cry; she just kind of squeaked. I vividly remember putting that featherweight on my shoulder when she fussed and singing to her quietly: *Hush-a-bye, don't you cry; go to sleep my little baby...*

In that moment, I was connected to my mother and my daughter; that intimate, tender expression of love and compassion bound us together as family. That song created and passed on an experience of belonging, of being loved, of being family.

Do you have something like that?

Intimate Delight Expressed In Song

Zephaniah 3:17 helped us look at the emotional experience of Joyful Delight back in Chapter 1. Remember, the delight words "rejoice" and "gladness" are balanced by the "jump for joy" woohoo word "exult." And the whole verse leads to song:

> [The LORD] will **rejoice** over you with **gladness**;
> he will quiet you by his love;
> he will **exult** over you with loud singing.
>
> *Zephaniah 3:17*, ESV

I really do love that verse. And for many years, this verse led me to imagine the God of the whole universe holding me tenderly like a mother holds an infant on her shoulder, and just as tenderly comforting me in love, calming my fears, and quieting my cries with a lullaby of joy.

"He will take great delight in you... he will rejoice over you with singing..." Can't you just imagine God holding you close and singing tenderly, *"Hush-a-bye, don't you cry; go to sleep my little darling...?"*

I love that verse; I love that image.

It turns out, Zephaniah 3 isn't about a mother and her infant; as we saw in Chapter 1, Zephaniah 3 is actually about a Mighty Warrior singing a song of victory! But while I imagined that particular verse in Zephaniah wrong, my image of a mother delighting over her child is thoroughly biblical. A more appropriate home base for that image would be something like Isaiah 46.

> "Listen to me, O house of Jacob,
> all the remnant of the house of Israel,

> who have been borne by me from before your birth,
>   carried from the womb;
> even to your old age I am he,
>   and to gray hairs I will carry you.
> I have made, and I will bear;
>   I will carry and will save."

Isaiah 46:3-4, ESV

God's words in Isaiah 43 push my image of a mother singing over a small infant back a few months... This is a mother, so full of joy, she sings over the baby in her womb! (Think of Mary, singing the Magnificat, while pregnant with Jesus.)

If it seems a little odd to use *in utero* imagery for grown adults, consider how the Almighty God take pains to make sure you know, this means you! "Even to your old age, I am he; and to gray hairs, I will carry you."

It doesn't matter how long ago you were born, your relationship with the God who delights in you is somehow mysteriously like the baby carried in the womb of a tender mother. "I have made, and I will bear; I will carry and will save." The focus is on God's heart and God's action, while the child passively receives.

I know my mom sang tender lullabies over me even before I was born. And I know that I don't know what it is like to be a mom or to carry an infant to term. I know not every mother has a great experience with pregnancy.

(I know one mom who couldn't shake the comparison to the movie *Aliens* the entire time she was pregnant: *there's this strange creature inside of me, and it's not me, and it is feeding on me, and I can't wait to get it out of me!!* That's not the best experience of pregnancy...)

In spite of the fact that not every woman enjoys carrying a child, and some pregnancies are really difficult, and some women never experience a desire to have a child, and some women who desperately long for motherhood struggle with complications—in spite of all of the ways our fallen and broken experience has from the beginning of sin's influence turned the *gift* of childbearing into a curse, for many moms **an experience**

of delight still belongs to the process of carrying a child.

I can't know that experience firsthand, but I have heard stories from my mother and sister and other friends. I have watched my wife—struggle, yes—but also *take great joy* in carrying the life that we created together in love. I've only experienced putting my hand on the outside of her belly to feel the baby kick—and believe me, I know at some point every mom gets tired of experiencing the kicking from the inside!—but I have been there when Miriam said, "Honey! Come quick! She's moving again! Can you feel that?"

I've seen my wife place a hand on her growing belly and stare into the middle distance with a smile on her face, lost in awe. (And I've also heard her cry and yell and call me all kinds of rotten names for doing something this terrible to her, again…)

So whether your experience of pregnancy is firsthand or secondhand or only from afar, whether your thoughts of pregnancy are full of joy or grief or pain, whatever complicates your own history with those wonderful and awful and terrifying and hormone-ridden months of growing another human being inside your body, I hope you know someone who at some point loved being pregnant and sang over the baby in their womb.

Because that's what God thinks of you.

The tender love and delight that only a mother carrying a baby can know is central to what God thinks about you and how you experience God.

In fact, that **tender love and delight is central to *who God is*.**

I know we typically call God, "Father." Indeed, both Old and New Testaments use "Father" and "King" as two of the most central ways for thinking about and talking about God. But the kind of tender love exhibited by a mother for her unborn child is not merely a side metaphor for God's love: tender love is a central aspect of God's nature.

At least, I am extremely suspicious that the Scriptures want us to consider that tender love of a pregnant mother as one of God's most central identity markers, a key to God's character and personality. The more I learn about *delight*, the more *tender love* and *compassion* make sense for the Almighty God.

A Mother's Tender Delight

I am suggesting that this delight of a mother carrying her child is *central to who God actually is*. I make this tentative suggestion not based only on Isaiah 46 or other mother metaphors for God in the Bible (there are a few, though Father and King are by far the more prominent), but also in light of one of the Hebrew words for God's mercy or compassion, and more specifically, where that vocabulary shows up in the story.

Moses, for example, in his farewell sermon to the people of Israel as they prepare to enter the Promised Land, contrasts God's wrath against sin with God's more characteristic attitude of grace:

> None of the devoted things shall stick to your hand,
> that the LORD may turn from the fierceness of his anger
>   and show you **mercy** and have **compassion** on you
>   and multiply you, as he swore to your fathers.
>
> *Deuteronomy 13:17*, ESV

David, at a key point in the story—in confession after his sin with Bathsheba comes to light—appeals to God's own nature:

> Have mercy on me, O God,
>   according to your unfailing love;
>   according to **your great compassion**
> blot out my transgressions.
>
> *Psalm 51:1*, NIV

The prophet Jeremiah, in the midst of his deep grief over fallen Jerusalem, still clings to the defining characteristic of Yahweh:

> The steadfast love of the LORD never ceases;
>   **his mercies** never come to an end;
>   they are new every morning;
> great is your faithfulness.
>
> *Lamentations 3:22–23*, ESV

After Ezra reads the Book of the Law to the people returned from Exile, Nehemiah leads the people in a lengthy prayer of confession and dependence on God for restoration. Nehemiah's prayer comes back again and again to the fundamental identity marker of who God is in relationship to God's sinful people:

> Because of **your great compassion**
> you did not abandon them in the wilderness…
>
> But when they were oppressed they cried out to you.
> From heaven you heard them, and in **your great compassion** you gave them deliverers…
>
> And when they cried out to you again,
> you heard from heaven, and in **your compassion** you delivered them time after time…
>
> But in **your great mercy**
> you did not put an end to them or abandon them,
> for you are a gracious and **merciful** God.
>
> *Nehemiah 9:19, 27–28, 31*, NIV

Each of these verses, taken from different key moments in the story of God's people—from entering the Promised Land, to the reign of King David, to the fall of Jerusalem, to the Return from Exile—all of these key moments refer to God's *compassion* and *mercy* as a central characteristic of who God is, an identity marker that is true even when God's people are false. When God has compassion or mercy, God is simply being true to who God *actually is*.

And in each and every one of these verses, **the Hebrew words translated as "mercy" or "compassion" are all directly related to the Hebrew word for "*womb*."**

God's character as Father is central to the way Scripture tells the story of salvation; and one central characteristic of this Almighty Father is the tender compassion God consistently shows to sinful people—the tender compassion most clearly understood as **the loving heart a mother has for the child in her womb.**

"Listen to me," God says to you again today, "you who have been borne by me from before your birth, *carried from the womb*; even to your old age I am the One..."

"I am the One who has loved you from your conception, carried you when you were unable to carry yourself. I am the One who all this time has provided for you, the One who freely gives of Myself for you.

"I am closer to you than you can imagine; I support you and surround you in ways beyond your understanding. You bring me joy you cannot yet begin to comprehend. And I give you life, every single day.

"Growing up and growing old can't change this intimate connection we share. To gray hairs I will carry you. I have made, and I will bear; I will carry and will save.

"It doesn't matter how old you are, you are still my baby; still carried by me; still dependent on me for everything you need, even when you don't know it.

"And I love it that way. You are mine and I delight in you. I will protect you and carry you and provide for you until I can welcome you finally into a face-to-face relationship, and introduce you to the rest of the family!

"Hush-a-bye, don't you cry; go to sleep my little baby..."

This tender compassion of a mother for the child in her own body is a central feature of God's character, a central feature of God's relationship with you. No matter how old or experienced you are, no matter how gray (or how absent) the hair on your head is, being **tenderly carried by God the way a mother carries her unborn child** is one of the most central and important ways the inspired Scriptures want you to experience your relationship with God.

You are not in control; in fact, there is more going on around you than you are even capable of comprehending. You are completely dependent on Someone Else for everything you need, even in ways you cannot articulate or understand.

That complete dependence is good news, because the Someone Else you are completely dependent on loves you, delights in you, rejoices over you. *Tender compassion* is central to your relationship. And your growth brings joy, even though you won't outgrow dependence until you enter a whole different experience of life. **You are still being carried, and that is both a relief and a delight**.

I don't know that Jesus had Isaiah 46 specifically in mind, but **childlike dependence** seems to be central to his teaching on what it means to be part of God's Kingdom. You know verses like, "Let the little children come to me, and do not hinder them, for the kingdom of God belongs to such as these" (*Luke 18:16*, NIV). But do you remember the context?

> People were also bringing **babies** [*brephos*] to Jesus
>   for him to place his hands on them.
>   *Luke 18:15*, NIV

Jesus is referring to babies when he talks about the kind of little children that are able to enter the Kingdom. These are infants, *who have to be carried by mom* if they are going to get there at all.

In fact, the Greek word for "babies" in Luke 18:15 (*brephos*; "People were also bringing babies to Jesus…") can mean a newborn infant, but the word just as likely refers to an embryo in the womb.

John the Baptist was a *brephos* in Elizabeth's womb when he leapt for joy at Mary's greeting (*Luke 1:41*); while Jesus was also a *brephos* when he was wrapped in cloths the night he was born and laid in a manger (*Luke 2:16*).

So *brephos* refers to *babies*, whether in utero or newborn; babies that must be carried, that must be given everything they need, babies that cannot do anything on their own or for themselves. And, according to Jesus, if you can't receive the Kingdom like a *brephos*, you can't get in at all (*Luke 18:18*).

Although there are plenty of times we get to be actively engaged in this discipleship journey and plenty of ways the Bible has for talking about the delight of actively developing our faith, there is a fundamental sense in which we are always and only the tiny child, in utero, who relies and depends on her mother's care in ways she is not even able to understand. Perhaps all of our growth in discipleship is simply coming to a clearer and clearer understanding of **our desperate dependence on Jesus for absolutely everything.**

That dependence on Jesus is a great gift.

That dependence is not intended as a burden, but as a joy.

The mother delights in her unborn child; the child kicks and jumps in the womb to hear her mother's voice; the two of them connected in intimate, personal, and mutual ways, marked by tender compassion and delight, and extremely difficult to capture in words.

That image of a child (*brephos*) completely dependent on her mother's compassion captures an essential element of your relationship with God. It's not the only essential element, but you need this image of delight to understand just how tenderly God takes care of you, provides for you, and carries you, even to your old age and tired faith and weary prayers.

Rest in that promise of being carried. Revel in your dependence. Rejoice in God's tender delight.

The Song Of The Mighty Warrior

The Scriptures provide us with a variety of images and concepts to help us get our heads around who God is and what God's delight means in our lives. God is both King and Father; and the tender compassion of a mother for her unborn child is also a central feature of God's character.

Going back to Zephaniah 3, it's easy to imagine this verse as a beautiful description of a mother with her baby: The LORD "will rejoice over you with gladness; he will quiet you by his love; he will exult over you with loud singing" (*Zephaniah 3:17*, ESV).

Remember, I told you that's how I always imagined it.

What changed for me? Well, I actually *read* Zephaniah 3 a little more closely in context. It's amazing how going back to a verse you think you know can open up all kinds of things you never imagined! (I think the joy of reading Scripture closely, in context, is related to what the Psalmist calls the "Delicious Delight" of meditating or chewing on God's Word.)

If we go back to this awesome verse *in its context*, we find not a mother singing over her infant, but a Father, King, and Mighty Warrior who rescues a beloved child and rejoices over her with singing. Let's take a closer look at this image of God's powerful song of joy in light of what leads up to it (a little more context…).

The book of Zephaniah is three short chapters you can read in one sitting. The book opens by giving us an idea *when* we are in the history of God's people: Zephaniah is writing during the reign of King Josiah, one of the few shining lights in the dark decline of the line of David. Josiah actually found a copy of the Scriptures during a Temple renovation project—it seems they had misplaced their only copies of the Bible(!)—and, reading God's Word for the first time in recent memory, King Josiah decided they might want to rethink their relationship with the God of Covenant and all the other gods of the nations around them.

While Josiah's reforms did some real good, they were too little, too late to prevent the nation from being carted off into Babylonian exile. God's people had utterly turned their backs on the God of Salvation. You can hear the pending doom drawing nearer in the first chapter of Zephaniah: judgment is ready to fall on God's people because they have turned away from worshiping the true God and gone after gods like Molech (the god you sacrifice your children to) and Baal (the god you typically worship through prostitution).

So, yeah; things weren't great. And like at the time of Noah, when the inclination of every heart was all evil, all the time, the devastating judgment of God is about to wipe out people who know they are sinning and refuse to repent.

Zephaniah Chapter 2 widens the scope to the sins of the surrounding nations, and their judgment as well. Then Chapter 3, the last chapter of Zephaniah, begins by returning to the way perversity has permeated the people of God: the leaders are like lions devouring their victims; the judges are like ravenous wolves feeding on the helpless; the prophets take bribes and tell lies; the priests are defiling the Temple.

Oof. All evil, all the time.

God laments the coming destruction and wonders aloud why these beloved people just won't listen or come back. God is trying to get their attention, because time is running out; and these people set their alarm clocks early so they can get a head start on the evil they have planned for the day.

Up to this point, the book of Zephaniah is pretty bleak. Intentional, relentless sinfulness, terrible judgment about to fall, and callous hearts that refuse to repent—not a happy combination for anyone involved (including God!).

Then, midway through the last chapter, the fire of judgment transforms into a fire of purification. Wonder of wonders, even the enemy nations are purified, and even foreign people abandon their foreign gods for a relationship with the one, true God. The haughty and stubbornly rebellious are removed, the exiles are brought home, and God's relationship with these people is restored. Judgment follows persistent rebellion; but *mercy* supersedes judgment.

That's the context of Zephaniah 3:14-17. The prophet is looking ahead, to a time of restoration when he exclaims:

> Sing, Daughter Zion;
>   shout aloud, Israel!
> **Be glad** and **rejoice** with all your heart,
>   Daughter Jerusalem!
> The LORD has taken away your punishment,
>   he has turned back your enemy.
> The LORD, the King of Israel, is with you;
>   never again will you fear any harm.
>
> *Zephaniah 3:14-15*, NIV

The people who had come under God's comprehensive judgment because of their comprehensive sin are now called *daughter*, a beloved part of the family! ("Zion," "Israel," and "Jerusalem" are all different ways to refer to the same people.)

God's people are pictured as a little girl, the daughter of the King (so I guess that makes her a princess...?). Daughter Zion was threatened on all sides by her enemies; she was captive, a prisoner. But her grief and fear have been turned into the jump-up-and-spin-around-and-start-singing-and-shouting variety of physical and emotional response we have called Joyful Delight.

The promise continues:

> On that day they will say to Jerusalem,
> "Do not fear, Zion;
>   do not let your hands hang limp.
> The LORD your God is with you,
>   the Mighty Warrior who saves.
> He will **take great delight** in you;
>   in his love he will no longer rebuke you,
>   but will **rejoice over you with singing**."
>
> *Zephaniah 3:16-17*, NIV

This is not the tender lullaby of a pregnant mother singing over the child in her womb; this is the boisterous battle song of a victorious champion! We get to see that moment when, still hot from battle, the Mighty Warrior finds his darling daughter through the fray. He rushes to her, picks her up in his arms, and twirls her around in her joy.

The battle took its toll; the Might Warrior is bruised and bloodied. He bears wounds in his hands and side. But the joy! The joy of being reunited with his darling makes it all worthwhile! The enemies have been defeated; the danger and the fear have fled. Now, finally, the embattled Warrior surrounds his daughter with loving arms. His delight overflows, until her song of joy is drowned out by the victorious hymn of the King!

Hold onto that image just a little longer. Watch the little girl weep in relief as she clings to his neck. See the upturned face of the King, beaming in delight. Notice the sweat and the blood from his forehead mingle with tears of joy, a ridiculous but contagious smile shining through his beard as he sings. Witness her hair pouring down over the armor on his shoulder; watch the sword of victory clatter to the ground as he tightens his embrace, for the battle is over. The victory is won.

The Father's longing—the long, painful longing—has finally passed. His daughter's fear has been replaced with joy.

She is no longer vulnerable, no longer captive, no longer afraid. And the King sings—oh, how he sings!—to have his darling in his arms again.

The Joy Of Being Rescued

In order to rescue his little girl, the Mighty Warrior has to defeat her enemies. In Zephaniah 3, those enemies seem to have two distinct origins. Some of the enemies are identified simply by the results of their actions: fear. These enemies cause hands to hang limp and hearts to tremble. They are external forces that lead to terror. Some of the enemies the Warrior King overcomes are the kinds of things that make you afraid.

But there is another enemy present in the promise. Maybe the context of the book of Zephaniah makes it a little more obvious, but some of the enemies in Zephaniah 3 appear to be internal, even well deserved: "The LORD has taken away *your punishment… in his love, he will no longer rebuke you…*"

Constant and persistent sin had turned God's people into God's enemies. They ignored God, denied God, doubted God, and mocked God. They gave up on God's promises and traded in their identity as God's chosen people. The first three-and-a-half chapters of Zephaniah make clear in no uncertain terms that the sinful rejection of God by these beloved people has started a blood feud; these people have made themselves God's archnemesis.

Then here, at the end of the book, when all hope seems lost, a great reversal takes place. The very sin that made me God's enemy, the very punishment I justly deserved, the rebuke that should rightly fall on my head gets turned into the real enemy. Although it was my sin, my own sin, my own most grievous sin that broke my relationship with God, that same sin gets cast as a captor. I am the beloved daughter, bound by a force too powerful for me to defeat. I have come under the ownership of the enemy. **And my dad is going to do something about it!**

Let that sink in for a moment. Your failure to love God or to love your neighbor, your failure to trust or believe, your willing rebellion and your eager unfaith—even when it was all your fault—*your own sin* is an enemy God is determined to defeat.

Even when that little girl was powerless against her enemies, even when she had given up hope in her exhaustion, even if she had cried herself to sleep cursing the Father who never seemed to come to the rescue—none of that could hinder the Mighty Warrior from coming to save.

Being sinful is no excuse for sin; there are plenty of passages that clearly show how my sin makes me an enemy of God. Yet there are also passages that see my sin as something distinct from *who I actually am* in Christ. My sin, even when it is my fault, can also be viewed as a captor, a kidnapper, an enemy. Knowing—and hating—my own propensity for weak faith and self-indulgent behavior, I can say with Paul:

> Although I want to do good,
>   evil is right there with me.
> For in my inner being I **delight** in God's law;
>   but I see another law at work in me,
>   **waging war** against the law of my mind
>   and making me **a prisoner** of the law of sin
>   at work within me.
> What a wretched man I am!
> Who will **rescue me** from this body
>   that is subject to death?
> Thanks be to God, who **delivers me**
>   through Jesus Christ our Lord!
>
> *Romans 7:21-25,* NIV

The sin for which I am personally responsible is also something I experience as an enemy; an enemy that God, my Warrior King, has promised to defeat.

The blood guilt that caused a blood feud will take a blood price to be removed, but the Mighty Warrior enters the fray, fully knowing the cost. And the result of the final battle is this: the enemies are scattered, the captives are set free, the King has his daughter back in his arms, and their mutual delight in loving and being loved overflows in a song of joyful reunion.

Already now, that's true for you. Already now, the death of Jesus on the cross has ended your blood feud with God. Already now, the resurrection of Jesus from the dead means sin and death have no final say over you. Your doubt, your sin, your rebellion, your faithlessness are all real enemies—*but they don't stand a chance* against the relentless pursuit of the Warrior King who was once crowned in thorns. Your sins are forgiven; your blood guilt paid for; your unfaith redeemed; your bitter tears of anger and doubt and shame have been wiped away.

Already now, you are forgiven. Already now, you have been brought home. Already now, your Father, the King, rejoices over you with singing.

Eternal Songs Of Eternal Belonging

Already now, and yet… now is not as good as it's going to get. Like so many images and promises from the Old Testament, Jesus *fulfills* the words of Zephaniah 3 in his life, ministry, death, resurrection, ascension, and sending of the Spirit. But Jesus won't *consummate*, bring to full completion, any of the Old Testament promises in any final or ultimate sense until he comes again in glory, the dead are raised, and God's will is done on earth as it is in heaven.

Already… and not yet.

I know our God has *not yet* had the full and complete victory promised in Zephaniah 3 for a couple of reasons. First, there are still things that make me afraid.

Aren't there still things that make you afraid? If you pick up the weekly prayer list at any local congregation on any given Sunday, you will find real and legitimate reasons to fear. A diagnosis that is still a question mark can bring real fear. The return of a cancer you thought was in remission can bring real fear. The prospect of losing your job and not finding another for months or years at a time legitimately brings fear for the whole family. Friends and loved ones serving in the military overseas during times of international uncertainty, projected paths of hurricanes or wildfires, news of another school shooting, the ongoing rise of an opioid epidemic, the threat of a recurring pandemic—just praying for people at your church or in your community can make your hands limp, your knees tremble, your heart melt.

Add to that prayer list your own fears, real or imagined: the dread that comes from expecting to hear at any moment, "It's terminal." "We're downsizing." "I want a divorce."

Zephaniah 3 can't have come completely true yet: the enemies that cause fear still circle around the gate. They act as if they have never heard of Zephaniah, and they certainly don't expect a Warrior King anytime soon. Illness, addiction, brokenness, loss—they all still have power over me, power to cause fear.

And if I'm honest, my own sin contributes to that brokenness; that fear. That's the other reason I know Jesus can't be done fulfilling Zephaniah 3: my own sin is one of my worst enemies, and that enemy still has power in my life. It's still so easy for me to doubt, so easy for me to think trusting is foolish, so easy to focus on my own will, my own ways, my own advantage, my own fear.

By faith, I am already the little girl in the arms of her victorious Rescuer; but by sight, day in and day out, I am surrounded by a world of fear and the reality of my own sin.

It's not always going to be like that.

As much comfort and joy as the promise brings, already now, **it gets even better**. Delight can be elusive while we wait, but **delight is the status quo of the reality for which we wait**. Already now, you have a foretaste of the feast to come; but the actual feast, *the feast to come*, will be consistent with the appetizers, and yet far exceed them.

Zephaniah 3 is already true because of Jesus; and Zephaniah 3 will be *even more true* when Jesus comes again.

Already now, you have your Mighty Warrior by faith; *on that day*, you will have your Mighty Warrior by sight.

Already now, even your sins can't keep you from his arms; *on that day*, you will be done with sin once and for all.

Already now, you have hope and courage in the face of fear; *on that day*, fear will be a thing of the past. *On that day…*

> *On that day* they will say to Jerusalem,
> "Do not fear, Zion;
>   do not let your hands hang limp.
> The LORD your God is with you,
>   the Mighty Warrior who saves.
> He will **take great delight** in you;
>   in his love he will no longer rebuke you,
>   but will **rejoice over you with singing**."
>
> *Zephaniah 3:16–17*, NIV

On that day, breath will fill your resurrection lungs, and you will join in New Creation shouts of praise in the very presence of your Mighty Warrior and King.

On that day, the Father's longing—the long, painful longing—will finally have passed. Your fear will be replaced with joy. You will no longer be vulnerable, no longer be captive, no longer be afraid. And the King will sing—oh, how he'll sing!—to have his darling back in his arms again.

On that day, **the only thing louder than the songs of saints and angels will be the song that rises from the throne itself,** as the Mighty Warrior sings for joy because you are home, home at last; home forever.

To know that Song, and to receive that Song, to have that Song sung over you means you have a place in the eternal family: you are loved; you are special; you belong.

That's the Eternal Song of Belonging Jesus is singing over you even now. You can hear it, even now, with the ears of faith.

But nothing you have now by faith will compare with the delight and the intimacy and the joy that will be yours when that faith is fulfilled, when the promise comes completely true, and Jesus sings you that Song of Eternal Belonging face to face.

For now, you still get to hum along.

For now, you can trust a Mighty Warrior is rejoicing over you with singing.

For now, you can rest in your dependence on Jesus, who

not only lays his hand of blessing on the little ones, but takes defenseless, dependent babies in his arms.

Already now, you are carried by Jesus.

And already now, that makes Jesus sing for joy.

GROUP DISCUSSION FOR CHAPTER 7

He Will Rejoice Over You With Singing

Pick one or two of the following questions to help you get to know a friend, family member, or small group better.

1. Talk about some ways you connected with your parents or grandparents. Did you have a special song for bed, or time spent reading or praying together?

2. Describe a tradition that might look odd from the outside but helps make your family unique.

3. How do you let new people know they belong to your family?

4. Invite any mothers in your group to share what they remember about carrying a baby. Every woman's experience is different, so there is no standard or judgment here. Just share something that helps others get a glimpse of what it was like.

Go a little deeper with someone you trust to point you back to Jesus. You don't have to reflect on all of the following, but spend some time on the ones that catch your spiritual attention.

1. How does a mother's experience relate to what God thinks about you? Come up with three promises from Jesus you are invited to trust based on that image.

2. In the scene of a warrior king rescuing his little girl, what resonates most for you? How do you see God differently through that lens?

3. Zephaniah 3 talks about God removing your punishment and rebuke, defeating your enemies, and removing your fear. What are some things that bring fear to your week? What might be some things that deserve God's rebuke in your week? Name some of the enemies that make you long for God's rescue.

4. If Jesus had three sticky notes on his desk that listed ways you make him sing for joy, what might those reminders say?

   Write one thing God loves about you down on a sticky note and put it in a place that will remind you how God delights in you. When you see that sticky note, take a moment to receive his delight and to rejoice in his rejoicing over you.

A Prayer For Delight

Come, Holy Spirit, draw me close to your heart.
Surround me with your love. Wrap me in
the strong embrace of your delight.

Hold me close, Jesus, and cause me to depend
on you. Comfort me in my anxiety and grief.
Protect me from dangers, known and unknown.
Provide for all I need or desire, and teach me to
desire you most of all.

As a warrior king rejoices over the daughter he
has rescued, hold me, Heavenly Father, in your
strong hands; let me experience your delight.
Since you are the King who takes away my
punishment, since you are the Mighty Warrior
who conquers my enemies, because you are the
God who saves, rejoice over me with
singing again today.

Let me know your love and your tender delight,
so I can rejoice in what you, my God,
have done for me.

Amen.

CHAPTER 8

I Am My Beloved's And My Beloved Is Mine

Reading Plan

Day 1

My Beautiful Wife

&

What's a Love Poem Doing In My Bible??

Day 2

The Bride: "I Am My Beloved's and My Beloved is Mine."

Day 3

The Groom: "There is No Flaw in You."

Day 4

The Confidence of the Bride

&

The Friends: "We Will Seek Him With You."

Day 5

The Bride, Already and Not Yet

&

Being Church

Day 6

Group Discussion

My Beautiful Wife

I don't think I'll ever forget the look on Miriam's face as she appeared from behind the massive pipe organ at the Chapel of the Holy Trinity on the campus of Concordia University, Ann Arbor. She was arm in arm with her father, a rather composed and dignified man in a conductor's tux, who was trying hard to keep it together as he escorted his baby girl down the aisle.

I even have a photograph to help me remember the event: Miriam, in her beautiful wedding dress with her hair piled up high—Miriam looked like a kid in a candy shop!

Miriam's eyes were open almost impossibly wide as she scanned the crowd. Her calla lily bouquet in one hand and her father's arm in the other, she rounded the corner to come down the aisle and saw her sister and my sister and select family and friends in rich, deep green dresses and black tuxedos standing in attendance on the slate tile stairs at the front of the sanctuary.

And there, surrounded by flowers and stained glass, she also saw her groom (me!) looking back up the aisle at her, waiting for her to walk down to the altar to make and receive promises, vows of love and commitment.

I don't think I'll ever forget the look on Miriam's face. Her countenance was a reflection of joy, wonder, and absolute delight.

I don't know what my face looked like just then—the camera man was rather busy with something else—but I do have a picture on my mantle of a moment from later in the worship service.

Miriam and I are facing each other. We are holding hands and I was just speaking tender words of promise to her as her groom, and she was just speaking tender words of promise to me as my bride. And I look…

Well, first of all, I look skinny.

I look awfully young.

I happened to be teaching at a private high school at the time, and the rules governing faculty facial hair back then (!) meant I was only allowed a mustache and not the goatee.

My hair was the floppy curl I wore back in college, and to my eyes now I look like I was about twelve.

But besides all that, I also looked absolutely in love, just head over heels; a little puppy dog with big, bright eyes and a black, swishy tail.

I can't tell you that every moment since has been just like that. You and I both know that, because we are in a fallen and sinful world, all of our relationships—our marriages included—all of our relationships are dysfunctional to one extent or another; some more, some less.

And whether you have ever been married, or never been married, or your marriage was a roller coaster, or a train wreck, or a celebration, or some combination of all of those, I want you to know that you don't have to carry your personal baggage with you into this chapter on delight. And I don't have to carry mine.

So you have permission not to have to think about your marriage (or your baggage) as you go through this chapter. This image of a bride walking down the aisle to meet her groom still holds something important for your life of faith. That moment of joy and intimacy and promise and anticipation and, yes, *delight* wrapped up with the best experiences of being bride and groom, husband and wife—all the best of who we are and what we experience is a window into God's heart for us.

Depending on the week you are having, it might be hard to relate to that image. You can come back to this chapter later if the topic is a little too sensitive right now.

But I want you to know that the brokenness of your experience does not, cannot diminish **what this image of mutual delight means for you in your relationship with a God who is unashamedly head over heels in love with you**.

So read on!

Your complicated experience with human relationships notwithstanding, the promise embedded in the image of bridegroom and bride is staggering.

And the *delight* is almost too much to take in.

What's A Love Poem Doing In My Bible?

Song of Solomon, that intimate love ballad of the Old Testament, seems almost out of place in a collection of holy writings. If you picked up this graphic expression of desire as a paperback, it would probably have an NC-17 rating and some partially exposed pomegranates on the cover.

In fact, tradition suggests that at one point this Song of Songs had an NC-30 rating: good Jews weren't supposed to read this part of the Bible until they were 30 years old. The logic for this prohibition seems to be expressed in the last chapter of book itself: "Don't excite love, don't stir it up, until the time is ripe..." (*Song 8:4*, MSG).

Nonetheless, this steamy love poem is a part of the library we call Scripture; not in the teen readers' section, for sure, but still part of the collection. So is there anything that this book can tell us about our relationship with God in Jesus Christ?

For some faithful readers throughout history, wanting Song of Solomon to say something about Jesus has led them to think it can't be saying anything about intimate, sensual love and desire. Faced with a text that clearly does touch on all of those themes, they have to say the author must actually *mean* something else. (This is where biblical interpretation can get a bit bizarre; but any time you try to make the author *not mean* what the text is obviously saying, you are going to get all kinds of strange results.)

Song of Solomon is certainly not *not* about intimate, sensual love and desire. On the other hand, this love ballad *is actually in your Bible*; so perhaps the Song is not *only* about intimate, sensual love and desire. In fact, the intimacy of the marriage relationship is used throughout Scripture as an image for the mutual relationship between God and God's people.

God seems to view the Covenant at Sinai as if the Almighty were the groom, speaking intimate words of love and promise, and Israel were the bride, speaking those tender words right back (*Hosea 2:14–23*). The prophets view idolatry not just as the breaking of a set of rules, but as the willing betrayal of a marriage relationship, the spiritual equivalent of going behind your spouse's back to spend quality time with the local prostitutes (*Exodus 34:15–16; Leviticus 17:7; Hosea 1:2; 2:1–13; 3:1*). "I, the LORD your God am a jealous God," (*Exodus 20:5; 34:14*) doesn't paint God as petty or emotional; it frames the bond between God and God's people as a committed, intimate, dare we say monogamous relationship.

The New Testament follows suit. Of course, Jesus tells parables of the Kingdom as a wedding banquet (see *Matthew 22:1–14; 25:1–13; Luke 14:7–24*), but even more specifically, John the Baptist refers to himself as the Best Man and Jesus as the Groom (*John 3:29–30*). Paul talks about the Church as the Bride of Christ, and in a section Paul himself admits is a little confusing, Paul talks about the relationship of husband and wife as an image of the relationship of Christ and the Church (*Ephesians 5:21–33*). In the closing chapters of the whole Bible, John describes the kicking off of an eternal party known as the "wedding feast of the Lamb" and God's people as a radiant Bride (*Revelation 19:7–9; 21:2, 9*).

Suddenly it doesn't seem so strange to think Song of Solomon has a place in the Canon of Scripture. That image of bridegroom and bride, of husband and wife loving and being loved, is all about an intimate, mutual, joyful, exclusive relationship of longing and delight. Read in that light, this Song of Songs is an amazing expression of God's intimate love for us and an invitation into an intimate, tender, passionate relationship with God.

Don't push that image too far; but do push it far enough. The Spirit intends for you to experience and understand God's love for you—and your love for God—through the lens of the intimate, mutual, playful, intense, passionate, exciting love relationship between an adoring bride and her adoring groom.

We experience that love relationship with God *together*: together as the Church, we are the Bride of Christ. That sense of community and corporate identity is an important part of biblical bridal imagery. And we also experience that love relationship with God as unique individuals: the personal character of this intimate image invites us all to receive this promise *personally*.

On the one hand, the Scriptures paint a picture of *communal* salvation in a way that may be surprising to people in our individualistic society; on the other hand, those same Scriptures paint a picture of salvation that is *personal, intimate,* and *individual* in a way that may have been surprising to people in the community-based society of the time.

When Yahweh declares, "As a shepherd **seeks out his flock** when he is among his sheep that have been scattered, so will I seek out my sheep, and I will rescue them," (see *Ezekiel 34:11–16*) the image is *communal*: the flock is rescued *as a flock*.

Jesus echoes that image when he talks about being the Good Shepherd: the sheep all together listen and follow and are brought in. There is "**one flock**, one shepherd" (see John 10). In both Old and New Testaments, we are loved and saved as a community and *into* a community.

At the same time, when King David expresses God's personal relationship to him as a person, the former sheep herder uses startlingly individualistic language: "The LORD is **my** shepherd, **I** shall not want; He leads **me**, restores **me**, comforts **me**."

In a time and culture where your identity was fundamentally tied to your community, the fact that the entire 23rd Psalm is written in the first-person singular is astounding!

Jesus picks up on that individual, personal aspect of salvation in the Parable of the Lost Sheep (sheep, singular and individual):

> If a man has a hundred sheep,
>> and one of them has gone astray,
>> does he not leave the ninety-nine on the mountains
>> and go **in search of the one** that went astray?
> And if he finds it, truly, I say to you, **he rejoices**—
>
> *Matthew 18:12-13*, ESV

[Another delight word! Rejoice, *chairo* (like "Cairo") is related to words we met back in chapter 1 on Joyful Delight: Joy, *chara* ("caress" with an "ah!") and Grace, *charis* ("caress" with an "iss!")]

> —he **rejoices** [*chairo*, Joyful Delight] over it more
>> than over the ninety-nine that never went astray.

So it is not the **will** [*thélēma*, Desirable Delight]
  of my Father who is in heaven
  that one of these little ones should perish.

Matthew 18:12–14, ESV

χαίρω (Chairo): to be glad, delight, rejoice (as a result of grace)

A single sheep is worth it. A single pearl can have immeasurable value. **Your personal God values you, personally.**

As an individual, you belong to the fellowship of believers, the whole Christian Church on earth, the Bride of Christ. And the Spirit also intends for you to experience and understand God's love for you as an individual—and your personal love for God—through the lens of the intimate, mutual, playful, intense, passionate, exciting love relationship between an adoring bride and her adoring groom.

You are saved **as an individual**, and you are saved **into a community**; grace upon grace, delight and even more delight. The Song of Solomon was written for you as an individual, and for us as the Church. We'll look at each of those in turn, but they are both true the whole time.

So as we raise a glass and the lights dim for dinner and the music starts to play, keep in mind that the guy in the tux leading you to the dance floor is head over heels in love with you as an individual; and, remember that all of us together as the Church belong to him, together and forever. Cheers!

The Bride:
"I Am My Beloved's And My Beloved Is Mine."

In Song of Solomon, chapter 6, the bride sums up her relationship with the groom:

> I am my beloved's
>   and my beloved is mine.

Song of Solomon 6:3, ESV

It sounds really cool in Hebrew. Next time you are whispering sweet nothings into your beloved's ear, try this one on for size: "Ah-KNEE leh dough-DEE, veh dough-DEE, LEE."

That's a sure winner every time.

אֲנִי לְדוֹדִי וְדוֹדִי לִי   anî le-dōdî, ve-dōdî lî

Seriously, though; if you repeat that phrase enough to get used to it, you begin to get a sense of the rhythm and flow of the Hebrew poetry. Shakespeare's iambic pentameter has nothing on the graceful, "ah-Knee leh dough-Dee, veh dough-Dee, Lee..."

OK. Trust me on this. The Hebrew poetry is beautifully rhythmic and balanced. And whether you can catch a glimpse of that beauty or not, even the English translation captures the balance and grace of the meaning: "I, my beloved's; and my beloved, mine."

That's what the bride says to the bridegroom in Song of Solomon: "I am my beloved's, and my beloved is mine!" That's a word of confidence. That's a word of surety. That's a word of joy and delight; a word spoken at the altar. *I am my beloved's, oh yes! And my beloved, he is mine!*

I know this to be true. I trust this must be true. I have seen this to be true: we belong to each other. I belong to him; and he belongs to me. *"Ah-Knee leh dough-Dee, veh dough-Dee, Lee!"*

Later in the Song, in chapter 7, the bride says the same thing even more strongly:

I am my beloved's,
and his desire is for me.

Song of Solomon 7:10, ESV

If you ever get to Song of Solomon, Chapter 7 in your Bible reading, this would be a good place to excuse the children for children's church…

But the point is this: the bride is so confident of the groom's love that she can even boast and brag about how much he desires her. And that confidence makes her desire him right back. They share a moment of mutual delight, where bride and groom unashamedly and unabashedly and unreservedly love and belong to each other.

That's the kind of confidence I think the Spirit of Jesus wants to invite you into today, a confidence that, no matter what else is going on in your life, you can say this one thing for sure and certain: "I am my Beloved's, and my Beloved is mine."

You belong to Jesus. You can have confidence in that. And, although we don't say it like that very often, there is a sense in which your Jesus belongs to you. It's not as if Jesus were your own personal possession and you can put him on a shelf and take him down occasionally to show off to your friends. (Any real love relationship isn't like that, either.) Rather, you belong to Jesus and Jesus belongs to you in a mutual relationship: the two of you just belong together.

Imagine what it would mean for you to say with confidence about Jesus: "I am my Beloved's, and my Beloved is mine!" Imagine the audacity of faith that would lead you to say, "I am my Beloved's and His desire is for me!" Yet that audacious statement is at the heart of the Gospel Promise. Jesus wants you to have the kind of confidence and faith in his love and commitment and compassion and delight that you would be able to boast in the Spirit: "Oh, yes, I am my Beloved's—I belong with Jesus. And Jesus—he loves me and delights in me and cherishes me. I know he belongs with me!"

What a beautiful moment of faith, to be convinced in your soul that the One you love most loves you most right back!

That beautiful moment can be as tender and as fleeting as promises of love spoken at the altar. Of course, Miriam doesn't walk around the house most days with that silly look of giddy love on her face. Of course, I look even less like Prince Charming than I did back then. But after 25 years, I still know that, even though I'm not perfect and she's not perfect, my favorite person in the whole world still thinks the world of me.

Usually. On most days.

It seems to me that the culture around us tends to hold up that fleeting feeling of head over heels love as the gold standard, the thing that is most important. And if you can't feel that with your spouse anymore, conventional wisdom seems to say it's OK to find it somewhere else.

That habit of chasing an emotional experience naturally leads you farther and farther away from any type of real relationship in which you could experience emotional connection fully and intimately, with the best kind of wonder and delight. **Chase the experience, and you end up without a relationship; chase the relationship, and the experience will follow**.

I think one of the temptations we face as followers of Jesus in our current cultural environment is to treat our relationship with Jesus that same way: to chase the experience. That fleeting moment of head over heels in love becomes the spiritual gold standard. Your emotions end up taking center stage, and if your worship service or your pastor or your denomination doesn't make you feel like you used to, it only makes sense to find that experience somewhere else.

One burden we put on ourselves is the *burden of expectation*. I expect following Jesus will feel the way everyone tells me it's supposed to feel: wonderful, and dramatic, and emotional, and sensational, and delightful *all the time*. When it doesn't work out like that in real life, I begin to doubt the authenticity of my experience. I begin to doubt the authenticity of my faith. I can even begin to doubt the authenticity of my God.

Just like the commercialization of romantic love can make Valentine's Day seem hollow, the commercialization of pious love can make Christian holidays feel forced or empty. Last

Christmas, a friend shared a Charlie Brown cartoon that expressed how he was feeling as the world around him says he should be having deep, meaningful, and emotional experiences of faith. Maybe you have seen the cartoon. Maybe you can relate.

Charlie Brown is leaning on a brick wall covered in snow. His head is propped in one hand and he's discussing life with Linus (who is wearing a green stocking cap, snuggling his ubiquitous blue blanket, and sucking his thumb). As large flakes gently drift down, Charlie Brown makes this lament: "I think there must be something wrong with me, Linus. Christmas is coming but I'm not happy. I don't feel the way I'm supposed to feel."

Wow. *"I don't feel the way I'm supposed to feel."* That says a lot, doesn't it? I think we can sometimes get caught up in the expectation of feeling a certain way when it comes to religion. And if Jesus feels distant, or the Spirit feels absent, or the Father feels disinterested, we pile guilt and shame on top of the loneliness and grief: "There must be something wrong with me… I don't feel the way I'm supposed to feel."

In this book on delight, in this chapter on intimate and passionate and almost giddy love, I want you to know that **the feeling of personal connection and spiritual joy is not the gold standard**. If your faith doesn't feel giddy right now, you aren't a failure. Jesus knows you and loves you and loves being with you even when you can't feel it, don't feel it, or don't even want to feel it.

The reality of Jesus' love for you is way bigger than what your emotions tell you about your faith. You can lay down the burden of expectation that comes with wanting to be a good Christian. You can just be who you are, because Jesus actually likes you— the real you—the complicated ball of emotions and expectations and needs and failure and joys and sorrows and desires and identity crises.

Jesus actually likes you, the real you; he's much less interested in the person you think you are supposed to be. I mean, you can talk to him about the person you think you are supposed to be; but Jesus thinks the person you are is way more interesting and delightful. **Jesus thinks you're awesome**.

You don't feel that right now? That's OK; it's still true. My wife doesn't have to be giddy in order to love me. I don't have to feel any certain way on any certain day to validate my love for her. Our relationship is not determined or grounded on the way we happen to feel at the moment.

And... if we *never felt anything*, wouldn't that also seem wrong? I don't judge my marriage by my feelings, but don't feelings of love and excitement and even giddy delight belong fundamentally to the intimacy of the marriage covenant?

If one of our temptations as followers of Jesus is to chase an emotional experience as a way of validating our faith, I think another temptation is to *avoid* all emotional experience, as if *not* having an experience were *a way of validating our faith*.

I've seen that; I've done that! I have sometimes thought (or acted like I thought) that *not* experiencing the grace of the Lord Jesus Christ, the love of God, or the fellowship of the Holy Spirit was a sign of strong faith.

After all, *feeling* like God's promises are true doesn't make them true: God's promises are true whether I feel like it or not! (So far so good.) Ergo, *not* feeling or experiencing God's promises must be true faith. (Now, wait a minute!)

That logic is good up to a certain point. I know my wife loves me, even when I don't feel like it, and even when *she* doesn't feel like it! That confidence is foundational to our relationship. I don't have to doubt every time one of us is less than giddy.

But push that too far and you end up in a relationship that only remembers love, and not in a love relationship. Emotions aren't a true litmus test for the relationship. But if I never feel like I love my wife? If she never feels a little head over heels still, once in a while, just a tiny bit? If our emotions—which can lie to us—never confirm the truth, wouldn't we want to work on that?

But not *work on the emotions* as if trying harder at feeling would bring authentic results. Rather, *work on the relationship*. **Chase the relationship and the experience will follow.**

I think following Jesus is like that.

I think it is good, meet, right, and salutary that you should at all times and in all places have the kind of confident faith that says, "I trust God's promises are true, even if I don't feel like it." And if you *never* feel like God's promises are true, Jesus wants you to long for something more.

Don't chase the emotions. Do chase the relationship.

And don't carry the burden of having to experience any particular emotion at any point on the journey. Are you grieving this Easter? Grieve. Jesus is with you. Are you sad this Christmas? Be sad. Jesus is with you. Jesus doesn't love some perfect and imaginary version of you that says and does and *feels* all the right things at all the right times. **Jesus love you**. **The real you**. The you that doesn't always live up to your own expectations of what faith is supposed to be like.

Don't give up on feeling deep and personal love in your faith walk. And *stop trying so hard* to have an experience of deep and personal love. Like all areas of discipleship, you can give your emotions (or lack of emotions) over to Jesus and let him deal with them. **You don't have to carry that burden**.

(Go ahead. Do that right now. It's not hard: "Dear Jesus, I give you my emotions. I don't trust them and I can't control them, but I trust your Spirit. Reign also in my feelings. Amen.)

I distinctly remember standing in a friend's kitchen and arguing about spiritual experience. I was in town for a conference, and three of us were talking about faith and experience and emotions and the Holy Spirit. I came down pretty hard on the "even if I don't experience it, I trust it is true" side of the equation, to the point of just about denying that I ever needed anything you could call a "spiritual experience" ever again. I don't think I was wrong exactly; but I don't think I understood delight. (OK; maybe I was wrong…)

I don't remember the details of the impassioned argument for or against emotional experience in the life of faith. What I do remember is worship at the conference gathering the next day.

While I was standing there with other worshipers, singing songs of praise and trust and confidence and joy, and going out of my way *not* to have a "spiritual experience," the Holy Spirit took me by the scruff of the neck and shook me, until I was weeping and laughing at the same time. Rarely have I felt such intimate connection or overwhelming delight in the presence of Jesus or the power of the Spirit.

My mind knew something to be true: my faith doesn't depend on my emotions. But my mind had forgotten something my heart learned again that day: my emotions are a part of my faith.

That palpable presence of the Spirit was a playful and joyful slap upside the head, a reminder that, while I can't dictate how I should experience Jesus, I can't keep him in a nice, tidy, sterile box, either. The irony of me—the one who had just passionately argued against needing an emotional experience—having such an *emotional experience* just added to the laughter and the delight. (I love that Jesus has a sense of humor.)

Let me say it again. **My faith doesn't depend on my emotions. And my emotions are part of my faith**.

That's why I want to explore this intimate delight a little more before we move on. I believe Jesus does love you intimately and personally and playfully. I believe it is good news that you don't have to manufacture an emotional response to that love.

What's more, I also believe that your emotional response is part of your relationship with Jesus. You don't have to feel giddy about it all the time; and more and more, as you get to know Jesus better and better, as the Spirit shapes and molds you, you just might have more of an emotional experience of your faith. In fact, I think you will *experience* the grace of Jesus and the love of God and fellowship of the Holy Spirit.

But don't chase the experience; chase the relationship.

The bride in Song of Solomon says with confidence, "I am my beloved's, and my beloved is mine." I want that confidence. And I want that confidence for you, too. To help us get there, let's look at what the groom says to the bride, and at some of the reasons we have trouble hearing that statement of delight from Jesus.

The Groom:
"There Is No Flaw In You."

At the beginning of Song of Solomon chapter 4, the groom says to the bride, "How beautiful you are, my darling! Oh, how beautiful!" (*Song 4:1*, NIV)

From there, he extols in graphic detail her eyes, her hair, her teeth, her lips, her temples, her neck… you get the idea. (The list could go on—and does!—but we're trying to keep it PG-13 around here.) After a wonderfully exhaustive inspection, the groom gives this verdict:

> You are altogether beautiful, my darling;
>   there is no flaw in you.
>
> *Song 4:7*, NIV

What a beautiful expression of delight! And that comprehensive delight gives me a window into what Jesus thinks about *me*, a single sheep worth saving, a pearl of immeasurable price!

I don't know about you, but when I imagine Jesus saying something to *me* personally like, "You are altogether beautiful, my darling; there is no flaw in you," I run into a problem. My immediate, knee-jerk response to that expression of divine delight is usually "Yeah, right!"

I mean, come on, Jesus! I know what my week has been like! I know the sin and the failure and the doubt and the shame that still cling to me. When I am not disappointed or disgusted with my own lack of faith or faithfulness, I am probably either ignoring it entirely or feeling kind of self-satisfied.

As David said, "I know my transgressions, and my sin is ever before me" (*Psalm 51:3*, ESV). As Isaiah pointed out, "All our righteous acts are like filthy rags" (*Isaiah 64:6*, NIV).

Jesus says he delights in me, but I know myself too well to think I'm beautiful.

It's funny, how your own self-evaluation affects how you receive love from other people. When my wife gets all gussied up for a night on the town, and her makeup is just right, and she's had her hair done, and she's wearing that new outfit because we're going on a date, and I say to her, "Girl, you look *good!*" she says with a smile and a wink, "Yeah; I know..."

When I tell her, "You are beautiful, my darling; you are altogether beautiful," and she *feels* beautiful, she can accept that compliment from me (and sometimes even return it!). But if it's been a long week and she hasn't showered in a couple of days and she's got on some grubby sweats and her hair is pulled back and she's wearing no makeup at all and I say, "Honey, you are *hot;*" she just rolls her eyes at me and goes back to folding laundry.

I think sometimes she thinks I'm just being a boy, and boys will say anything. (I mean, she's not wrong...) But I also think that she doesn't quite understand how she can be drop-dead gorgeous, even when she's wearing sweatpants and a sweatshirt and hasn't washed her hair in three days and isn't wearing any makeup. She just doesn't believe I can find her absolutely lovely. Sometimes she just doesn't get how beautiful she is, and how beautiful she is *to me.*

I wonder if that's what happens in my relationship with Jesus.

Jesus says, "You are altogether beautiful, my darling; there is no flaw in you," and it's natural for me to say, "Yeah, but I haven't washed my hair in three days and I'm wearing grubby sweatpants and I don't have on any makeup!"

I know the reality of my sin. I know my week and my weaknesses. I know I am anything but "altogether beautiful." There are days when I don't know why anyone would even *like* me, let alone want to be with me; there are days when I don't like being with me, myself.

I'm sure I could give you a hundred examples of times when I don't like being me, of times when my own sin makes me disgusted with myself. And maybe you could give me a hundred examples of the kinds of things that make you ashamed to be you. But here's one example—a rather safe but revealing example— an ordinary example from my ordinary life of the brokenness that infects my heart and my relationships.

I sat down with a dear friend of mine to have an important conversation about our direction and our future as a congregation.

I knew it was an important conversation and had the potential to be a difficult topic, so I told myself ahead of time that I wasn't going to respond in anger or frustration. I didn't want my personal feelings to leak out onto my friend, because I knew the situation could legitimately be seen from more than one perspective, and anyway, none of this was my friend's fault.

This is my good friend. None of this is his fault. I told myself I wasn't going to let my anger or frustration damage our relationship. But that's exactly what I did.

I told myself I wasn't going to do it before I did it; I knew what I was doing while I was doing it; and afterwards, I knew I shouldn't have done it.

I remember thinking, "Yeah; that wasn't great… Maybe I should apologize to him…" But then I just figured, the next time I saw him I would make sure it wasn't a big deal; I thought I'd just let it blow over. Truth is, I didn't really want to deal with it, because dealing with it meant admitting to myself (hard) and to Jesus (easy) and to my friend (hardest) that I am a stinking sinner. So I just ignored my actions and told myself I had every right to be a little testy.

That's the kind of stupidity and frailty and fear that drive me crazy! I walked right into a trap I set for myself. I hurt someone I care about. And then I convinced myself it wasn't really that bad.

And Jesus says, "You are altogether beautiful, my darling; there is no flaw in you." And I want to say, "Who are you looking at, Jesus?? Because I know it's not *me*."

In one sense, I am right. In one sense, I know (and you know) that even though we are redeemed, even though we are baptized, even though we are part of God's family, even though we are forgiven and covered and made holy—even though all of that is true of us, it's also true that, as long as we still live in this broken and sinful world, we bring our brokenness and sinfulness to this world, too.

In that very real sense, Isaiah 64 is true of you and me: even on our best days, even on our best behavior, even our most righteous acts are like filthy rags.

But that's not the whole story. That's not the only real

perspective. That's not the only truth true of you and me, even now.

Isaiah 64 may describe our present reality, but so does Isaiah 62. Do you remember Isaiah 62 from Chapter 5: Desirable Delight? Maybe you remember the Desirable Delight word we used was *chephets* (*che-* pronounced Kay: KAY-fets).

חֵפֶץ (Chephets): delight, pleasure, desire, longing

> You shall no more be termed Forsaken,
>   and your land shall no more be termed Desolate,
> but you shall be called **My Delight** [*chephets*] Is in Her,
>   and your land Married;
> for the LORD *delights* [*chephets*] in you,
>   and your land shall be married.
>
> *Isaiah 62:4*, ESV

Isaiah 62 is a promise already fulfilled in Jesus, and that promise is going to be fulfilled completely and without remainder when Jesus comes again. Already now, Isaiah 62 is true of you; and Isaiah 62 will be finally and ultimately true of you when Jesus returns in glory. Now, Isaiah 62 is yours by faith; then Isaiah 62 will be yours by sight.

Already now, God declares his *chephets* over you: you are a Desirable Delight that makes Jesus say, "Yes, please!" Already now, God declares divine sus over you (like "Dr. Seuss"): you are a Joyful Delight that makes Jesus go, "Woohoo!"

שׂוּשׂ (Sus): exult, rejoice, take delight in, make mirth, be glad

Just look at the next verse in Isaiah 62:

> As the bridegroom **rejoices** [*sus*] over the bride,
>   so shall your God **rejoice** [*sus*] over you.
>
> *Isaiah 62:5*, ESV

Isaiah is using the same wedding imagery we find in the Song of Songs: God's people receive a new name, "My Delight Is in Her." The Land of Promise is now a Land called "Married." The Almighty God finds you delightfully desirable and wants your present and your future the way a groom delights in and longs for his bride. The same rejoicing, mirth, celebration and delight that belong to a wedding feast define your relationship with Jesus. Jesus looks at you, jumps up, spins around, and sings his happy song!

Jesus is head over heels in love with you, and Jesus loves being in love with you; **your relationship with Jesus brings Jesus joy**.

The Confidence Of The Bride

When Jesus says to you, "You are altogether beautiful, my darling; there is no flaw in you," he actually means it. **What Jesus says, Jesus intends you to believe**.

Jesus expresses his love to you so you can receive his delight, and then return his delight. Jesus wants you to experience a relationship with him defined by a Spirit-led "Yes, please!" and punctuated by a Spirit-given "Woohoo!"

Of course, you aren't "altogether beautiful" in the same way you will be in the resurrection of the dead and the life of the world to come. Of course, you are not yet without flaw in the complete sense of the promise that will be yours on the Last Day. Of course, you are still a sinner, but that's not what Jesus is talking about right now!

Jesus wants you to know how completely, how thoroughly, how over the top wonderful he thinks you are. Jesus thinks you are awesome! Jesus absolutely loves being in a relationship with you! You bring Jesus joy!

And don't give me any, "I haven't washed my hair in three days and I'm only wearing grubby sweatpants" excuses. Your self-evaluation or the unrealistic standard you have in your mind does not get to overturn the verdict of Jesus' delight.

Of course you aren't perfect, *but that's not what we are talking about right now!!!*

Real contrition, real sorrow over your sin, real repentance and forgiveness all have a place in the life of faith. You need to know you are a sinner, and you need Jesus to deal with your sin. *And* you need to know that you are altogether beautiful, that you are a delight, that you are loved and cherished and celebrated like a bride on her wedding day.

You! You make Jesus smile and laugh and dance and sing for joy! You can have confidence in that promise, even when you feel less than beautiful.

The groom says: "You are altogether beautiful, my darling; there is no flaw in you!" And the bride says, "I am my beloved's, and his desire is for me!" The two go together.

In fact, you can't have one without the other. The bride is not boasting about her good looks. The bride isn't making a statement about how objectively appealing she is or how much all men everywhere find her attractive. There is only *one* man, *one* opinion she cares about, and because she is confident of *his* love and *his* delight, she can say with confidence, "I am my beloved's, and his desire is for me!" Because she trusts his love, she can say, "I am my beloved's, and my beloved is mine!"

Do you see the confidence, the freedom that comes from actually believing Jesus when he says to you, "You are altogether beautiful, my darling..."?

I don't have to pretend to be perfect, I don't have to hide my sin, I don't have to make sure I never go out of the house without my hair done up just right, dressed to the nines, with a professional makeup job to make me shine (talk about putting lipstick on a pig!).

I don't have to make myself look like a perfect version of myself so Jesus will love me; he *already* thinks I am altogether beautiful! And he wants *me* to believe that!

With confidence that Jesus already thinks I am awesome, I don't have to cover up my failures or sins. I don't have to justify my actions. Why do I think I need to look perfect all the time? My beloved already thinks I am delightful!

That confidence has real-life consequences. Remember the kind of week I am having? Remember the friend, whose toes

I stepped on even after I told myself I wasn't going to, and then knew it while I was doing it, and then chose to ignore it after it happened? (Yeah; not so awesome.) That friend sent me an email a couple of days later. He shared some of the hurt I had caused. He pointed out something I knew was wrong but wanted to ignore. He pointed to my sin, and to the brokenness I had caused.

At that point, I have a couple of options. If I feel like I have to be perfect, so other people will like me, and above all God will think I am OK, or at least better than some other people I could mention—if I have to have my makeup just right and my hair styled so I can feel good about myself, then I cannot afford to let this guy make me look like a jerk. I am obligated to point out the circumstances that led up to this conversation, circumstances that were, by the way, at least partially his fault. I have to demonstrate how my response was natural and reasonable (compared to other people), and considering how much I have put up with the failures and dysfunctions of people around me, my actions were not only understandable, my actions were better than most other people.

I must justify myself in my own eyes, even if he doesn't buy it, even if it causes further damage to our relationship, because I can't afford to look in the mirror or to imagine for one second that I might not be the amazing and godly person I am pretending so hard to be.

That's one option, an option driven by fear and doubt and self-justification. Thankfully, that's not how it played out.

If I am confident in this statement, "I am my beloved's and his desire is for me," then I don't have to make sure I appear to be perfect. I already have all the attention and approval I need.

I don't have to justify myself, because I know my Beloved justifies me, and already now thinks I am beautiful. I have acted in less-than-delightful ways, but I have confidence that Jesus' delight is not fickle, not dependent on how closely I can resemble a supermodel.

Jesus quite simply loves me. The real me. Not some made-up version of me. Just me.

So when I get an email from a friend that points out my failure, my selfishness, my hurtful words, my sin, I don't have to panic. Confident that Jesus already loves me and that I don't have to make myself look perfect, I can respond differently. I don't have to excuse or justify. I can use a simple formula I think I first learned from Tim Timmons: "I was wrong. I'm sorry. And I love you."

I was wrong. I'm sorry. And I love you.

That's what I emailed back to my friend. Because I am my Beloved's and my Beloved is mine, I don't have to pretend. I can be me, the real me, the real me who messes up; the real me who is forgiven. The real me; the one Jesus thinks is altogether beautiful.

The bride's confidence doesn't come from what everyone at the wedding feast thinks of her. The bride's confidence doesn't come from her own evaluation of her dress or her hair. **The bride's confidence comes from the promise of the groom.** Because he says, and believes, "You are beautiful, my darling; you are altogether beautiful," she can believe it, too. That confidence gives her the right to boast: "I am my beloved's, and his desire is for me."

Jesus says to you,—and he actually means it, he actually believes it, he actually wants you to believe it!—

"You."

"You are beautiful, my darling."

"You are altogether beautiful."

The Friends:
"We Will Seek Him With You."

The bride says with confidence, "I am my beloved's, and my beloved is mine!" Her confidence flows from the bridegroom, from what he says about her: "You are altogether beautiful, my darling; there is no flaw in you." And her confidence gets a little help from her friends...

When I think of the Song of Solomon, of course I think of the bride. And of course I think of the bridegroom. But sometimes I forget other characters also play a role in this story, friends of the bride and groom—the best man, and maid of honor, and the whole wedding party there to help celebrate the big day. And these Friends say to the bride:

> "Where has your beloved turned,
>   that we may seek him with you?"
>
> *Song of Solomon 6:1*, ESV

It's similar to the situation when, at the reception, the groom has stepped outside, and the bride is like, "Where'd he go?? They're clinking the glasses!" and the maid of honor says, "Oh, I know where he is! Come on; I'll take you to him!"

It's sort of like that. Only, this is a Middle Eastern wedding reception from around 300 decades ago, so they have different rules and different customs and different timelines and different ways of celebrating. In this case, there seems to be what amounts to a game of hide-and-seek during a week-long party. Or something like that. The details are somewhat obscured by time and culture.

What is clear is this: the groom is absent and the bride is on the hunt for him. And in that context, their mutual friends say to the bride, "Where did he take off to now? We want to help you look for him. We want to seek him with you. **We want to help you find the one who delights in being found by you**."

You see, the groom isn't hiding because he doesn't want the bride to find him, because he does! He can't wait to be found by her! And the friends are there to help make that happen!

When Miriam and I got married, we each chose a maid of honor; my sister stood by my side and Miriam's sister stood by her. We also chose a best man, a mutual friend who had been part of our relationship before we even started dating. Those important people were committed to us. They celebrated with us. They nurtured our relationship and promised to keep nurturing it. Our relationship would not have been the same without them.

So it was natural, when our sisters chose the attendants for their weddings, that I would stand for my sister and Miriam would stand for hers. Miriam was the *bride* at one wedding, and

the *matron of honor* at another. I think something like that is
going on in this Song, at least as it applies to individuals as well
as to the Church, the one sheep *and* the whole flock.

Recall that the various cultures we find represented in the
Bible share a view of community that makes it amazing good
news for God to love and save not only *a people group* together
as a group, but unique individuals as *individuals*. In contrast,
most of our contemporary cultures are so individualistic that we
can sometimes miss the fact that God loves and saves not only
unique *individuals*, but individuals as part of a *community*.

This both/and is Good News and More Good News: God
loves *you*, singular *and* God loves y'all (or, as my Texas friends
would say when they *really* meant community: *all y'all*).

As we look through the lens of the Song of Solomon to see
our relationship with God in Jesus Christ, we get both a *you* and
an *all y'all* perspective. You, as a unique individual, are cherished
by Jesus as if you were his one and only; *and* you, as part of a
community, are the Church, and the Church *as a community of
believers* is the bride, the Bride of Christ.

You. And all y'all.

All of which means you get to be bride, *and* matron of honor.
You get the joy of knowing you are individually loved and
cherished. *And* you get the joy of being the friend of the bride
who helps her seek and find the groom. **The bride's joy is one
kind; the best man's is another. And you get both!**

Although you as an individual are *loved and saved*, you are
never loved and saved *as an individual* ; you are always loved and
saved *as* and *into* a community.

You have been given the gift and blessing of a wedding party,
designed by God to help you seek and find your Beloved.

And you have been given the gift and blessing of being a
member of a wedding party, designed by God to give you the joy
of helping your friends and family seek and find their Beloved.

You get play the part of the friends who say, "Where is
your beloved gone? We will help you look for him! We'll keep
searching until we find him! I think I heard him over there; let's
go see!"

You.

And all y'all.

So this image of Jesus and his love for *individuals* is also an image of Christ and his love for *the Church*. After a wonderfully exhaustive inspection, the groom gives this verdict to the Church as a whole:

> You are altogether beautiful, my darling;
>> there is no flaw in you.
>
> *Song 4:7,* NIV

What a beautiful expression of delight! And that comprehensive delight gives me a window into what Jesus thinks about the Church!

I don't know about you, but when I imagine Jesus saying something to the Church *I know* like, "You are altogether beautiful, my darling; there is no flaw in you," I run into the same problem I had when Jesus was talking to me, personally. My immediate, knee-jerk response to that expression of divine delight in the Church as a community of believers is usually, "Yeah, right!"

I mean, come on, Jesus! I know what my church is like! I know the sin and the failure and the doubt and the shame that still clings to us. When I am not disappointed or disgusted with our lack of faith and faithfulness, I am probably either ignoring it entirely or feeling somewhat self-satisfied. As David said, "Everyone has turned away, all have become corrupt; there is no one who does good, not even one" (*Psalm 53:3,* NIV). As Isaiah pointed out, "All of us have become like one who is unclean, and all our righteous acts are like filthy rags; we all shrivel up like a leaf, and like the wind our sins sweep us away" (*Isaiah 64:6,* NIV).

Jesus says he delights in the Church, but I know us too well to think we are beautiful.

And yet, the Church is also the Bride of Christ, altogether beautiful, the place where I find friends who love me and relentlessly point me back to Jesus and his love for me.

Already now, the Church is the Beautiful Bride ahead of the

New Creation, because her Jesus is present with her, already now, and working in and through her; and the Church is *not yet* the Beautiful Bride she will be, when the New Jerusalem comes down out of heaven from God, as John says, "prepared as a bride adorned for her husband" (*Revelation 21:2*, ESV).

Part of our calling as the Friends of the Bride is to help each other keep a firm grasp of both sides of that already-but-not-yet equation. We need each other.

The Bride: Already And Not Yet

A couple of summers ago, I found myself on a leather couch in a ranch house overlooking the Rocky Mountains. Lounging on chairs and couches accented with denim and other Western décor, like antlers, other presenters for the gathering that would start the next afternoon had formed a rough circle; we had all been invited to come out a day early to talk and share and worship and pray. That kind of openness and engagement was a mark of this particular event every year, and I leapt at the chance to participate.

I was sitting next to Miriam on my left, and on my right was one of the other speakers, Idelette McVicker, an amazing woman, leader, author, and presenter who was on her way to becoming a friend.

As the group talked, Idelette shared an image that moved me deeply. The scene came from an experience she had while in Taipei, Taiwan. She was covering a story for *The China Post* on The Garden of Hope, a non-profit combating human trafficking and the practice of taking "child brides." As part of a press conference, they set up a dramatic representation of their mission to reach girls caught in a cycle of sexual abuse, sexual exploitation, and domestic violence.

A young woman was dressed as a child bride (many of whom are fifteen years old or younger). Instead of a pure white, her bridal gown was dirty and torn. She perched on the very edge of a high overpass, dangling her adolescent legs over a knot of traffic in the middle of one of the busiest roads in Taipei. You can imagine the noise and the dust and the traffic; you can imagine the sense of imminent and rising danger.

The girl was so young and so vulnerable; she didn't belong in that dangerous and precarious position. It was just plain wrong. The wedding dress, a symbol of love and joy and promise, didn't belong on this young girl; the promise for her future was as tattered and stained as the dress. It made you want to do something about it.

In the wake of #metoo and #churchtoo movements, but also in the face of all of the statistics on violence against women, that image of the child bride dangling over traffic became for my friend Idelette a way of thinking about the Church.

As she put it, "I can't help but think that our Bride of Christ is wearing a wedding gown that is tattered and torn. She's not safe yet... She's not the beautiful bride she is meant to be. Too many who make up the Body of Christ are like that young child bride—violated, abused, a victim of a system that does not protect the vulnerable. But Jesus reminds us of the Bride— that one day she will be radiant and beautiful. We have much work to do."

I need that image. I need that reminder. I need that sense of urgency, the motivation to make a difference. I need people who will capture my heart with images that remind me real people are being hurt in real ways, and somebody has to do something about it. And that someone, at least in part, *has to be me.*

I need to hold onto the fact that the Church is not yet the Beautiful Bride she is meant to be, and to receive that image of brokenness **as an invitation to action, not to despair**.

In that same circle of presenters I shared the image that had captured my mind and heart, the image I also shared with you at the very beginning of this book: a parent—it could be a mom or a dad—holding a child up in the air so their faces almost touch, and swinging that little child around and around until both parent and child are laughing at each other and with each other in delight.

I remember, that was one of the first times I tried to verbalize that image of delight. I had just begun the initial research on delight vocabulary in the Bible, and I shared some of what I had discovered about Joyful Delight and Delicious Delight and Thoughtful Delight; I shared some things that make you go "Whee!" and things that make you go, "Wow!" And I talked about the intimate and mutual delight of a bridegroom and his bride. I talked about individuals as well as the Church as not yet, but already "altogether beautiful."

I learned that day that, as much as I needed Idelette's image of a vulnerable bride to *motivate* my own heart, my new friend also needed my image of a radiant bride to give her heart *peace*. She needed that reminder. She needed that sense of delight.

She needed to hold onto the fact that the Church is already the Beautiful Bride in whom Christ delights, and to receive that image of wholeness as an **invitation to trust, not to complacency.**

We need both. We need the image of the *vulnerable bride* that moves us to *action*, and we need the image of the *radiant bride* that moves us to *delight*. And we need each other. As Friends of the Bride, we help each other keep a firm grasp of both sides of that already-but-not-yet equation.

Being Church To Each Other

Because I know the Church, the Bride of Christ, is not yet perfect the way she is going to be, and yet I also know that the Bride of Christ, the Church, is his beloved, treasured possession, and Jesus delights in her and considers her altogether beautiful— because *I know both of these things at the same time*, I don't have to expect from the Church (and you don't have to expect from me) that we're going to follow Jesus together perfectly.

I can try to *help you* find the Jesus who delights in being found by you, and I don't have to get hung up on being perfect as I do. I know I'm not going to be a perfect Friend of the Bride to you. I know I am a stinkin' sinner. But we're not really talking about that right now.

If I waited until I was *sinless* until I tried to help someone follow Jesus, I'd never try to help anyone follow Jesus!

When I look for someone to *help me* delight in taking a next step, I don't have to hold them to an impossibly high standard. I know they aren't going to do a perfect job of helping me find the Jesus who delights in being found by me.

If I waited to find a *sinless* friend before I entered into a relationship that helped me follow Jesus better, I'd never get any help following Jesus!

The friend who emailed me about our conversation—you know, the conversation where I told myself I wasn't going to be a jerk, and then was a jerk, and then told myself being a jerk was fine and I should just forget about it—that conversation… The friend who emailed me didn't have to make sure he got the email exactly right before he sent it. In fact, the email wasn't perfect at all. My friend is a stinkin' sinner, so of course an email that pointed out someone else's wrong wasn't going to be free from sin.

But that's OK! He sent it anyway. Because it's not about being the perfect Friend; he was still my Best Man, pointing me back to the Jesus I had kind of forgotten was looking for me to find him.

And when I said, "I was wrong. I'm sorry. And I love you," he immediately wrote back: "You're completely forgiven and there is no baggage between us." I wasn't a sinless Friend. He wasn't a sinless Friend. And yet, in being Church to each other, we could point one another to Jesus (even though we didn't do it perfectly).

That's your role as a Friend of the Bride. You get to be the Maid of Honor, the Best Man. You get to help others seek the Jesus who delight in being found.

You get to say to people in your family and in your workplace and your neighborhood: "Did I just hear the Groom's voice? Was that his footstep outside the window? I know you are looking for Jesus, and I know it's hard to see him sometimes, and I'm here to help you find him. I am sold-out committed to this. I want to celebrate your relationship with your Beloved, and I want to strengthen that relationship in any way possible. You two belong together! And I love being your Friend!"

When Miriam and I got married, our family and friends were

right there with us. Why did we do that? I think it's because **those people belong to our relationship, too**. The people who stood up and made toasts at our reception were important to us; our relationship with each other as bride and groom, husband and wife, would not have been the same without them.

You get the joy of being a Maid of Honor or Best Man. You get to point people back to Jesus without expecting perfection from them or from yourself.

We aren't going to get this church thing right, but we are going to keep following Jesus together. You'll get your toes stepped on. And you'll step on other people's toes. And you will desperately need Jesus in your faith relationships, just like you desperately need Jesus in every other area of your life.

Your calling as a member of the already-beautiful-but-sinful-and-fallen Body of Christ that is the Church is to say to your Friends, "Where is your Beloved, that we may seek him with you?"

Your calling as a follower is to fall in love afresh with the Jesus who says to you, "You are altogether beautiful, my darling; there is no flaw in you."

With your Friends by your side and the promise of your Bridegroom ringing in your ears, you get to sing the Song of Solomon's Bride, loud and clear, with confidence and joy: *"ah-Knee leh dough-Dee, veh dough-Dee, Lee…"*

"I am my Beloved's, and my Beloved is mine."

I belong to my Jesus. And my Jesus belongs to me.

What a delight!

GROUP DISCUSSION FOR CHAPTER 8

I Am My Beloved's And My Beloved Is Mine

Pick one or two of the following questions to help you get to know a friend, family member, or small group better.

1. Talk about a memorable wedding you have been to. How did the bride and groom respond to each other? What was the role of the friends?

2. Have you ever been to a wedding in a different culture? Describe similarities and differences. What do you remember about the bride, the groom, and their friends?

3. If you were going to be married to the love of your life next week, and cost and time were no issue, where would you hold the service? The reception? Who would be invited? Who would give a toast?

   How does delight relate to those decisions?

Go a little deeper with someone you trust to point you back to Jesus. You don't have to reflect on all of the following, but spend some time on the ones that catch your spiritual attention.

1. In the Song of Solomon, the friends delight in the relationship between the bride and the groom. They also help sustain and celebrate that relationship; they even help the bride find her beloved!

   a. In what ways have your friends delighted in your relationship with Jesus?

   b. In what ways have your friends helped sustain or celebrate that relationship?

2. Take a moment in prayer to consider your friendships in the presence of Jesus and in the presence of his Spirit.

   a. Who in your life could use some help seeking the Jesus who delights to be found?

   b. Whose relationship with Jesus can you help sustain or celebrate this week?

3. Write down the names of one or two friends here:

   Brainstorm five ways to affirm their relationship with Jesus this week. Do two of them.

A Prayer For Delight

Lord Jesus, thank you that I am yours.

Thank you for delighting in me, for desiring me, for falling head over heels in love with me. Your tender words of promise have changed my life.

Lord Jesus, thank you that you are mine.

Pour out your Spirit on me, so I can delight in you, desire you, and fall head over heels in love with you. Let my words of promise, though often broken, lead me back into a deeper and more intentional relationship with you.

Lord Jesus, put people in my life who regularly help me seek you. Strengthen and increase my relationships of faith. Give me opportunity to help others seek after you, Lord, trusting that you delight to be found.

Give me the faith to rest in these words: "I am my Beloved's, and my Beloved is mine."

Amen.

SECTION 3

Your Adventure Of Delight

Welcome To The Adventure Of Your Life

God delights in people. God created, redeemed, and continues to sustain real, live human beings; and God loves it when these people feel the same way about their Creator, Redeemer, and Sustainer. That mutual delight in loving and being loved has been the central theme of this book.

We started in Section 1: The Architecture of Delight with a look at some of the biblical vocabulary that helps define a scriptural framework of mutual delight. Then in Section 2: God Delights in Us, we looked at some of the unique and powerful ways the Scriptures talk about God's heart for God's people. You are God's treasured possession; God delights over you with singing; Jesus is head over heels in love with you (and with y'all).

In this last section, we get to turn our attention to the other side of that mutual delight equation, as the Scriptures invite you to experience your relationship with the Father, Son, and Holy Spirit, already now, with delight that is visceral, emotional, intellectual, and playful, all at the same time.

To turn the page and talk about your adventure of delight does not mean we have stopped talking about God's action, and now we get to talk about how you can hold up your end of the bargain. Quite the contrary! Just as God's delight in us is grounded in God's work *for* us, our delight in God is grounded in God's work *in* us; it's still God's work!

And that is such good news! As we shall see, you don't have to manufacture your own delight in God's will or God's Word or God's ways. You don't have to pull yourself up by your own spiritual bootstraps so you can experience more fulfillment as a follower of Jesus. You don't carry the burden of fulfilling the expectations of being a *good Christian*; you get to delight in what God is up to in your life as the Spirit shapes delight in you.

This is an adventure of delight.

For me at least, the word adventure is exciting. An *adventure* can take you places you didn't expect for reasons that weren't clear at the time. There may well be a sense of movement or progress on an *adventure*, but any destination you reach is just a next step in the journey; and even going backwards can propel the plot forward.

On an adventure, you never know what twists or turns are around the next corner, which characters will be introduced in the next chapter, or what new information will cause you to reevaluate everything you thought you knew so far.

An adventure can have a goal or a timeline, but as any adventurer knows, you have to hold your plans loosely and see what happens on the road.

To be on an adventure is to be committed to a process you know you can't control but you also know will bring new knowledge, new discoveries, new risks and new rewards.

I firmly believe that **your delight in following Jesus is tied directly to a spirit of adventure**, a willingness to courageously embark without knowing the final destination and discover the meaning of the journey on the way.

Following Jesus is the most difficult thing you will ever do. And following Jesus is the most exciting, challenging, engaging, heart-breaking, frustrating, meaningful, scary, fun, delightful thing you will ever be part of.

Finding delight in who God is and what God is up to in your life is an *adventure*. It can be dangerous as well as exhilarating. And it is not for the faint of heart.

But you also follow a Jesus who will not "break a bruised reed or snuff out a smoldering wick." Even adventurers get exhausted, lonely, lost, and confused. And Jesus is there for that part of the adventure, too.

So buckle up, hold on tight, and let the adventure begin!

CHAPTER 9

God's Will Directs Your Adventure

Reading Plan

Day 1
Expanding Our Definition
&
God's Will and God's Pleasure

Day 2
Jesus and God's Delight

Day 3
Suffering, Obedience, and Jesus

Day 4
Suffering, Obedience, and You

Day 5
Praying for God's Delight
&
A Simple Way to Pray

Day 6
Group Discussion

Expanding Our Definition

Way back in the Introduction, I referred to a traditional, corporate confession of sins that actually gives the reason we want God to be active in our lives of faith:

"Forgive us, renew us, and lead us,
    so that we may delight in Your will
    and walk in Your ways,
    to the glory of Your holy name. Amen."

That delight is a gift of God and a product of the Spirit's work in your life. That delight flows from God's action of forgiving, renewing, and leading. That delight is connected to God's will, and results in walking in God's ways. **God's will directs your adventure of following Jesus.**

Delighting in God's will is like striking a chord on a guitar: the strings are in tune with each other, the fingering establishes the right relationships between the strings, and the vibration of the strings together produces a resonance, amplified by the instrument, for the delight of those who play and those who hear. The music that results in striking that delight chord is like walking in God's ways: God's will being played out in the diverse rhythms and chord progressions of countless beautiful lives in different ages and cultures around the world.

To delight in God's will is to walk in God's ways; and more than that, to delight in God's will is to delight in God's *delight*.

Thinking of God's *will* as God's *delight* seems very foreign to me. For me, the concept of "God's will" can seem hard, or cold, or even calculating. I was surprised to find that the Greek word for "will" fits comfortably in the biblical word cloud for Delight.

When I hear people talk about "God's will," I don't get the impression they have *delight* in mind at all. But the Bible actually does overlap the concepts of "pleasure," "desire," "delight," and "will." That overlap challenges how I typically imagine what it means to hope or pray or act for God's will to be done.

"God's will" isn't the only concept in our thinking about life with God that needs some reimagining. As I see it, we have also shifted the central meanings of such important ideas as **"the Law," "justice," "righteousness,"** or even *"obeying **God's commands**."* That sort of shift happens slowly and naturally over time, and can really be confusing. Some Scripture verses can seem awkward or unintelligible to us simply because the meanings of key vocabulary words have migrated; sometimes a little, sometimes a lot.

We don't get these words completely *wrong*; it's more like we put the em-PHA-sis on the wrong syl-LA-ble. The parts of the meaning we emphasize and minimize end up modifying the core concept to the point that, although we keep using those words, I don't think they mean what we think they mean. Or at least, **those words don't carry a sense of *delight* any more.** And I think they really should, because I think at one time they really did.

These concepts that need more delight are so important to the biblical witness that shifting our focus even a little has the potential to change how we imagine our lives as followers of Jesus. So it's worth going back to some of the original vocabulary of Scripture to try and hear the resonance of delight.

Stick with me if the original languages aren't your cup of tea. I really hope this comes together in a way that makes you reimagine God's will (and God's delight!) in your life. The idea that God's will/delight actually directs your faith adventure should come as astoundingly good news. This is not an academic exercise!

And we do kind of need to dabble a little in Greek and Hebrew to get there. I'll make it as painless as possible … which also means I won't be nearly detailed enough. Remember, my goal is not to prove or convince, but to help you catch a glimpse of something you didn't know was there before. I want you to pick up delight-tinted glasses to look at things you thought you knew about God and Christian living. I want to alleviate the burden of being a good Christian with the adventure of being a follower. I want you to begin to experience delight in God's will as you walk in God's ways, to the glory of God's holy name.

Let's start with the concept of "God's will." We'll reimagine a few other Bible words along the way, but most of them tie directly back to God's will being done and what that means for us.

Back in Chapter 4, we met the Hebrew word for "pleasure" or "desire." *Chephets* (the *che-* is pronounced Kay: *KAY-fets*) refers to something that you *desire* because it brings you pleasure or *delight*.

חֵפֶץ (Chephets): delight, pleasure, desire, longing

In Chapter 5, on Desirable Delight, we talked about how *pleasure* and *desire*—although they sometimes carry negative connotations for us—belong to the biblical Word Cloud of delight. Desirable Delight makes you say, "Yes, please!!"

We even noted that this Desirable Delight isn't a *sinful* pleasure, it's a *good* pleasure. Indeed, one way to translate the Hebrew word *chephets* is "Good Pleasure." And God's "good pleasure" is nothing less than "God's will," the thing God wants done because it brings such delight.

It's no wonder that the Hebrew word for "desirable delight" (chephets) often came across in the Greek translation of the Old Testament as the Greek word for "good pleasure" or "will" (*thélēma*, pronounced THELL-aye-ma).

θέλημα (Thélēma): good pleasure, will, delight

You might not remember all of the vocabulary words from Chapter 5, but perhaps you remember some of the Bible verses that helped establish the idea that, biblically speaking, **God's will** and **God's pleasure** overlap in meaning.

Do you remember Psalm 1:2? "Blessed is the person whose *delight* is in the *law of the LORD*." Already back in Chapter 5 we talked about how the word "law" usually has a negative connotation as a set of rules that shows us how sinful we are. Of course, "law" *can* mean that in the Bible, but often "law" is a broad concept that **includes not only commands and restrictions, but promises, relationships, and the story of God acting in human history to save.** "Law" in the Hebrew phrase "the law of the LORD" or the "Torah of Yahweh" means much more than we mean by "law" in the phrase "Law and Gospel" (or even in the phrase, "I fought the law, and the law won"). The "Torah of Yahweh" is the whole history and promised future of God's gracious interaction with God's people.

Psalm 1 talks about delighting in the story of God's saving relationship with God's people (which includes commands and blessings and promises and saving actions). When we talked about Desirable Delight in Chapter 5, we noticed that the specific vocabulary in the Hebrew and Greek versions of Psalm 1 sheds some light on delight:

> Blessed is the person whose *chephets* [Hebrew]
> is in the law of the LORD...

> Blessed is the person whose *thélēma* [Greek]
> is in the law of the LORD...

Both versions of Psalm 1:2 are talking about a desirable delight that makes you say, "Yes, please!!" Then we noticed that the Greek version of Psalm 119:35 makes the same translation decision.

> Direct me in the path of your commands,
> for there I find *chephets* [Hebrew]

> Direct me in the path of your commands,
> for there I find *thélēma* [Greek].

Again, both versions are talking about a desirable delight in God directing the journey of faith. While the Hebrew word *chephets* leans toward "pleasure" or "desire," the Greek word *thélēma* begins to shade toward "will." But they definitely overlap in meaning: both are talking about a delight that makes you say, "Yes, please!!"

It seems the Greek word *thélēma* can translate the Hebrew word for Desirable Delight; but when we translate the Greek into English, we get the word "will." Translating *thélēma* as "will" isn't *wrong*, but certainly carries little or no sense of delight.

I mean, when I think about God's "will," I'm not usually

thinking "Desirable Delight," are you? When I hear someone evoke "God's will," it usually refers to something I know I won't like, but I have to take, because it will ultimately be good for me, even though I find it repulsive now (like cough medicine).

And yet, the Greek version of the Old Testament that was being read in Jesus' day was able to translate the Hebrew word for "desire," or "pleasure," or "pleasurable delight" with a word that means "will." I suspect that the way "will" and "delight" overlap in the Old Testament is different from how "will" and "cough medicine" overlap (at least for me) in English.

That insight leads me to wonder: if the word "will" overlaps with the concept of "Desirable Delight" in the Greek version of the Old Testament, the version *being read when the New Testament was being written*, maybe the Greek word for "will" in the New Testament is also steeped in delight.

The Bible intertwines the Hebrew *chephets* and the Greek *thélēma*, and then we translate *thélēma* into English as "will." I wonder if "**delight**" **gets lost in translation**. Perhaps we need to look at expanding our definitions.

God's Will And God's Pleasure

If we want to "delight in God's will and walk in God's ways," then how we understand "God's will" is essential. God's "will" and God's "pleasure" overlap in significant ways in the Bible. But when we read those different words, I'm pretty sure we understand very different things.

Take Revelation 4:11 as a test case. Revelation, chapter 4 describes a scene of heavenly worship, a hymn that includes these words of praise:

> "You are worthy, our Lord and God,
>   to receive glory and honor and power,
>   for you created all things,
>   and **by your will** they were created
>   and have their being."

Revelation 4:11, NIV

Of course, the phrase translated "by your will" includes the Greek word *thélēma*. When I read that verse, I typically think of God's will as "the thing God wanted to get done." God wanted it that way, so it was that way, because *God*. God gets what God wants. And you don't have to like it.

I don't actually think of God as a two-year-old throwing a tantrum, but I also don't sense any resonance of *delight* in God's *will* being done: just as that two-year-old may or may not be pleased even if they get what they want, "God getting what God wants" might describe God's *will*, but not necessarily God's *pleasure*.

At least that's my sense of the word "will;" are you with me, or am I by myself?

The people who made translation decisions for the King James Version of the Bible decided on a different emphasis in Revelation 4:11. I take this difference as at least anecdotal evidence these translators from the early 1600's were aware of a *connotation of delight* in the Greek vocabulary word *thélēma*.

> Thou art worthy, O Lord,
>> to receive glory and honour and power:
> for thou hast created all things,
>> and **for thy pleasure**
> they are and were created.
>
> *Revelation 4:11,* KJV

If you compare those English translations carefully, you'll notice that even the first line has some minor variation: "our Lord and God" in the New International Version is simply "O Lord" in the King James Version. (That type of small disparity comes from the fact that the different Greek manuscripts the translators were looking at had minor variations at that point. Those kinds of minor textual hiccups between different handwritten manuscripts are pretty common, and actually go to show how reliable the text of the New Testament actually is; but that's an interesting discussion for a different time…)

The most significant change is not a variant reading, but two different and legitimate ways of translating *thélēma*. The phrase could mean "by your *will*" (NIV) or it could mean "for your *pleasure*" (KJV), because thélēma means, roughly, "a Desirable Delight that makes you go, 'Yes, please!!'"

I don't know about you, but those two different translations of the same phrase give me very different ideas about this heavenly hymn. The first, "by your *will* all things were created," makes me think *God got what God wanted*, and things are set in place because God said so; which is still good news for me, but from a rather theoretical distance. Everything is ordered exactly, down to the last detail. I imagine the music of that hymn to be beautiful, but also complicated and ethereal, a Latin chant with lots of contra-tenors and counterpoint.

The second translation, "for your *pleasure* all things were created," makes me think of a party. A pretty wild party. With lots of dancing. At a zoo. All kinds of creatures are darting back and forth and flying around and cavorting about, trumpeting and buzzing and stampeding in joy. In my imagination, that party is not exactly *out of control*, but it is not exactly *orderly*, either. I see God smiling as all creation plays, and dances, and enjoys life. The music accompanying this version of the hymn is much closer to a salsa than a Gregorian chant. And God's delight in that scene puts a smile on my face.

Maybe I am making too much out of that minor translation decision. Maybe I am stating the difference in exaggerated terms. While those two different takes on the text are honestly a good description of my own personal experience with the different translations, you may not experience the differences the same way.

So let me put it this way: even if the difference between "by your will" and "for your pleasure" doesn't seem as stark to you as it does to me, *if you sense any difference in meaning or implication at all*, you have seen my point. I am extremely suspicious, after looking at how the ancient Greek translation of the Old Testament handles the word for "pleasure," that when a New Testament author read or wrote the word "will" in Greek, it meant something closer to "the pleasurable delight I desire" than our English word "will" ever does. "Good pleasure" might get close; but not "will."

I think we need to be careful that our more modern tendency to divorce "will" from any emotion at all doesn't lead us to misread the Bible. Scripture, it turns out, conflates "will" and "pleasure." And that's good news for us.

Look how the author of the letter to the Hebrews closes the benediction of that book:

> Now may the God of peace...
> equip you with everything good
>   for doing his **will** [*Yes, please!!*],
> and may he work in us
>   **what is pleasing** [*Wow!*] to him,
> through Jesus Christ,
>   to whom be glory for ever and ever. Amen.
>   *Hebrews 13: 20-21*, NIV

God's will—God's Desirable Delight—is parallel to that which is pleasing to God—God's Thoughtful Delight. This isn't just "God getting what God wants;" this is God *wanting* what brings God *delight*. Desirable Delight and Thoughtful Delight are working together in God, in a way that leads God to work in us. The Spirit is equipping you for doing things that make the Father go, "Yes, please!!" and working in you things that make the Father go, "Wow!" All for the sake of Jesus.

Here's a similar example of how the New Testament uses the Greek word *thélēma* to mean more than our English word "will" can account for. Maybe "good pleasure" gets close? But I'm thinking this is Desirable Delight we are talking about.

Philippians 2 puts the verb that comes from thélēma in close proximity to one of our vocabulary words for Thoughtful Delight from back in Chapter 2: eudokéō (oi! + dough-KEH-oh) "to think well of, approve, delight in."

εὐδοκέω (Eudokéō): be pleased with,
think well of, approve, delight in

The Father uses that Thoughtful Delight word of the Son at Jesus' baptism: "You are my Son, the beloved; with you I am *well pleased* [*eudokéō*]." Philippians 2 uses the noun that comes from that delight verb to talk about what God thinks about *us*:

> Work out your own salvation with fear and trembling,
> for it is God who works in you,
>> both to **will** [*thélēma*, Desirable Delight]
>> and to work for his
>> **good pleasure** [*eudokía*, Thoughtful Delight].
>
> *Philippians 2:12-13*, ESV

I can't wait for Chapter 10 on God's work! But for now, notice that God is working in you, so that you say, *"Yes, please!!"* to the thing that makes God go *"Wow!"* God is creating a Desirable Delight in you so that you hold onto, and put yourself under, and work for the thing that gives God Thoughtful Delight. God wants your will/good pleasure to align with the work that brings God delight/good pleasure.

When we pray, "Forgive us, renew us, and lead us, so we may delight in Your will and walk in Your ways..." we are *not* asking our Heavenly Father to make us get on board with the cold and calculating way the Eternal Creator has ordered all things so that God gets what God wants.

Instead, we are asking God to work in us a holy and pleasurable desire to do what puts a smile on the Father's face, and makes the Spirit do a little jig, and causes Jesus to sing his happy song. That's what God's will is: absolute delight.

To desire God's will is to delight in God's delight.

You were created (and continue to exist) not because of some uncaring and well-ordered mathematical equation tied to God's abstract and impersonal will. You were created (and still exist) because *your ongoing existence brings God delight*.

And you are invited to delight in God's delight.

Isn't that just awesome?

Cue the salsa music.

Jesus And God's Delight

Did I mention I can't wait for Chapter 10 on God's work? Here's a little appetizer (spoiler alert!): the Spirit is working in you, to shape you, mold you and empower you to delight in God's delight and to joyfully engage the work of the Kingdom (to delight in God's will and walk in God's ways). And the master design this Sculptor Spirit is shaping you towards is, quite simply, *Jesus*.

Anointed with the Spirit, Jesus fulfills his mission (to do God's will/delight) in the power of the Spirit, and pours out that same Spirit on those who follow him. **The Spirit, who fills Jesus with the joy of doing God's delight, now dwells within *you*.**

You can see the joy of Jesus clearly connected to the Spirit's presence and the will/delight of the Father in Luke 10. Jesus sent seventy-two hand-chosen followers out in pairs to prepare people for his imminent arrival. When these seventy-two return with "great joy" (*Woohoo!* Joyful Delight) because of their success, Jesus instructs them to have Joyful Delight not in what they have accomplished, but in the fact that their names are entered into the rolls of the Kingdom. In both cases, Jesus and the disciples use the Joyful Delight word we have gotten to know in Greek (*chara*, like "caress" but with an –ah!).

χαρά (Chara): joy, delight, gladness (as a result of grace)

Then the Spirit fills Jesus with delight:

> At that time Jesus, full of **joy**
> [Joyful Delight, *Woohoo!*]
> through the Holy Spirit, said,
> "I praise you, Father, Lord of heaven and earth,
> because you have hidden these things
> from the wise and learned,
> and revealed them to little children.
> Yes, Father, for this is what **you were pleased**
> [Thoughtful Delight, *Wow!*] to do."
>
> *Luke 10:21*, NIV

At the beginning of this verse, the Joyful Delight of Jesus is described with a word we haven't met yet: *agalliáō* (if you said, "Ah, golly!" and added an "AH-oh" at the end, you wouldn't exactly be speaking Greek, but you'd be close...)

ἀγαλλιάω (Agalliáō): to jump for joy, delight greatly

This word is a jump-up-and-spin-around-*Woohoo!* word, much like the Hebrew *gil* (sounds like *feel*) we met back in Chapter 1: "He will exult [gil] over you with loud singing" (*Zeph. 3:17*). Jesus is definitely experiencing Joyful Delight in the Spirit.

Just as the Father was well pleased (*eudokéō*) with the Son at his baptism, the Father now takes Thoughtful Delight (*eudokéō*) in revealing the Kingdom to little children. And that Thoughtful Delight makes Jesus jump up and spin around and go, *"Woohoo!"* in the Spirit.

In these few short verses, we have three different Greek words for delight: *chara, agalliáō, and eudokéō.* Add our English translations into the mix and you get even more layers. Where the NIV has "Jesus, full of joy through the Holy Spirit, said..." the ESV translates, "He rejoiced in the Holy Spirit and said..."

(OK. Maybe that one's not so bad. The NIV just took the *verb* "to rejoice" and made it the *noun* "joy." They must have thought it sounded more natural that way. But the next one is significant.)

Where the NIV translates, "Yes, Father, for this is **what you were pleased to do**," the ESV puts the same Greek words into English like this: "Yes, Father, for such was your **gracious will**."

Now, wait one minute here! The Greek word for *will* we have been working with is *thélēma* and translates the Hebrew *chephets, Desirable* Delight *(Yes, please!!).* But this is *eudokéō, Thoughtful* Delight *(Wow!)* suddenly being translated as "gracious *will!!*"

What gives?

You might not be bothered by this. I understand. But I am trying to build a coherent system of how the Bible talks about delight and how we typically understand (or misunderstand) that concept. And these words and meanings are not easy to nail down! Translating from Hebrew to Greek, or Greek to English, or Hebrew to English, the concepts and vocabulary words get somewhat slippery sometimes (let alone making nouns into verbs or verbs into nouns).

I think this verse just goes to show that you can't plug your translator machine into a mathematical equation or line up your Super Hebrew–Greek–English Decoder Ring to make a magic translation pop out the other end. Context, nuance, changing usage over time, and typical patterns for different authors and different translators all play significant roles in getting meaning across the lexical divides of history and culture.

I also think we're dealing with a very natural phenomenon we talked about in the very beginning of our discussion of delight: the biblical Word Cloud for delight is complex and multifaceted and does not overlap exactly with the English Word Cloud for delight, let alone your own personal experience with the concept.

But don't throw up your hands or throw in the towel just yet! **Despite the differences, some things are actually really clear**: *delight* as a category of experience in the Bible is rich enough to include Joyful, Thoughtful, Playful, Delicious, and Desirable Delight; and **God's *will* is directly related to God's *delight***.

So the Spirit fills Jesus with Joyful Delight *(Woohoo!)*, with the result that Jesus aligns himself with the delight/will/good pleasure of the Father. Now, as little children to whom the secrets of the Kingdom have been revealed according to the Thoughtful Delight *(Wow!)* of the Father, you also are filled with the same Spirit who fills Jesus. The result? **The Spirit also fills you with a Joyful Delight in the delight of the Father**. You delight in God's will and walk in God's ways to the glory of God's holy name.

Jesus expects something like that Spirit-led delight to happen. Jesus tells his disciples on Maundy Thursday (*Chara* Thursday?) that they will put themselves under the words of the Father and do the same kind of work Jesus himself has been doing. Why? Because Jesus will ask the Father to send the Spirit. **The Spirit will enable the followers of Jesus to do the work of Jesus**. Part of the work of Jesus is saying *Woohoo!* to the things that make the Father go *Wow!*

"I speak just **as the Father taught me**," Jesus said, "and he who sent me is with me. He has **not left me alone**" (*John 8:28-29*). Or again: "It is the Father, living in me, who is doing his work" (*John 14:10*). Or again: "These words you hear are not my own; **they belong to the Father** who sent me" (*John 14:24*). Or again: "**I love the Father** and do exactly **what my Father has commanded me**" (*John 14:31*).

Jesus is *hearing* the Father and *doing* the delight of the Father in love. That same *hearing and doing in love* is made possible by the presence of the Spirit in you.

Jesus says: "Whoever believes in me will **do the works I have been doing**, and they will do even greater things than these ... If you **love me, keep my commands**. And I will ask the Father, and he will give you another advocate to help you and **be with you** forever—the Spirit of truth... you know him, for **he lives with you and will be in you**" (*John 14:12, 15–17*)

Filled with the Spirit, Jesus delights in the Father's will and walks in the Father's ways. Filled with the Spirit, so do you. Filled with the Spirit, you actually get to say *Woohoo!* to the things that make the Father go *Wow!* You get to delight in the Father's delight.

I can almost sense you beginning to believe, or at least *wanting* to believe, that the Spirit who fills you can also enable you to delight in God's will and maybe even walk in God's ways. I can almost feel your heart opening up, or wanting to open up, to the presence of the Spirit, the *Woohoo!* of the Son, and the *Wow!* of the Father. And I think I have an idea of what might be holding you back, at least a little; keeping you from jumping for joy; throwing water on the ember that had just begun to catch fire.

Or maybe it's just me.

I want so badly to believe and live out this Joyful Delight that is a gift from the Spirit and connects me both to Jesus and to the Father—I want so badly for you to see *delight* as a core attribute and defining characteristic of any Jesus follower—I want so badly for delight to have meaning in my own, personal, everyday life... And then: cold, hard reality strikes, and I am back to dealing with loss and failure and disappointment and fear and sin and shame.

In the cold, hard, *real* world, God's will seems distant and calculating. God's will works behind a divine curtain in a way I never get to see or understand.

God's will allows suffering, most of it worse than mine, but all of it terrible; and if *suffering* fits into God's will, then it seems like *delight* just can't. Do you see how that thought, that *reality*, can stifle delight?

I imagine I can sense you just beginning to open up to the possibility of delight in your life as a follower of Jesus; and I imagine that timid opening to delight is closed down quickly by the reality of suffering.

I want to lean into that reality, because the kind of delight Jesus experienced—the kind of delight Jesus wants you to have— is strong enough, and deep enough, and big enough **to hold even suffering in the hands of faith before the throne of grace**. For anyone filled with the Spirit—like Jesus; like you—suffering is safely held under the umbrella of God's delight.

Suffering, Obedience, And Jesus

You can see the struggle between God's delight and suffering even in the life of Jesus; not only in the cross, but also in his struggle in the wilderness and in the garden. As soon as Jesus receives the guiding presence of the Spirit and the Father's Verdict of Delight, Jesus is led into the wilderness to be tempted by the devil. Still dripping wet from his baptism, Jesus heads to the desert region, a place of testing and temptation. And if his baptism in the Jordan establishes this Jesus as God's Son, in whom the Father delights *(Wow!)* and in whom the Spirit dwells, then the temptation in the wilderness challenges *what it means* to be God's Son.

"If you are the Son of God..." the tempter whispers. Three times, Satan invites Jesus to alleviate or avoid his own suffering *because* Jesus is the Son. Satan tries to redefine sonship to mean getting what you want, when you want it. Jesus, on the other hand, holds to a core identity marker of the beloved Son: obedience.

There's another one of those Bible vocabulary words I think we just don't have a good handle on. We send pets to "obedience school"; how robust can our concept of obedience really be? (As if God said, "Sit!" and Jesus said, "Woof!") Of course our concept of "obeying" extends beyond pets, to things like "obeying your parents" or "obeying the law." But I think what you and I typically mean by "obeying" misrepresents what the Bible means by "**hearing and holding onto God's will and God's delight**."

You see, the Greek word for "obey" combines the action of *hearing* and *holding onto tightly*, and in that sense, *doing* or *putting into practice*. To obey is first to hear, and then to put yourself under what you have heard and hold onto it for dear life.

I think that's one reason Jesus, filled with the Spirit, quotes Scripture in the face of temptation; **Jesus hears and holds onto God's Word**.

Three times, Satan says, "If you are the Son of God (and let's say for the sake of argument you are), then define sonship by getting what you want." Three times, Jesus responds, "*It is written...*" Jesus hears the Father and, filled with the Spirit, holds onto what the Father has said. Jesus submits his own actions to the words of the Father. Jesus *obeys*. And in so doing, Jesus shows what it really means to be the beloved, obedient Son.

Just as God's people were tempted in the wilderness, God's Son goes into the wilderness to be tempted; just as Adam and Eve had an opportunity to hear and hold onto God's Word in the Garden, so Jesus, the New Adam, goes into the Garden to do the will of the Father and thereby crush the Serpent's head. Where we failed to be faithful, Jesus proves true.

The book of Hebrews says:

> Son though he was,
> he learned *obedience*
> from what he *suffered*.
> *Hebrews 5:9*, NIV

I'm sorry, but when I read that, it seems to me like we have gone even beyond doggie obedience school: this feels like the dog is being beaten with a stick until it learns how to behave. (I always appreciated the office sign: "Beatings will continue until morale improves.") Of course that can't be right; but doesn't "learning obedience through suffering" sound awful? How dare we suggest we have a God of love if God does something like that?

A closer look at the Garden of Gethsemane only makes it worse. Jesus, in utter anguish, prays three times (like the threefold Temptation in the Wilderness) that the cup of suffering would be removed. "If there is any other way," he prays, "I choose that one." And then God's will and human suffering come head to head:

> "*Abba*, Father," he said,
> "everything is possible for you.
>> Take this cup from me.
>> Yet not what I will,
>> but what you will."
>
> *Mark 14:36*, NIV

Jesus, as Son, seems to think the Father *could* do something different. But it is God's *will* for Jesus to go to the cross. We're back to God's will being hard, cold, calculating, almost Vulcan. And our exploration of Delight will find things getting worse before they get better.

The word for "will" here is the same Greek word used to translate Desirable Delight in the Old Testament. In this case, if you divorce God's will from God's delight, the text actually seems to make *more* sense. But the cost of that sleight of hand is to create a concept of God's will that can be cold, and distant, and calculating, and not delightful at all.

Thankfully, I don't think the biblical witness allows us to go there. While the Greek word for *will* might not overlap completely with the Hebrew for Desirable Delight, both the Greek *thélēma* and the Hebrew *chephets* shade the concept of "will" towards "delight."

And that's a problem. At least here in Gethsemane. And at the cross. Listen to what Isaiah says about the Suffering Servant of Yahweh, the chosen and anointed one:

Yet it was **the LORD's will**
[*chephets*, Desirable Delight]
to crush him and cause him to suffer,
and though the LORD makes his life an offering for sin,
he will see his offspring and prolong his days,
and **the will of the LORD**
[*chephets*, Desirable Delight]
will prosper in his hand.

Isaiah 53:10, NIV

Yep. That's *chephets*. The Hebrew word for desire or pleasure; something *I set my will on* because it brings me *delight*. The King James Version makes the tension even clearer:

Yet **it pleased the LORD**
[*chephets*, Desirable Delight]
to bruise him; he hath put him to grief:
when thou shalt make his soul an offering for sin,
he shall see his seed, he shall prolong his days,

and the **pleasure of the LORD**
[*chephets*, Desirable Delight]
shall prosper in his hand.

Isaiah 53:10, KJV

Somehow the suffering and death of Jesus brings the Father *pleasure*. That offends me. That seems to make the Father a sadist, or the Son a masochist, or both. That goes against what I have been taught about love and family, let alone about good and evil.

If the Father can take pleasure, can desire, can *find delight* in the suffering of the Son, I'm not sure I want that Father after all. In fact, some people have rejected the message of Scripture precisely because the cross can be seen as a form of divine parental abuse, and rejecting parental abuse seems to require rejecting the God of the Bible. And I kind of get it. The existence of suffering in general, let alone the will of the Father for the suffering of the Son, is enough to make atheists out of true believers.

So we need a way of thinking about suffering, and sonship, and obedience, and God's will that helps us see how and why it makes sense to say God delights in the suffering and death of Jesus. You could just chalk it up to God's will being cold and abstract and beyond our understanding, but then you are left with God's *will* devoid of *delight*. And that's not how the Bible talks.

So **let's lean into suffering and God's will**, because on the other side is a **clearer understanding of God's delight**.

First, let's go back to that problematic text in Isaiah 53. This is the Suffering Servant, who will be wounded for our transgressions and pierced for our iniquities. This is the Servant of Yahweh on whom God will place our sins so that our sins can be removed from us.

Notice that when the text talks about God's Desirable Delight in the death of this Suffering Servant, the *life* of the Suffering Servant is also right there in view. In fact, even though he becomes a sacrifice for sins in his death, he will still see the light of life.

What's more, the Desirable Delight of God will prosper in his hand, even after the sacrifice has been made:

> Yet it was **the LORD's will** [Desirable Delight]
>   to crush him and cause him to suffer,
> and though the LORD makes his life an offering for sin,
>   he will see his offspring and prolong his days,
> and the **will of the LORD** [Desirable Delight]
>   will prosper in his hand.
> After he has suffered,
>   he will see the light of life and be satisfied;
> by his knowledge my righteous servant
>   will justify many,
> and he will bear their iniquities.
>
> *Isaiah 53:10–11*, NIV

According to Isaiah, the thing that pleases the Father is **not the suffering and death of the Son** *in isolation*; rather, the obedient suffering, sacrificial death, and victorious resurrection of the Son—and all that brings about—is the true Desirable Delight of the Father. After the bruising and crushing and dying comes the light of life; after the offering is complete, the living Son will accomplish the Delight of the Father.

Jesus' suffering and death are central to the story of salvation, but they are never *alone* **in the story of salvation.** I think we are more faithful to Scripture if we imagine this as a single event, as the "obedient-suffering-and-sacrificial-death-and-victorious-resurrection-for-the-purpose-of-justifying-sinners-and-accomplishing-God's-Delight."

That's what the Father delights in. Not the suffering of the Son in isolation, but the obedience of the Son unto death for the purpose of bringing God's loved but estranged children back home forever.

Understanding death/resurrection as a single event helps me understand how the Father can bear to let the Son go to the cross, let alone delight in what's taking place.

Quick aside: I think that's what I always misunderstood about Abraham and Isaac. On the surface, it looks like a father willing to take the knife to his son "because God said so." What kind of faith is that? What kind of *God* is that? No thank you.

But then you realize God has made an explicit promise about this Isaac, who had been miraculously born when both mom and dad were not physically capable of having kids. God said Abraham's offspring would come from this son of promise, so when Abraham obeys God and goes to sacrifice the son whom he loves, Abraham is **hearing and holding onto (obeying) the** *promise* **as well as the command**. As the book of Hebrews puts it:

> Abraham reasoned
>   that God could even raise the dead,
>   and so in a manner of speaking
>   he did receive Isaac back from death.
>
> *Hebrews 11:19*, NIV

The story makes a different kind of sense if you hold promise-sacrifice-death-and-resurrection together as a single event.

What was true of that son of promise is also true of Jesus, the

Son of Promise. **Jesus hears and holds onto both the promise and the command**. According to Jesus, the definition of being the Beloved Son is not using your power or status for your own advantage; rather, being the Son means being *obedient*, hearing and holding onto the Delight of the Father.

Read in that light, the obedience of the Son unto death makes more sense. Or maybe we should call it, the Son's hearing and holding onto the Delight of the Father unto *death-and-resurrection*. Go back to Hebrews 5 with that thought in mind:

> During the days of Jesus' life on earth,
>   he offered up prayers and petitions
>   with fervent cries and tears
>   **to the one who could save him from death,**
> and **he was heard**
>   because of his **reverent submission.**
>
> Son though he was,
>   **he learned obedience**
>   **from what he suffered** and,
>   once made *perfect*,
>
> he became the source of eternal salvation
>   for all who **obey** him.
>
> *Hebrews 5:7–9*, NIV

In Gethsemane, the Son prays fervently to the Father, who can *and who will* save him from death. Because Jesus *submitted* himself to the will/delight of the Father, that is, because Jesus heard and held onto (obeyed) God's delight, the Father in turn heard and answered his prayers: "he was heard because of his reverent *submission*."

The suffering and death of the Suffering Servant is not the end; the Vindicated Servant will see the light of life, and the Delight of God will prosper in his hands.

Jesus "learned obedience from what he suffered," because **hearing and holding onto God's delight is not a theoretical thing, but something that gets lived out in real life.**

God, who knew at least theoretically how much Abraham trusted the promise, could say only *after* Abraham raised the knife, "Now I *know* that you fear God, that you submit yourself to hear and hold onto God's promise and command."

In the same way, the Son was theoretically committed to the Father's plan for salvation, but going through with it *showed* that Jesus held onto the Father's word of promise and command. Jesus obeyed, and in that hearing and holding onto, was brought to a place of fulfillment or completion as God's beloved Son. (That's what the word "perfect" means in Greek; made complete or brought to fulfillment.)

Delighting in God's will/delight means walking in God's ways. Obeying God's will/delight means hearing and putting yourself under the commands and promises that stem from God's delight, and then holding onto those promises in real life.

God's delight encompasses even the suffering and death of Jesus. But God does not delight in suffering and death of and by themselves; rather, God delights in the [obedient-suffering-and-sacrificial-death-and-victorious-resurrection-for-the-purpose-of-justifying-sinners-and-accomplishing-God's-Delight] of Jesus.

Suffering, Obedience, And You

Because Jesus was obedient unto death-and-resurrection, Jesus became the source of salvation to all who *obey* him, to all who hear and hold onto his words of command and promise. Once the unique and divine sonship of Jesus was brought to fulfillment in the Son's obedient suffering-and-sacrificial-death-and-victorious-resurrection, Jesus became the firstborn of many brothers and sisters. That's another sense in which the suffering of Jesus does not happen in isolation. God delights in the suffering-death-resurrection of Jesus because of what it accomplished; because of *you*.

Our conversation about the treasured possession back in Chapter 6 finds its fulfillment (is perfected?) in the mystery of God's delight in the cross and empty tomb. Just as the merchant jumps up and spins around and shouts, *Woohoo!* and *sells everything he owns* to buy that one, precious pearl, so the Father considers what it will take to bring you, beloved, back home.

The Father's Delight sends Jesus to the cross. God does not delight in the suffering of Jesus by itself; God delights in the obedient suffering, sacrificial death, and victorious resurrection of Jesus because of what it accomplishes: God gets *you* back. **And *you* are the focus of God's Desirable Delight**.

Having been brought back into God's family, we now find in Jesus the source of our salvation. In fact, **we now *obey* Jesus; that is, we hear his words of promise and command and hold onto them for dear life**. Jesus' submission to the will/delight of the Father becomes our submission to the will/delight of the Father. Jesus' willingness to face suffering and death in light of promise and resurrection becomes *our* willingness to face suffering and even death in the confidence of promise and resurrection. Jesus' *obedience* becomes our *obedience*, as we hold onto both promise and command; as the adopted status of beloved child is brought to fulfillment in us through the challenges and temptations and sufferings of our own wilderness and garden.

Jesus says as much in some key places in the Gospels. In this chapter, we've already spent time sitting with Jesus in the Upper Room right before his arrest and trial and crucifixion. These passages in John capture the last extended teaching before Jesus puts obedience unto death-and-resurrection into practice. No wonder, then, that obedience is on his mind.

We already looked at the surprising Joyful Delight (*chara*) of that Maundy Thursday, but look at how that *delight* is found in the midst of *obedience*:

> As the Father has loved me, so have I loved you.
>   Now remain in my love.
> If you **keep my commands**, you will remain in
>   my love, just as **I have kept my Father's commands**
>   and remain in his love.
> I have told you this so that my **joy** [*Woohoo!*]
>   may be in you and that your **joy** [*Woohoo!*]
>   may be **complete** ["*made perfect*"].

> My **command** is this:
>   Love each other as I have loved you.
>   Greater love has no one than this:
>   to lay down one's life for one's friends.
> You are my friends if you **do what I command**.

John 15:9–14, NIV

If you are thinking doggie obedience school, all this talk of commands just doesn't make sense. But this can't be some blind obedience to the rules: for Jesus, **doing what God commands flows from a love relationship**. This is Jesus delighting in and doing the delight of the Father, and inviting the disciples to delight in and do the things that bring the delight of Jesus to complete fulfillment.

You aren't slaves; you are friends. You aren't being asked to sit up and roll over for a treat if you amuse your master. You are being invited to participate in a love relationship that includes hearing and putting yourself under delight, holding onto commands and promises even when that means obedience unto death-and-resurrection.

It's hard to understand words like "obedience" or "commands" in this context of love and friendship and joy. It sounds like Jesus must be preaching Law, but some of it sure feels like a Gospel invitation rather than a condemning burden. That might be because Jesus is talking about law in the absolute broadest sense of the word, the story of God's action in human history to save, which includes Thou Shalt and Thou Shalt Not, but also includes promise and rescue and blessing.

In John 15, Jesus commands you to hold onto "God loved the world in this way: God gave the Beloved Son, that whoever believes in him would not perish, but have eternal life" (*John 3:16*).

Jesus commands you to hold onto "Whoever drinks the water I give them will never thirst. Indeed, the water I give them will become in them a spring of water welling up to eternal life" (*John 4:14*).

Jesus commands you to hold onto "Just as the Father raises the dead and gives them life, even so the Son gives life to whom he is pleased to give it" (*John 5:21*).

Jesus commands you to hold onto "All those the Father gives me will come to me, and whoever comes to me I will never drive away" (*John 6:37*).

Jesus commands you to hold onto "I am the light of the world. Whoever follows me will never walk in darkness, but will have the light of life" (*John 8:12*).

All of these passages belong to what Jesus has instructed, taught, and *commanded* his disciples; his disciples are now to *obey these commands*: hear, put themselves under, and hold onto these instructions and promises.

You are not left on your own to muster up a little more faithful obedience this week (even if "obedience" is broader and more delightful than you once imagined). The same Jesus who received the Spirit, pours out the Spirit, with the result that the same Spirit who filled Jesus now fills you:

> God sent the Spirit of his Son into our hearts,
>   the Spirit who cries out, *"Abba*, Father."
>
> *Galatians 4:6*, NIV

> The Spirit you received does not make you slaves,
>   so that you live in fear again;
> rather, the Spirit you received brought about
>   your adoption to sonship.
>   And by him we cry, *"Abba*, Father."
>
> *Romans 8:15*, NIV

Your obedience is not the obedience of a slave, who has no relationship or status in the family. Your obedience is the obedience of a beloved daughter, of a beloved son; in fact, your obedience is the obedience of *the* Beloved Son, the Son who sends the Spirit to form the prayer of the Beloved on your lips, too: *Abba*, Father. Just as Jesus prayed in the Garden, you pray in your garden, in your wilderness, in your place of testing or confusion or wandering or doubt: *Abba*, Father: Your Kingdom, come; Your Delight be done, on earth as it is in heaven.

Of course, *suffering* is not delightful, and you are not supposed to delight in the *act of suffering*; as one who belongs to Jesus, sealed with the Spirit, adopted into an *Abba* relationship with the Father, you delight in the *midst of suffering*. As Peter, the friend who fell asleep in the Garden of Gethsemane and shortly thereafter denied knowing Jesus three times—as Peter, who knows the risen Christ, says:

> In all this you **greatly rejoice**
> [*agalliāō*, Joyful Delight]
> though now for a little while
> you may have had to suffer grief
> in all kinds of trials.
>
> *1 Peter 1:6*, NIV

Agalliāō ("Ah, golly! AH-oh"): that's the same variety of jump-up-and-spin-around joy Jesus experienced in the Spirit when he saw the Thoughtful Delight of the Father at work.

ἀγαλλιάω (Agalliáō): to jump for joy, delight greatly

Peter doesn't say you should think the suffering is *fun*. Peter declares our living hope based in the resurrection of Jesus from the dead; Peter looks forward to the coming of Jesus when our genuine faith will result in praise and honor and glory for Jesus; and in light of the hope- and confidence-giving sacrificial-death-and-victorious-resurrection-and-final-saving-return-at-the-Last-Day of Jesus (all one, big, accomplished reality), Peter can say, even suffering in all kinds of trials can be met with a hopeful and confident, "Woohoo!"

(Incidentally, Peter seems to have practiced what he preached. Peter was one of the apostle in Acts 5 who, after they were flogged for teaching and healing in the name of Jesus, "left the Sanhedrin, **rejoicing** because they had been counted worthy of **suffering** disgrace for the Name.")

This rejoicing is not, "Thank You for the pain." Rather, this sacred rejoicing in the midst of trials and persecutions and struggles and suffering says, "Thank You that this experience of pain is **tied up in a bigger reality** that means this pain is not the first or the final word. Thank You that hope and faith and victory and promise are stronger than death. Thank You that my present is tied directly to Jesus' future. Abba, Father, Your Delight be done."

Like the suffering of Jesus, your suffering doesn't happen in a vacuum. As real and terrible and all-consuming as your suffering is, it is not the first, the last, or the most important thing about you.

Oh, your suffering is real; all too real. Don't pretend it's not. And don't listen to people who tell you that true believers don't suffer. We've been talking about delight a lot in this book, and I have tried to show at least a little of why I think delight is not just a marginal experience for a follower of Jesus, but a defining characteristic. The biblical delight I have in mind is not an "ignorance is bliss," "ignore your pain," "don't worry, be happy" kind of sappy sentimentalism.

The delight of Jesus-followers echoes the delight of Jesus: it resonates with harmonies and overtones rich enough to encompass dissonance and resolution. Delight in God's delight means embracing suffering, but not suffering in isolation; suffering as a part of a bigger story, a story that began *before* suffering and continues on *through* suffering, to the other side.

Your obedience and suffering are tied up in a sacred and insoluble tangle with the obedient suffering, sacrificial death, victorious resurrection, and return in glory of the Suffering Servant of Yahweh. You can rejoice in the midst of your suffering because God's Delight is so much bigger than your suffering. Your suffering is real and painful and almost unbearable; and **your suffering ties you to Jesus**. It was God's delight not to stay far away from your suffering, but in Jesus, to draw near and stay near to you. "I am with you *always*," Jesus promises; even in your suffering.

Just recently, our youngest climbed into bed with my wife and me in the middle of the night. He is almost too big for that now; but he had a bad dream, so he wanted to be near Mom and Dad, where he felt safe and warm and protected and loved. I grieve that one of these nights will be the last time he seeks comfort in snuggles; he's growing up so fast…

When my father-in-law came home from the hospital for the last time, we put him in his own bedroom, in his own bed. We gathered as family and sang and prayed and kept vigil over those final days of decline. I remember my mother-in-law climbing into bed next to him when he was no longer conscious; snuggling close, embracing his failing body, to let him know even beyond words that he was safe and protected and loved.

When I hear Jesus pray, *"Abba*, Father, if there is another way, let this cup pass from me," it's hard for me to understand why an all-powerful and all-loving God couldn't snap those omnipotent fingers and remove the cup of suffering from Jesus. What kind of vindictive Father lets a beloved Son go to the cross?

And then I realize, the thing that required Jesus to enter into suffering was not God's will *for Jesus to suffer*, but God's will *to be near to sinful humans in the midst of their suffering*; God's Desirable Delight to be close to *you*.

When Jesus set out to rescue fallen humanity from the sinful mess we had gotten ourselves into, Jesus didn't keep a safe distance. Jesus came near. We made our bed, and Jesus chose to lie in it with us. Jesus snuggled up close and embraced us, even in our mortality.

Jesus knew hunger, for you. Jesus knew thirst, for you. Jesus knew exhaustion, for you. Jesus knew temptation, for you. Jesus knew grief, for you. Jesus knew suffering, for you. Jesus knew death, for you.

It cost Jesus everything to draw near to you so he can be with you always. He will not turn you away in the night. He will not shun even your deathbed. Jesus' suffering and death belong to the Delight of Jesus holding you in his strong embrace, to let you know even beyond words that you are safe and protected and loved, now and forever, no matter what.

For the joy set before him—for you—Jesus counted the cross a ridiculously small price to pay. The incarnation-life-baptism-temptation-teaching-healing-suffering-death-resurrection-ascension-and-Return of Jesus (one, big, unified reality) gives

Jesus the delight of saying to *you*: "Behold! I am with you always; even to the end of the Age."

The promise of the ongoing presence of Jesus is part of what is known as the "Great Commission." After the cross and empty tomb, just as Jesus is about to be taken up bodily into heaven with the promise to return in the same way, Jesus gives this last benediction wrapped in marching orders:

> Go therefore and make disciples of all nations,
>   baptizing them
>   in the name of the Father
>   and of the Son and of the Holy Spirit,
>   teaching them to **observe**
>   all that I have **commanded** you.
> And behold, I am with you always,
>   to the end of the age.

Matthew 28:19–20, ESV

I like how the English Standard Version chooses the phrase, "*observe* all that I have commanded you." I understand why the New International Version goes with "*obey* everything I have commanded you." That translation isn't *wrong*. It's just that if we take our knee-jerk understanding of "teaching people to *obey* everything," I think we tend toward a list of rules or strict laws you can't break under penalty of death.

"All that Jesus commanded us" certainly does include rules and laws. It even deals with the penalty of death. But "all that Jesus commanded us" covers so much more.

When we as Church go to *disciple* the nations—that is, when we walk with people of all ethnic groups in a way that helps them know and follow Jesus—when we disciple the nations, we baptize and teach. We teach them to observe everything Jesus commanded, including marching orders like "Baptize and teach," but also including promises like "Behold! I am with you always!"

This is another one of those whole-story type of commands that includes hearing and holding onto God's delight, not as a theoretical thing, but as something that gets lived out in real life. "Observing everything Jesus commanded" means **holding onto**

promises and putting into practice the life and teachings of the one who, filled with the Spirit, pours out the Spirit on those who hold onto his promises and put his teachings into practice.

This command to observe (obey, hold onto, put yourself under and live out) the teachings of Jesus echoes what Jesus said at the end of the Sermon on the Mount: "Therefore everyone who *hears* these words of mine and *puts them into practice* is like a wise man who built his house on the rock" (*Matthew 7:24*, NIV). Hear and put into practice. That's at the heart of what it means to obey.

It seems obvious that you can *obey* commands like, "Do not judge, or you too will be judged" (*Matthew 7:1*, NIV). But "obeying a command" doesn't fit as well with "Ask and it will be given to you; seek and you will find; knock and the door will be opened to you" (*Matthew 7:7*, NIV). Yet both come at the end of the Sermon on the Mount, just before Jesus says you have built your house on a rock if you hear his words and put them into practice.

If you go back to the beginning of the Sermon on the Mount, the contrast gets even starker between our concept of obeying as following rules (without relationship) and a biblical understanding of hearing, putting yourself under, holding onto, and putting into practice. You can teach disciples from all nations to *obey* the command "Do not judge," but how do you *obey* "Blessed are the poor in spirit, for theirs is the kingdom of heaven; blessed are those who mourn, for they will be comforted; blessed are those who hunger and thirst for righteousness, for they will be filled"? (*Matthew 5:3–4, 6*, NIV).

When Jesus commissions us to teach all people, regardless of their nation of origin, to "obey everything he commanded," he intends for us to teach them how to put themselves under, hold onto, and live out:

> Blessed are you when people insult you,
> persecute you and falsely say all kinds
> of evil against you because of me.

> Rejoice [*chara*] and be glad [*agalliáō*, Joyful Delight],
>> because great is your reward in heaven,
>> for in the same way they persecuted
>> the prophets who were before you.
>
> *Matthew 5:78*, NIV

"Blessed" could go into our biblical Word Cloud of delight somewhere near *chara*: joyful on account of grace. When we obey, put ourselves under, embrace and hold onto, trust and live out the words, commands, promises, exhortations, and blessings of Jesus, we have built our house on a solid foundation that no storm can shake. We can face suffering with confidence. And, according to Jesus, we will know Delight:

> Now that you know these things,
>> you will be *blessed* if you do them.
>
> *John 13:17*, NIV

> These things I have spoken to you,
>> that my joy [*chara*, Woohoo!] may be in you,
>> and that your joy [*chara*, Woohoo!] may be *full*
>> [made complete or brought to fulfillment].
>
> *John 15:11*, ESV

Our job, then, as disciples and as *disciplers* is to obey the blessings, promises, and commands of Jesus, as we, filled with the Spirit, discern the Delight of the Father: the Father's good, pleasing, and perfect will.

Jesus himself teaches us to *pray for* that sort of joyful obedience, that we may delight in God's will and walk in God's ways, to the glory of God's holy name.

Praying For God's Delight

How many times have you prayed the Lord's Prayer in your life? How many times have you *paid attention* as you prayed the Lord's Prayer in your life? Don't answer that. And don't feel bad about it, either. Focused prayer is really hard; that's one reason we pray again and again and again…

I remember an anecdote about Martin Luther. Brother Martin reportedly bet that his friend couldn't get through the entire Lord's Prayer without his thoughts wandering. Luther let the man into a closet, shut the door and promised not to distract him. Luther was so confident of victory, he bet his own horse.

When Luther's friend came back out, he was shaking his head. With a rueful smile the friend reported that the prayer went really well. He got all the way to "For Thine is the Kingdom," when he began to wonder if the horse came with a saddle…

Sustained, focused prayer is hard. *Meaning* what you pray is hard. Meaning even the Lord's Prayer ain't easy, in part because you pray it all the time.

But *what do you mean* by the Lord's Prayer? Let's start there. What do you think you are doing when you pray the Our Father? What kind of prayer is "Thy *will* be done on earth as it is in heaven"?

If I imagine "God's will" as that cold, calculating, good-for-you-but-you-won't-like-it pill you have to swallow, then "Thy will be done" usually means something like, "Go ahead and have what you want, God, even though I know I won't like it."

But God's *will* is tied directly to God's *delight*.

What if we prayed, "Our *Abba* in heaven, Your Kingdom come; Your *Good Pleasure* be done…"? What if we prayed, "Our Father, Your *Desire (Yes, Please!!)* be done…"? What if Jesus is teaching us to pray, "Our Father, Your Kingdom Come, Your *Delight* be done, on earth as it is in heaven…"???

Let's take a brief look at the prayer Jesus taught us. It takes on new meaning when you know you are praying for *delight*.

You are asking God to do *the things God actually delights in doing*. You are inviting the Spirit to shape you to *delight in and do the things God delights in.* The Lord's Prayer teaches us to delight in God's will and to walk in God's ways, to the glory of God's holy name.

Our Father who art in heaven...

Jesus begins his prayer with relationship: *Abba*, Our *Father* in heaven, hallowed be Thy name. Jesus is placing the same *Abba* prayer on our lips that he prays in the Garden of Gethsemane. This prayer for delight is *grounded in relationship*. You are not a slave; you are a beloved child. And you ask for God's delight to be done in your life as a darling child asks their loving Father. You are also praying for obedience, but the obedience that flows from relationship, the obedience of delight in God's will as you observe God's ways to the glory (and hallowing) of God's holy name.

Thy kingdom come, Thy will be done...

Just as the Beloved Son prays, "Father, your will be done," he teaches beloved daughters and sons to pray, "Our Father, Thy kingdom come; Thy will be done."

Praying for God's Kingdom to come *is* praying for God's will to be done, on earth as it is in heaven. And praying for God's *will* (*Yes, please!!*) to be done is praying for God's delight to be a reality in us and through us. "Thy Kingdom come, Thy *Delight* be done."

God actually *delights* in saying yes to this prayer. This is exactly what filled Jesus with joy in the Spirit and made him jump up and spin around and go, "Woohoo!" The Father *delights* in revealing the kingdom not to the wise and learned, but to the little children. (This means you!) Or, as Jesus says to us in another place,

> Fear not, little flock,
>   for it is your Father's **good pleasure**
>   [*Wow!*, Thoughtful Delight]
>   to give you the kingdom.
> *Luke 12:32*, ESV

The apostle Paul puts it this way:

> This is good, and it is **pleasing** [*Wow!*]
>   in the sight of God our Savior,
>   who **desires** [*Yes, please!!*]
>   all people to be saved
>   and to come to the knowledge of the truth.
>   *1 Timothy 2:3–4*, ESV

God's Thoughtful Delight and Desirable Delight is to bring people into the eternal kingdom. When you pray for God's kingdom to come, you are praying for God's delight to be done. But it doesn't stop there.

Give us this day our daily bread...

When you ask God to supply for your daily needs, you don't come as a beggar. Your Father loves to daily and richly provide all that you need to support this body and life. You are asking God to do what God loves to do, and would do even if you didn't pray.

But when you *pray* for your daily bread, the Spirit works in you an attitude of dependence. You receive your daily bread with open hands and a thankful heart in a way you miss if you receive the same daily gifts with no thought for the Giver.

And God delights in that dependence. Jesus himself is dependent on the Father for everything he needs; as the Spirit shapes that daily dependence in us, it delights the Father.

Forgive us our debts as we forgive our debtors ...

When you go to your Heavenly Father burdened by guilt, you are not facing a cold, calculating, impartial judge who only begrudgingly lets you off if the evidence against you is not sufficient. No! You come to a God who loves to forgive! You come to a God who takes no delight in the death of the wicked, but who loves it when sinners turn back. You have a God who *celebrates* when the prodigal returns, a God who absolutely loves forgiving *you*!

And you are praying for the Spirit to shape that joyful forgiveness in your heart, too. Forgiving someone else 70 times 7 often feels like 489 times too many for me. But our God delights when we show mercy; when we let go of the burden of debt that comes from sin against us.

"Forgive us… as we forgive…" puts what we *do* and what we *receive* together in one beautiful symphony of relieving burdens and erasing debts. As we forgive, we are playing in tune with the music of *who God is*. As we seek forgiveness, we are asking to be put in the right key. As we forgive and receive forgiveness, we are resonating with the delight of the Father, who delights to forgive.

Deliver us from evil…

God absolutely loves delivering you from evil. Evil certainly includes sin, death, and Satan. And "evil" is a broad enough biblical concept to include all kinds of bad stuff; whatever is wrong in this fallen and sinful world, God loves setting it right.

King David appeals to God's Thoughtful Delight even as he calls out for rescue from his enemies:

> **Be pleased** (*ratsah*), O LORD, to deliver me!
> O LORD, make haste to help me!
>
> *Psalm 40:13*, ESV

God's *ratsah*, or Thoughtful Delight, is what God approves, what makes God go, "Wow!" God thoughtfully and joyfully approves of coming to the rescue, of saving the helpless, of delivering people from their enemies! (Rah, rah-TSAH: kick 'em in the other knee!)

רָצָה (Ratsah): approve, accept be pleased with, delight in

In fact, that delight in rescuing is part of God's core identity:

> Let the one who boasts boast about this:
>   that they have the understanding to know me,
>   that I am the LORD, who exercises *kindness*,
>   *justice* and *righteousness* on earth,
> for in these I **delight** [*chephets*, Yes, Please!!].
>
> *Jeremiah 9:24*, NIV

Kindness (or covenant love and faithfulness), justice, and righteousness: all three are about God setting right things that have gone so terribly wrong in this world. This is God delivering us from evil; it's just part of who God is. Doing justice, righteousness, and covenant faithfulness brings God Thoughtful and Desirable *Delight*.

God's delight—that is, God's *will*—shapes our adventure as followers of Jesus who are shaped by the Spirit to do the things that delight the Father.

> He has shown you, O mortal, what is good.
> And what does the LORD require of you?
> To *act justly* and to *love mercy*
> and to *walk humbly* with your God.
>
> *Micah 6:8*, NIV

God delights in kindness and justice and righteousness; and God loves it when you act justly and love mercy. "Walking humbly with your God" is a rough equivalent of "observing everything I have commanded you." You are putting yourself under God's Word of command and promise (and direction and exhortation and comfort and warning); and then holding onto those words as if your life depended on it. That's walking humbly with your God. That's obeying everything Jesus commanded you. That's the Spirit of the obedient Son shaping obedience in you. That's taking pleasure in doing God's Good Pleasure. That's delighting in God's will and walking in God's ways to the glory of God's holy name.

For Thine is the kingdom... forever and ever. Amen.

This final coda of the Lord's Prayer, added later by the Church, reminds us that this kingdom we are praying for comes to us ahead of time; but it is still an eternal kingdom, a kingdom that will not be complete or fulfilled in its most ultimate sense until Jesus comes again in glory.

It's like tacking on a part of the Hallelujah Chorus to the end of your prayer: "The kingdom of this world... will become... the kingdom of our God... and of his Christ (and of his Christ)...

and he shall reign forever and ever. Hallelujah. Hallelujah. Hallelujah! Hallelujah!"

One Day, God's Kingdom will come *completely* and God's delight will be done *perfectly* on earth as it is in heaven. And until that Day, every time you receive your daily bread with a thankful heart, every time you ask for forgiveness or offer forgiveness, every time you see God delivering you from evil or inviting you to set this world right in a way that brings your Father delight—every time you pray and live out the Lord's Prayer, you experience the Eternal Kingdom already present now, in Jesus.

Jesus delighted in the Father's will. Jesus walked in the Father's ways. Jesus brought and still brings the Eternal Kingdom. And one Day soon, the creation will finally and completely be set right. God's Kingdom will come and God's delight will be done once and for all, and justice and righteousness and mercy and kindness will have the final and eternal word on all of our brokenness and suffering and failure. We pray for that day. We long for that day. We delight to participate in that coming kingdom already now, ahead of time.

God's will—that is, God's *delight*—sets the course for this adventure of faith. As a result, we get to delight in God's will and walk in God's ways, to the glory of God's holy name.

A Simple Way to Pray

The Reformer, Martin Luther, was once asked by a barber how to pray. In a warm and friendly letter, Luther suggests that we all need a way to focus our prayer time, just like the barber needs to focus on the hair he is cutting, even if he is holding a conversation at the same time. So Martin shares a simple method that allows him to focus his thoughts in prayer.

Luther says he himself regularly uses this structure to pray from the Ten Commandments or the Apostles' Creed or from a biblical text. You could also use it to spend some focused time going through the petitions of the Lord's Prayer; this simple method works with a variety of texts for meditation. Luther's basic approach looks like this:

1. Notice what God is like and how God acts in the text.
   What is he teaching you?

2. Offer thanks based on the text.
   What has God done for you?

3. Confess your sins based on the text.

4. Use the text to say a prayer for strong faith
   or discipleship growth.

This structure is not supposed to be a straitjacket: Luther goes out of his way to say that if the Holy Spirit begins "preaching" to you as you pray, let your fixed pattern go and pay attention to what the Spirit is doing.

That kind of openness to possibilities makes Luther's fourfold process a good prayer experiment to run. Practice his approach over the next few days and see what you learn.

Prepare for prayer by inviting the Holy Spirit to open your heart and mind. You could pick any Scripture text to focus your meditation, but for the purposes of this chapter, sit with the words of the Lord's Prayer.

You might want to have the Lord's Prayer in front of you so you can read it slowly and take your time. Sometimes we rush through prayers we have memorized, or even have trouble starting anywhere besides the beginning. (I still have to sing the whole alphabet song to alphabetize anything ...)

You can write out the Lord's Prayer yourself, or you might find it in the front of a hymnal or prayer book, or look it up in your Bible in Matthew 6:5-15 or Luke 11:1-13, or see the version I know, below.

Once you have the Lord's Prayer in front of you, consider Luther's four keys to prayer for each of the petitions of the Lord's Prayer. How does, "Our Father, who art in heaven" teach you something about God that is different from "give us this day our daily bread"? How might "deliver us from evil" cause you to rejoice, or to confess? What changes if you hold onto delight as you pray, "Thy kingdom come, Thy *will* be done..."?

As you pray, pay attention to what the Spirit is doing in you through this Word. Jot down some notes or prayer requests if you like. And, as Luther said, if the Spirit guides your thoughts and prayers in a different direction, accept the Spirit's invitation, and follow where the Spirit leads!

Our Father, who art in heaven,
    hallowed be Thy name,
    Thy kingdom come,
    Thy will be done on earth as it is in heaven.
Give us this day our daily bread;
    and forgive us our trespasses
    as we forgive those who trespass against us;
and lead us not into temptation,
    but deliver us from evil.
For thine is the kingdom and the power and the glory
    forever and ever. Amen.

GROUP DISCUSSION FOR CHAPTER 9

God's Will Directs Your Adventure

Pick one or two of the following questions to help you get to know a friend, family member, or small group better.

1. What is the most adventurous thing you have ever done? Where were you? What happened?

2. When and where did you first learn the Lord's Prayer? Do you know or could you guess who taught it to you?

3. Would you prefer to listen to salsa music or Gregorian chant? If you had a choice, what style of music would you listen to?

Go a little deeper with someone you trust to point you back to Jesus. You don't have to reflect on all of the following, but spend some time on the ones that catch your spiritual attention.

1. "Obey," "command," "perfect," "God's will."

   How are those words defined differently in this chapter than the way you normally use them?

   Which were most similar? Most different?

   Do these differences matter?

2. "God's will is clearly and directly related to God's delight." Discuss.

3. What difficulty or suffering have you experienced in your life, or seen in the lives of others? Did this chapter give you any new ways of looking at suffering?

4. Have you had a chance to try Luther's *Simple Way to Pray*? If so, how did it go?

   If not, what got in the way?

CHAPTER 10

God's Work Shapes Your Adventure

Reading Plan

Day 1
God Delights to Shape You

Day 2
God Delights in Your Full Engagement

Day 3
God Delights in Your Rest

Day 4
God Delights in Your Play
&
Wear Your Helmet and Go Have Fun!

Day 5
Jesus Near You and Formed in You

Day 6
The Prayer of Examen
&
Group Discussion

God Delights To Shape You

If you've ever watched a potter, live or on YouTube, then you know the clay can have a tough time of it. I have seen a potter take a lump of clay and slam in onto her workspace as hard as she could, and then punch it—literally, punch it!—and knead it, and just beat that clay up one side of the table and down the other. The entire time, I was thinking, "I'm sure glad I'm not that clay!"

I found out later that the potter *has* to knead all of the air out of the clay before she starts shaping it. That intense process is actually necessary for the clay: any air still in the clay will cause the pottery to explode during the firing process. So what seems like rough treatment from the potter is actually the only way to protect the clay.

Which is why I am not quite sure how I feel about the biblical imagery of God as the Potter and me as the clay. I don't like being clay. **Being clay means you are not in control.** Being clay means getting the air beaten out of you. Being clay means being shaped to a design not your own, being sculpted with dangerous-looking tools that cut and trim and leave marks. Being clay means eventually being fired and baked and becoming both beautiful and useful according to the Potter's plan.

Well, I guess being beautiful and useful isn't all bad—I just wish I could skip over the rest of the process! If I had it my way, I would avoid all the shaping and molding and sculpting, especially anything to do with working defects out the clay or firing a glaze at 1,650°F. The thing is, if I got my way, I would end like I started—a cold, shapeless lump. Sigh.

Being shaped by the very hand of God means letting go of my plans, my control, my agenda, my own will for my faith life and for my usefulness in the Kingdom. I don't like it. My culture teaches me independence and self-determination as core values. The mythical caricatures of an independent woman and a self-made man are set up on pedestals as ideals. I have been enculturated into the idea that I should be the one in charge of my life.

My first day as a freshman in high school I was assigned an essay on a line of poetry from William Ernest Henley, "I am the master of my fate: I am the captain of my soul." According to years of funeral director polling, one of the songs most often requested for funeral services in my lifetime has been "My Way" by Frank Sinatra.

That song was played at the funeral of rapper Nipsey Hu$$le after he was gunned down in South L.A. two years after it was played at the inaugural ball of President Donald J. Trump, making self-determination one core value to bridge cultural divides and cover the gamut of American experiences from coast to coast.

"*I did it my way…*" The song and the sentiment are both quintessentially American. Maybe even quintessentially Western (the top funeral song in the UK is also "My Way").

And that sentiment is antithetical to following Jesus.

I am not in control of my own adventure of discipleship; **God** is. And sometimes that truth has to take me down a notch, put me back in my place, knock me off the throne of my own Western heart and humble me in the presence of the Almighty God who properly claims preeminence over *all* things, my heart and my destiny included.

Both the Prophet Isaiah and the Apostle Paul use the potter and clay image to bring us back down to reality. Who are you, *clay*, to talk back to God? Will the clay tell the Potter how to make a pot, or what type of vessel to form? Self-determination? I don't think so.

But change your perspective on that reality ever so slightly, and those harsh words become overwhelmingly good news!

The fact that God is in charge of shaping my life of following is such a relief! I don't have the skill, design or perspective to produce something beautiful, meaningful, and useful out of my own life. I carry a burden: I am supposed to produce results. I am supposed to "have an impact" or "make a difference." I'm even told I have to reach my potential, or be my best self, or reach for the stars. Talk about pressure! All that self-actualization can be like clay trying to shape itself according to its own design.

My culture tells me *I* have to work hard and make something of my life. But both the design and the sculpting are beyond me; I don't trust my own life plan, and I have little power to put it into effect.

The ideal of the self-realized individual is a persistent fiction that burdens the conscience and drains the joy out of your everyday life by always comparing your present reality with a standard impossible to meet. For those who know the burden of unrealized potential and unreachable expectations, the image of the potter and the clay comes as really good news.

I don't carry the responsibility of shaping my own life into something useful or beautiful; that's God's job description, not mine. *God's job* as the potter is to shape me and mold me according to a meaningful and artistic divine design. The pressure is off. I can stop trying to run my own life or get my own way. I don't have to make something of myself and pretend to be satisfied with what I get. The burden of making something of my life gets nailed to the cross of Jesus and drowned in the waters of baptism:

> "I have called you by name; *you are mine.*"
>
> *Isaiah 43:1*, ESV

> "You are *not your own*; you were bought at a price."
>
> *1 Corinthians 6:19–20*, NIV

> "Your steadfast love, O LORD, endures forever.
> Do not forsake *the work of your hands!*"
>
> *Psalm 138:8*, ESV

Of course, as clay, I will sometimes need to get the air bubbles kneaded out of me. That process can make me feel confused, out of control, or even under attack. But knowing that God is the potter and I am the clay is a comfort even when—*especially* when—I don't understand what God is doing in my life.

If you have ever watched a potter work on clay, then you know that those moments that seem like the most radical or unexpected to an outside observer are treated by the potter with the most care. I have seen a potter slice off the top third of a clay pot with a wire. And I thought the potter was crazy! Just when I thought the pot had taken its final shape, when it was better than I could ever have done myself, the artist took drastic measures and eliminated part of the clay I was sure belonged to the original design. But it didn't. It had to go. And the result was a design far better than the one I had in mind.

I have seen a potter take a fork, of all things, to wet clay spinning on the wheel. I have to say, I was not only curious; I was a little concerned. Forks don't seem to me to be tools appropriate for working with clay. But in the hand of an artist, even a fork can create a design: ever so slowly, and ever so carefully, that potter applied just the right pressure with the fork to create a pattern of wavy lines on the pot without ruining the clay. Against my expectation, the fork ended up making the pot more beautiful, not less. But only because an expert artist knew how to use even an unexpected tool to get the intended result. It took great care and concentration, but the result was beyond my expectation or imagination.

If you get a chance to see a potter work, on YouTube or in person, watch the potter's eyes: those eyes are focused on the clay, completely attentive. If the potter grabs a wire or a fork, you can bet their focus and care only increase. When the divine Potter allows something important to be removed from your life, when God allows suffering or struggle or loss to leave their mark, God is not ignoring you. God has not forgotten you. In times of radical or unexpected change, the Potter's eyes are all the more carefully focused on you. The Potter uses utmost intention and care to shape the clay. The Potter's eyes and heart and skill and imagination and cunning and experience are all brought to bear most clearly in that moment the clay comprehends least. God has those potter's eyes focused on you, especially when your life seems most confusing.

God is the potter; you are the clay. And that's good news.

Just as a potter cannot sculpt clay from a safe distance, your God does not stay comfortably remote from a creation wracked by brokenness and sin. Look at the potter's smock: that work apron is covered in spatters from the wheel. Look at the potter's hands: those strong hands are coated and stained from engaging the clay. Your God does not pull a few strings from behind the curtain and keep the messiness of human existence in quarantine. Your God rolls up potter's sleeves and personally, intimately, joyfully engages the clay.

You have a loving God with dirty hands.

That's what the message of the incarnation is all about. As God shapes and molds the lives of real people, God ends up with dirty hands. Jesus was born of the Virgin Mary, just like you were born; in the same messy way. And his dad probably wiped baby Jesus off and picked him up by the feet and spanked him on the butt to make him cry. Jesus came into the world just like you did.

Jesus *walked*. That's what he did! Jesus didn't have an angel chariot that whisked him wherever he wanted to go! Jesus didn't even have a bike. Jesus walked everywhere he went, and his feet got dirty, and his legs got tired, and he got hungry; even, at times, exhausted.

Jesus knows what it's like to bury a father; Jesus knows what it's like to stand at the graveside of a friend and weep; Jesus knows what it's like to be betrayed by someone you trusted. Jesus was willing to get his hands dirty.

Jesus got his hands dirty when he touched a woman who was ceremonially unclean because of an illness she had carried in her body for years; *Jesus got his hands dirty* when he made mud and put it on the eyes of a man born blind, in order to heal. *Jesus got his hands dirty* when he knelt down and washed his disciples' feet; *Jesus got his hands dirty* when he allowed Roman soldiers nail them to the rough wood of a cross.

God was not willing to play remote control with your discipleship walk from a distance. In Jesus, God stepped into human history to save. By the power of the Spirit, God still steps into human history, into *your* story, and in Jesus touches your life to mold you and shape you in love. At times, God's presence will seem near and real and comforting; at times God will seem to you to be distant, aloof, uncaring, or even absent. But throughout the range of your personal experience, this truth remains constant: you have a loving God with dirty hands.

God is the potter, and you are the clay. And that's *good news*. You are not in control, and the One who is in control has the skill and the talent and the experience and the design to create a masterpiece of unique beauty and usefulness out of your life. The times that seem most difficult to you are times when the Potter is most focused on your life. You have a loving, personal, intimate God with the strong, careful, and dirty hands of a potter who delights to shape the clay.

The potter's *delight* is my new favorite part of this biblical image of the potter and the clay. Have you ever done something, something you do *really well*, and it turned out just the way you wanted? Then you know something of what God feels when that divine potter takes a moment to stop and see how your life is starting to shape up.

I can just imagine God sitting back from the potter's wheel with a smile of pride and delight.

> Thou art worthy, O Lord,
>> to receive glory and honour and power:
> for thou hast created all things,
>> and **for thy pleasure**
>> they are and were created.
>
> *Revelation 4:11*, KJV

That's God's *Desirable Delight* in creating and sustaining you.

> It is God who works in you,
>> both to will and to work
>> for his **good pleasure**.
>
> *Philippians 2:13*, ESV

That's God's *Thoughtful Delight* in the way you are turning into a masterpiece, beautiful and useful and delightful.

God is up to something in your life. God is molding and shaping you. God is using even the most difficult and confusing experiences in your life to create a divine design. The careful, beautiful, intentional work the Father is doing in your life is an absolute *delight*.

> But now, O LORD, you are our Father;
>> we are the clay, and you are our potter;
>> we are all the work of your hand.
>
> *Isaiah 64:8*, ESV

God Delights In Your Full Engagement

God absolutely loves saving you. I mean, really. Like really, *really*. God's *Desirable Delight* is to give you the Kingdom as a gift. God's *Thoughtful Delight* is for you to be saved. God rescues you and picks you up and swings you around in an intimate embrace and with *Joyful Delight* exults over you with singing. God absolutely loves saving you.

And God loves giving you everything you need for salvation as a gift, without any merit or worthiness in you. If you live in a merit-based society, that's rather hard to wrap your mind around; but God loves giving undeserved gifts. God delights in your complete dependence. Your dependence allows God's grace to shine.

As an heir of the Reformation, things like Grace Alone and Faith Alone have been drummed into me from a young age. Perhaps the first Bible verse I learned was in Ephesians 2:

> For by grace you have been saved through faith.
>> And this is not your own doing;
>> it is the gift of God, not a result of works,
>> so that no one may boast.
>
> *Ephesians 2:8–9*, ESV

Salvation is a gift, and even the faith that receives the gift is, *wait for it...* a gift. That's Paul; but it's also Jesus: "Blessed are the *poor in spirit*—the bankrupt in spiritual currency—because theirs is the Kingdom without paying for it; as a gift." "Have no fear, little flock, for it is the Father's Good Pleasure to *give you* the Kingdom." "Unless you turn and become like this *little child*—who has nothing but dependence to bring to the relationship—then you can't get into the Kingdom." According to Paul, according to *Jesus*, God loves to give the free gift of salvation; which is good news for us, since there is no other way to receive the Kingdom.

The image of the potter and the clay emphasizes this passive receiving of the Kingdom gift. The clay can't tell the potter how to sculpt; in fact, the clay brings nothing to the table at all. A lump of clay is completely passive during the sculpting process, almost painfully so; and only when a pot is fully formed and fired does it begin to be useful for other people.

As great as that image is for breaking me of the habit of trying to shape and mold my own faith journey, the process of discipleship is a little more complicated than that. Scripturally speaking, God delights in **your complete dependence**. And, scripturally speaking, God also delights in **your full engagement**.

If all you had was the image of clay being shaped by a potter, you could reasonably assume that you can sit back and relax and let salvation be done to you from the outside. And while there are some important things right about that thought—salvation is by grace, from the outside, for the sake of Christ, not because of you or your work—still the Bible thinks it's a bit more nuanced than that.

Often, the verses that talk most about how we passively receive salvation in *complete dependence* go right on to describe how *actively engaged* we get to be in the process. It's like someone got peanut butter on my chocolate…

> For **by grace** you have been saved **through faith**.
>   And this is **not your own doing**;
>   it is the **gift** of God, **not a result of works**,
>   so that **no one may boast**.

So far, so good. But Ephesians 2:8–9 is followed directly by Ephesians 2:10.

> For we are [God's] **workmanship,**
>   **created** in Christ Jesus **for good works,**
>   which **God prepared beforehand,**
>   that we should walk in them.
>
> *Ephesians 2:10,* ESV

Did you know Ephesians 2 verse 10 came right after Ephesians 2:8–9? Or is that new to you? No matter how often I see those verses back to back, I still get a little jolt of surprise! Salvation is, on the one hand, by grace, through faith, given as a gift, and not a result of works; and in the next breath, Paul says we are the work of the divine Craftsman. The result of God shaping and molding and forming us is that we end up walking in the same good works that were not able to earn salvation in the first place. You are completely passive; and, as God's workmanship, you are completely engaged.

Notice, though, when it comes to your complete engagement, **even your active participation is framed as God's work in you**: God saves and shapes you for a purpose, and the good works you walk in as a result were laid out in front of you by God's intention and design. Your complete dependence and your active engagement in the things that bring God delight both result in no boasting, because both originate with God.

You can see that dynamic of complete dependence and active engagement in the Philippians 2 passage we have looked at before:

> Therefore, my beloved,
>   as you have always **obeyed,**
>   [*heard and put into practice*]
>   so now, not only as in my presence
>   but much more in my absence,
>   **work out** your own salvation
>   with fear and trembling,
>   for it is God who **works in you,**
>   both to will [*Yes, please!!*] and to work
>   for his **good pleasure** [*Wow!*].
>
> *Philippians 2:12–13* ESV

Did you know Philippians 2 verse 13 came right after Philippians 2:12? No matter how often I see those verses back to back, I still get a little jolt of surprise! You are *completely engaged* in the process; you are even supposed to work out your salvation! (The fear and trembling relates to what we saw about Jesus in the Garden of Gethsemane: this is submitting yourself to God's will, holding onto and putting yourself under God's commands and promises.)

And, at the same time, even while you are working, God is also working: God is working in you to shape both what you delight to do (your will) and the work you do, the work that results in God's delight. **Even when you are most actively engaged in God's work,** *God is actively engaged,* **working in you**. God delights in your full engagement; and God shapes that engagement in you.

I love that Paul puts down the duality of *your work* and *God's work* in you so clearly while writing to the followers of Jesus in the city of Philippi. Paul got to see something happen in Philippi that I think captures the essence of active engagement coupled with complete dependence. The story takes some time to tell, and it needs a little setup to be clear, but stick with me; the story of Paul and Lydia perfectly captures the delight of being actively engaged in following Jesus while God remains completely in control of the process.

By the time we get to Acts 16, where our story is recorded, Paul is on his second missionary journey around the Mediterranean. This time, Paul is traveling with a guy named Silas (yes, there's a backstory …) and these partners in the Gospel have just picked up a young gun named Timothy. Paul and Silas and Timothy have a plan: they want to go preach the Gospel in the Roman province of Asia. (No, not China; the Roman province of Asia, the western half of what we know as Turkey.) This Asia includes cities like Philadelphia, and Sardis, and Thyatira; not Beijing, Shenzhen, or Shanghai.

So Paul wants to go preach in Asia and, get this, *the Holy Spirit won't let him.* I know; right? What's up with that??

Instead, Paul and Silas and Timothy head out on a two-and-a-half-week hike cross-country to find out where God actually wants them to go next. They think they've got it figured out as they get to the western end of Turkey. They want to go north, up into a region called "Bithinia." But Acts 16 says again, very explicitly, that *the Spirit of Jesus would not allow them* to go into the region of Bithinia.

These missionaries don't go into Asia per plan A; they don't go into Bithinia per plan B. Instead, they end up in a port city called Troas, where they pick up a guy named Luke (yes, the Luke who wrote the Gospel of Luke, and, incidentally, the book of Acts, including Acts 16: if you look closely at the text, you can see the narrator starts using "we" at this point in the story).

Are you with me so far? Paul and his companions are working pretty hard here. But one thing is painfully clear: although they are completely and actively engaged in this missionary journey, God is the one in control.

In the city of Troas, God gives the assembled team clear marching orders. In a divine dream, Paul sees a person from the region of Macedonia asking for their help. Macedonia is just across the Aegean Sea, so Paul and Co. board the first available ship and set sail, blown by the guiding wind of the Spirit of Jesus.

Which is how they end up in the city of Philippi, the capitol of the province of Macedonia. Whew. Deep breath. They have finally arrived.

It seemed a little dicey there for a moment, but Paul and the boys are back in business. After being guided (let alone deterred) by the Spirit, they are now ready to do their part.

But not so fast.

You would think Paul would do what he *always* does when he enters a new city. But Paul can't follow his standard playbook in Philippi. You see, whenever Paul visits a new city, he typically goes to the synagogue on the Sabbath and proclaims Jesus as the fulfillment of the OT scripture; if they listen, he teaches more. If they don't listen, he goes to the Gentiles. That's just Paul's MO.

But *there is no synagogue* in the Roman colony of Philippi, so Paul can't follow his standard operating procedure. Instead, Paul and his companions end up at a riverside prayer meeting and women's Bible study. That's where Paul runs in to a woman named Lydia.

Maybe you've never heard of Lydia. That's OK; we don't actually know a whole lot about her. But here is what we do know: Lydia is from the city of Thyatira. Not Shanghai. Not Beijing. Thyatira! Right smack dab in the middle of Roman Asia, which is where Paul was trying to get at the very beginning of this Acts 16 misadventure, but the Spirit wouldn't let him!

We aren't given the details on how Lydia ended up in this exact place at this exact time. We know that Lydia is a dealer in purple cloth or perhaps the purple dye that made Thyatira world-famous. But we don't know what she was doing in Philippi. Probably something to do with her trade? But this is no simple business trip: she has a local address and local real estate with accommodations large enough for multiple guests.

As the head of her own household, she was fairly well-off; most likely, that means her husband left her the family business when he died. Lydia is also the name of a geographical region, and it was common practice in Paul's day for freed slaves to take their name from the region of their release. So it may well be that Lydia was a slave set free by the man she married before he died and left her (and her slaves) in charge of running Lydia's Purple Dye Imports and Emporium.

Of course, that's reading between the lines, but it's not too far of a stretch to pull together a reasonable account of her history that fits the facts we know. We know she is a woman of means. We know she is a dealer in purple. We know her husband is not mentioned. And we know her name is shared by local geography.

We also know she was a God-fearer, that is, a Gentile who believed in the God of the OT. But we don't know who first told her the stories of the God who created in love, who promised Abraham his offspring would bless the whole world, who took a chosen people out of slavery in Egypt and cut covenant with them at Sinai, who went with them into the wilderness wandering, planted them in the land, promised David a Son who would rule the nations in peace—we don't know where Lydia first heard those stories of promise. We know the gods she grew up with were dangerous and fickle. We know idols always take and never give. We know false gods always expect more and more of you until you are exhausted in their service. They always tear down your relationships, destroy your self-esteem, burden you beyond what you can bear, and maximize despair, self-centeredness, and burden in your life.

And we know Lydia came to believe that the God of Abraham, Isaac, and Jacob was somehow *her* God, too. Lydia is on a journey of faith, and God is the one in control of the journey.

So to recap: Paul is not where he intended to be, doing something he never does, and Lydia is not where she is supposed to be, for reasons we'll never know. If you didn't know any better you would get the impression that this is a complete coincidence, a chance meeting, a random event.

But as you look at the text more carefully you see very clearly Who is in charge of this situation. The Spirit of Jesus leads Paul very clearly not *there*, or *there*, but *here* instead. Paul has an appointment with a woman from Thyatira; he just can't go to Thyatira to find her.

And when God brings Paul way out of his way to meet Lydia, God doesn't sit back and relax. God still shows up and delivers. God is still the one in control. The text says, "God opened Lydia's heart to pay attention to Paul's message."

Oh, Lydia is a God-fearer, for sure; but she doesn't *get credit* for that. Paul is a great missionary, but this was not a part of *his* plan. There by the riverside, God shows clearly who is ultimately in control, and Paul and Lydia and Lydia's entire household are caught up and swept away by the mighty current of the river of God's grace.

Riding a mighty river current is actually a pretty good description of your journey of faith. Of course some river rides are intended to be slow, safe, and lazy. I've even been to a "Lazy River" at waterpark: you float slowly in a big circle and don't actually go anywhere.

While that's fun for a hot, lazy afternoon with your toddlers, that's not exactly what the life of faith is all about. **God delights**

in your complete dependence. God is the one completely in control (just ask Paul and Lydia).

And God also delights in your full engagement. Your life of faith is not a lazy Sunday afternoon floating in circles. Your life of faith is much more like taking a kayak through whitewater rapids: you certainly aren't in charge of your direction or destination, but you are buckled in, paddling furiously, soaking wet and loving every active, engaged minute of it!

Just ask Paul and Lydia! Lydia isn't in charge of her faith life; God even opens her heart to receive Paul's message! But Lydia is certainly fully engaged in the ride! As soon as she comes to faith, Lydia grabs her paddle and gets soaking wet: she and her whole household are baptized.

Lydia makes her home the new center of Gospel outreach in the city of Philippi and the region of Macedonia. She opens her house and her life to Paul and Silas and Luke and Timothy and the Gospel of Jesus. When Paul and Silas get out of prison, they return to their home base at Lydia's house to meet with the believers.

Which reminds me! Paul and Silas aren't in control of this missionary journey; God is! But Paul and Silas are paddling furiously, completely, physically and emotionally involved in what God is doing. They start Acts 16 with a hike that probably took them almost three weeks. They gather fellow travelers on the road, take a ship across the Aegean, walk from a port city up to Philippi, have to improvise a new plan when they find there is no synagogue in the city, and then they set up shop at Lydia's place, preach the Gospel, cast out an evil spirit, get dragged in front of an angry crowd, are stripped, beaten with rods, and put in stocks in prison, where they live through an earthquake, save the jail warden from suicide, baptize his whole household, go back to jail, and refuse to let the local authorities sweep their case under the rug before they eventually get back to Lydia's house for some encouragement. And that's just chapter 16!

Whew! That doesn't sound like a Lazy River to me! And that's just chapter 16 in the book of Acts! But that's just the way it goes with followers of Jesus. **You are not ultimately in**

charge of your faith life. You are along for the ride. But what a ride it is! Knowing you are not in control, **you get to live a fully engaged life of faith with abandon!** You get to strap on a helmet and start paddling furiously, expecting to get wet from head to toe! You might even experience some bumps and bruises and moments of exhilaration or even panic along the way, but one thing you are not is a passive observer.

You are completely, actively involved in this journey of faith where you completely, passively receive everything you need for the journey. You don't get credit for being a God-fearer. You don't get credit for listening or believing the Gospel. You don't get credit for opening your heart and your home and your life to following Jesus. But who cares about credit? You are on the adventure of a lifetime! To God's delight and yours, you are not in control of your faith life; and you are 100% actively involved in the adventure of following Jesus.

It is God who **works in you**, both **to will** and **to work** for his **good pleasure**. Woohoo! Yes, please!! Wow!!!

God Delights In Your Rest

God delights to shape you, which is good news, since you don't have the skill to design and shape a beautiful and useful masterpiece out of your own life. And God delights in your full engagement in the process of being shaped; followers of Jesus don't float down the Lazy River of life, going in a slow circle that leads nowhere. No, the river of God's grace has you on the adventure of your life. Buckle up and start paddling! God is in control of your journey and destination, but you get to be a fully engaged, whole person, all in explorer on this journey of faith.

That active engagement is intended as a delightful gift from your Heavenly Father. And, like all delightful gifts in a fallen world, that active engagement can become a burden.

We don't just have an "I did it my way" culture, we have a "What have you done for me lately?" culture. In that kind of performance-driven environment, it's easy to start out excited to grab a paddle and get actively engaged in your life of faith, and then get pretty exhausted pretty quick. When we get tired, we tend to just try harder. The Spirit's work in us fades into the background as our effort and our productivity begin to take center stage. Trying harder to be shaped by God just doesn't work. So we paddle faster and faster, hoping the current will pick up any minute. After all, we aren't on a Lazy River ride! If you can't see any progress, you better paddle a little faster! The less you feel like you're moving, the more you feel like you have to try harder, until following Jesus is like paddling upriver towing a sack of rocks. You can do it! Just paddle harder! (Exhausted yet?)

The gift of being actively engaged in the adventure of faith is not supposed to be a burden of maximizing your own potential. This is certainly no Lazy River ride; fully engaged discipleship is not for the faint of heart. Yet, if the river is in charge of the process as well as the destination, then you should expect some quiet pools or still waters right along with the exhilarating rapids. Rest and refreshment are part of the journey. **You are supposed to enjoy the ride**.

In a culture that makes an idol out of personal production, it's easy to turn even the work of discipleship into a burden. A scriptural perspective on growth includes both work and rest. See the opening verses of Psalm 127 as an example.

> Unless the LORD builds the house,
>   those who build it labor in vain.
> Unless the LORD watches over the city,
>   the watchman stays awake in vain.
> It is in vain that you rise up early and go late to rest,
>   eating the bread of anxious toil;
>   for [the LORD] gives to his beloved sleep.
>
> *Psalm 127:1-2,* ESV

Has anxiety ever kept you from falling asleep? Has your task list ever startled you awake in the middle of the night? Do you ever get to the end of a long day with more to do than when you started? Yeah; me, too.

Psalm 127 puts our work in the proper relationship with God's work. Because the Spirit is working in you both to will (Desirable Delight) and to do that which is pleasing (Thoughtful Delight) to God, you work under the umbrella of God's work. If the Lord is building the house, your labor to build is not in vain. If the Lord is watching the city, those who watch are working the night shift for good reason: they are participating in the ongoing work of God in the world.

Notice how the anxiety that drives your day from early morning emails to late night meetings doesn't have a place in this rhythm of grace: just as God gives the gift of work, God gives the gift of sleep. You receive the gift of rest because God loves you.

The rhythm of rest and work establishes an ongoing dependence on God and an ongoing participation in the Spirit's work. You get to be actively engaged and soaking wet on this whitewater discipleship adventure; and precisely because you are not in control, the river gets to show you quiet, refreshing pools as well as exhilarating rapids. Without one, the other becomes a burden; both work and rest can become idols. Dependence on Jesus means receiving both work and rest as a gift.

You can see the delightful rhythm of rest and work in the teachings of Jesus, especially when he uses images from agriculture or home life. The Kingdom of God is like some guy who plants a seed: the farmer can't work to make it grow. While he is sleeping God produces abundant crops. The Kingdom of God is like some woman who adds leaven to her dough; yes, she combines the right ingredients and kneads the dough, but the real work takes place when she lets the dough rest. That's when growth and abundance can happen. (Both of those images are found in Luke 13:18–20.)

A more familiar image may be the Vine and Branches in John 15. You know how that teaching goes: "I am the Vine, you are the branches; apart from me you can do nothing." That captures God's work in our work—or perhaps better to say, that captures our work in God's work. But do you remember what comes next? "I am the Vine, my Father is the Vinedresser. Any branch in me that does not bear fruit he cuts off. And *every branch that does bear fruit, he prunes, so it can be even more fruitful.*"

Whoa! Hold on a second!

You can't bear fruit or be productive in the Kingdom unless you are connected to Jesus. OK, I've got that.

You don't *work hard* at producing fruit; fruit is a natural result of being connected to the Vine. OK; I don't *like* it (I just want to try harder to pop out a few more grapes), but I guess I *get* it. My work on my own is not what Jesus wants; Jesus want his work in me and the fruit that comes from dependence on him. Fine. I'd rather be in control, but I am coming to understand that *me being in control* is the worst possible outcome for my faith life. OK. Fine, Jesus. Have it your way.

But then Jesus goes so far as to say that *when I do produce fruit, even then* I don't get a blue ribbon. I get the pruning knife instead. Say what?

If you have ever tended roses or cut back raspberry bushes or deadheaded flowers or pinched suckers off of tomato plants, you know what Jesus is talking about. Bearing fruit comes after a long, dependent process of growth. But it's not the end of the process. You cut back the vine so it produces more fruit. You trim the rose bush so it will flower again. You let the field lie fallow so that its yield can increase. Times of producing fruit in your life are balanced by times of rest and inactivity.

Healthy pruning belongs to the process of bearing fruit. Good work includes good rest. Pouring out demands receiving.

You see that delightful rhythm of rest and work, receiving and pouring out, not just in the teachings but in the life of Jesus. Before he chooses the 12 disciples, Jesus spends alone time with the Father and the Spirit in prayer. In the midst of his active preaching and teaching, Jesus tells the disciples, "Come away with me to a quiet place to get some rest." (They don't actually get to rest at that point, because 5,000+ people crash their retreat center and Jesus has compassion on the crowds.)

After he feeds those 5,000+, Jesus sends the crowds away so he can recharge in solitude and prayer. Not long after, the Transfiguration occurs on a mountain where Jesus had taken three of his closest friends for some alone time, not for a *vacation* exactly, but for rest and spiritual renewal. In fact, Luke tells us Jesus *was in the act of praying* when he was transfigured before Peter, James, and John. And of course, on the night he was betrayed, preparing for arrest and torture and humiliation and death, Jesus spends extended time in the seclusion of the Garden of Gethsemane for the purpose of prayer.

One of my favorite moments of rest in the life of Jesus comes in the midst of a storm. You remember the story. Jesus is asleep on a cushion in a boat when a sudden storm gets so violent that even career fishermen are shaking from fear, but Jesus sleeps on.

The disciples, out of their minds with terror, finally wake Jesus up with cries of, "Don't you care if we drown??"

At which point Jesus calls the winds and waves to heel, and the resulting calm strikes new terror in the hearts of these fishermen. Who but God could calm the storm? Who is this Jesus, *really...*?

I've heard this story used to show Jesus was fully human and exhausted; and rightly so. I have heard this story used to show that Jesus was fully divine, commanding the storm; and rightly so.

But don't miss this point: sleep is **fundamentally an act of trust**. Jesus is actively entrusting his life and his situation to his Heavenly Father. The obedient Son could sleep securely in the midst of the storm because Jesus knows and trusts the One who holds the power of the wind and waves. Jesus not only puts himself under the authority of the Father in his ministry, Jesus trusts the authority of the Father with his life.

When Jesus finally does wake up, his response is not, "Whoa! Look at that storm!! You should have gotten me sooner!" Instead, in the midst of that fearful gale, Jesus asks the disciples, "Where is your faith?" Faith enables sleep even while the storm rages.

Jesus was simply putting into practice the attitude of the heart expressed in Psalm 4:8, "In peace I will lie down and sleep,
for you alone, LORD, make me dwell in safety."

Sleep is a gift from God. Sleep is an act of trust. You can sleep securely, like Jesus in the storm, because your Heavenly Father is still in control, even when you are not. In fact, part of your work in the Spirit is rest in the Spirit. The Father prunes even the fruitful branch. Living in dependence on Jesus means experiencing both moments of productivity and moments of repose.

You might plant or water, but God gives the growth. You might knead that leaven into the dough, like a potter kneads the clay, but you've got to let it rest.

Part of the faithful work of followers of Jesus is refusing to let work or rest become idols that demand all of your attention and time. **In Jesus, you work and rest both to the glory and increasing delight of the God who is in charge of seedtime and harvest, night and day, labor and sleep.**

God delights in your work. And God delights in your rest. Both work and rest belong to the adventure of following Jesus.

God Delights In Your Play

God delights in your work. God delights in your rest. A third experience somewhere between work and rest also puts a smile on God's face. *Play* involves active engagement, like work, and results in rejuvenation and refreshment, like rest. From the beginning of creation to the restoration of creation, your God delights in play.

We met Playful Delight back in Chapter 3. The Hebrew word *sha'a'* can refer to anything that makes you go, "Whee!!" It also refers to the species of joy you experience as you engage God's Word (we'll come back to that idea in Chapter 11). Psalm 119 describes the *fun* we have exploring God's Word, but that's not the only place we see Playful Delight in the story of Scripture.

שָׁעַע (Sha'a'): sport, take delight in, play

You remember the opening of the Gospel of John: "In the beginning was the Word, and the Word was with God, and the Word was God…" John says, Jesus is the Word made flesh who took up residence among us, who *tabernacled* among us.

The passage is clear: Jesus, as the Word, was present even from before the very beginning of creation. As God *spoke* the universe into existence, *the Word* was right there, actively participating:

> All things were made through him,
>> and without him was not any thing made
>> that was made.
>
> *John 1:3*, NIV

Jesus, as God's active Word, has been actively at work from the very beginning. Paul would later write:

> By him [Jesus] all things were created,
>> in heaven and on earth, visible and invisible,
>> whether thrones or dominions or rulers or
>> authorities—all things were created
>> through him and for him.
> And he is before all things,
>> and in him all things hold together.
>
> *Colossians 1:16–17*, ESV

Jesus was present and active from the beginning of creation. And that's where the fun begins! In the last chapter, we already saw how one way of reading the hymn in Revelation 4 gets at the salsa party of creation:

> "Thou art worthy, O Lord,
>> to receive glory and honour and power:
>> for thou hast created all things,
>> and for thy pleasure [*thélēma*] they are
>> and were created."
>
> *Revelation 4:11*, KJV

One reason I think the King James gets this verse right is because of a similar passage in the Old Testament Wisdom book of Proverbs. Proverbs is a collection of wise saying from the perspective of someone who knows and fears God (and also knows the ways of the world). One of the key features of the book is Lady Wisdom, the personification of one central aspect of God's character.

It's not entirely clear all the time how poetic the language is, or how we are supposed to relate Lady Wisdom to God, or to God's Spirit, or to God's Word, but Proverbs says enough about Lady Wisdom to invite us to keep her as a clear and unique feature of who God is and what God is about.

Proverbs 8 hangs together with John 1 and Colossians 1 to give us a beautiful mosaic of Lady Wisdom with God the Creator, Spirit, and Redeemer at work (and at play) from the dawn of creation.

> When [God] established the heavens,
>   I [Wisdom] was there;
>   when he drew a circle on the face of the deep,
>   when he made firm the skies above,
>   when he established the fountains of the deep,
>   when he assigned to the sea its limit,
>   so that the waters might not
>   transgress his command,
>   when he marked out the foundations of the earth,
> then I was beside him, like a master workman,
>   and I was daily his **delight** [*sha'a'*],
>   **rejoicing** before him always,
>   **rejoicing** in his inhabited world
>   and **delighting** [*sha'a'*] in the children of man.
>
> *Proverbs 8:27–31*, ESV

The Maker of Heaven and Earth is experiencing Playful Delight in this personification of Wisdom; the Creator delights in Lady Wisdom. And Lady Wisdom is rejoicing (a new *playful delight* word in Hebrew) in the presence of the Creator.

Lady Wisdom also rejoices (takes Playful Delight) in the inhabitants of creation (cue the salsa music) and even knows the Playful Delight of spending time with Adam and Eve. I love the thought of Lady Wisdom throwing a Garden party in Eden. What a playful delight!

That same *"rejoicing with playful delight"* vocabulary word shows up again in the Old Testament. This time, however, the promise of the New Creation is in view.

As Zechariah images the restoration of Jerusalem and of the whole world at the coming of the Day of Yahweh, this detail makes me want to throw back my head and sing for joy:

> This is what the LORD says:
> "I will return to Zion and dwell in Jerusalem.
>
> Then Jerusalem will be called the Faithful City,
>   and the mountain of the LORD Almighty
>   will be called the Holy Mountain.
>
> The city streets will be filled
>   with boys and girls **playing** there."
>
> *Zechariah 8:3, 5* NIV

One mark of the restoration of creation: boys and girls will be laughing and playing and just plain having fun. "There'll be dancin'; dancin' in the street!" *Rejoicing with playful delight* is the new status quo of the New Creation.

I think God had fun in the process of creation. I think Jesus had *fun* with his disciples. I think the Spirit thought Pentecost was just plain awesome.

You serve a God who made the blue whale as well as the platypus. You have a Savior who turned gallons and gallons and gallons of water designed for following strict religious rules into more of the best wine than could be drunk in a month full of weddings. You have received the Spirit who wouldn't let Paul go to Asia just so he could meet a woman from Thyatira, and then opened Lydia's heart the message of salvation.

Play, like rest, is an act of trust, trust that God is in control and your ongoing work is not necessary to keep the planet spinning. God likes play. God created play. God loves it when you play, in part because you can't be worried about everything else if you are enjoying God's good gifts with delight.

As a human being, you were created in the image of God. You

therefore have a calling to image God to the rest of creation. You certainly do that in your work and labor, as a steward of God's creation; and you also image God in your play, as you delight in God's creation.

When you receive them with delight, and in dependence on Jesus, **your rest, your work, and your play all move you into deeper relationship with God**, your Creator, Redeemer, and Sustainer. And that makes God rejoice with playful delight!

Wear Your Helmet And Go Have Fun!

I rode my bike a lot when I was a kid. I still remember the steel blue frame, and the black banana seat, and all the shiny chrome. You could do some pretty amazing stunts on that bike! And we did! We raced on dirt tracks, and popped wheelies on every curb, and jumped every incline, no matter how small, and tore across trails to go cross-country to Dine-O-Bite Donut Shop where you could sit in that cool, sweet-smelling air and pump quarters into Centipede or Pac-Man. Ah, the good old days…

I don't think I even saw a bicycle helmet until I had kids of my own. But we still had safety rules. The kids had full reign of the trails and tracks in the backyard, and our neighbors had driveways right next to each other that made an awesome race course, but you never, ever, ever rode your bike out onto West Court Street. The speed limit there was 55 mph, and back in the '80s, Sammy Hagar wasn't the only one who couldn't drive 55. That street was not safe for kids on bikes. And we still managed to have all kinds of fun, and scrape some knees, and lose some teeth…

I didn't think about safety rules nearly as much as a kid as I did once I had kids of my own. Suddenly, helmets and kneepads and elbow pads (and shin guards and mouth guards and miniature suits of armor) all became very interesting.

Parenting taught me a lot about the relationship between risk management, safety, and delight. Depending on how you were parented, or how you parent, you have also had different experiences with risk management and delight.

Perhaps you can imagine the parent who bundles their kid up in so much protective equipment, the poor child can hardly peddle their trike around the cul-de-sac. Or perhaps you can imagine the parent whose disinterest results in their kid playing in the busy street. My guess is you are somewhere in between. But where exactly? And how do you make that call?

We've been talking about delight and being fully engaged in this adventure of discipleship. We've been talking about rest as well as play, and how much fun it actually is to follow Jesus. And there is some danger here. But I want to capture the heart of the kid who loves riding that bike on one wheel uphill and down (even without a helmet) and who also knows you don't ride your bike into traffic.

I want to be aware of the danger, but not let the danger hinder the delight. I want you to know that playing in traffic is really dangerous—you can even get killed! But I don't want you looking over your shoulder all the time to make sure you are following all the rules. Because **the fear of failure sucks joy**. If you have to get every detail of riding your bike right, or else, you will never find delight in riding your bike.

So I want you to know: you are going to mess up. You are going to get the balance of rest and work and play wrong more often than you get it right. You are going to scrape your knee, or fly over a curb into the bushes, or get stuck in a pileup with other kids and their bikes in a tight corner. You might even lose a tooth or break an arm.

Stay out of the traffic.

And go have fun.

Any fun worth having involves some risk. Discipleship is no different. When you fall down, get back up, dust off, and get back in the saddle seat.

Sometimes you might need a Band-Aid or some comfort from mom; but don't let the fear of getting it wrong prevent you from flying down the hill at top speed.

(And stay out of the traffic!)

To know where the danger lies, you need to know what the busy road looks like. Of course, you could fall down and skin your knee at any time; but try to avoid playing in traffic on purpose…

The danger in rest, work, or play stems from a natural human inclination: even in the Garden of Eden, we humans have had **a tendency to focus on the gift at the expense of the Giver**. Rest, work, and play are no different.

Of course, if you take 48 weeks of vacation, your job is going to suffer. And of course, if you take 0 weeks of vacation, your job is also going to suffer. Play can become an idol we set up and enjoy not with God, but against God, and against God's calling on our lives. That danger is real. You see something like that in Amos 6.

> Woe to you who are complacent in Zion…
> You strum away on your harps like David
>   and improvise on musical instruments.
> You drink wine by the bowlful
>   and use the finest lotions,
>   but you do not grieve over the ruin of Joseph.
> Therefore you will be among the first to go into exile;
>   your feasting and lounging will end.
>
> *Amos 6:1, 5–7* NIV

God loves a good party; but idle feasting while the innocent suffer becomes *idol* feasting—worshiping at the altar of Sloth when God has given you good work to do, for your good, your neighbor's benefit, and God's glory. Sleep is an act of trust; lounging on your couch all day, every day is ignoring God's gift of the day. I think God thinks *improvising on musical instruments* is the bomb; God even commissioned choirs and musicians as well as artists and craftsmen right besides priests and Levites for holy service in the Temple. Turned toward God, music is one of God's greatest gifts; but separate the gift from the Giver, and you get music tuned in on itself. **Play is a gift; and any gift can become an idol**.

Rest follows the same pattern. Rest can become a burden as well as an idol. The book of Proverbs has this to say about too much rest:

The lazy person claims, "There's a lion on the road!
Yes, I'm sure there's a lion out there!"
As a door swings back and forth on its hinges,
so the lazy person turns over in bed.
Lazy people take food in their hand
but don't even lift it to their mouth.

Proverbs 26:13–15, NLT

It's gotten pretty bad when you are so lazy you can't be bothered to get the scoop of ice cream out of the bowl and all... the... way... up... to... your... mouth. Sigh. I need a nap...

Play and rest, if unchecked, take over your whole life and drive you to focus on yourself at the expense of those around you. **Just like work**. If you work and work and work and work and tell yourself you are too important to take a vacation, too busy to lose a weekend, too essential to get sidetracked by other people, then you will tend to focus on work at the expense of relationships, with other people and with God. You can work so much that your faith and your family suffer.

It is in vain that you rise up early and go late to rest,
eating the bread of anxious toil;
for [the LORD] gives to his beloved sleep.

Psalm 127:1-2, ESV

So you face real danger. But don't let that suck the joy out of this adventure of following Jesus. You aren't going to rest, work, or play perfectly; but focusing on your own effort is a sure way to lose hope as well as joy. Wear your helmet, sure; but go have fun! Go race around the trails! Go pop a few wheelies! Go see how fast you can fly down that hill with both feet in the air and no brakes! Just stay out of the traffic....

How do you balance the fear of failure with the delight of trying? I think **relationship is key** whether we are looking at rest, work, or play. God takes a day of rest, a Sabbath, as soon as creation is complete. God's people are supposed to follow suit. But Jesus has to remind even the most religious people of his day, "Sabbath was created as a gift for human beings; human beings weren't created just so someone could follow the rules of Sabbath!" It's about relationship, not just following rules.

I was stunned to find that Sabbath rest is actually talked about as a covenant in the Old Testament. God rests, and so God's people rest, and that **rest binds them together in relationship**:

> The Israelites are to observe the Sabbath,
>   celebrating it for the generations to come
>   **as a lasting covenant.**
> It will be a sign between me and the Israelites forever,
>   for in six days the LORD made the heavens
>   and the earth,
>   and on the seventh day he rested and was refreshed.
>
> *Exodus 31:16–17*, ESV

God delights to shape the rhythm of rest, work, and play into the creation in ways that reflect our relationship with God. Although we have the capacity to abuse them, rest, work, and play are good gifts, fun gifts, gifts you are meant to take out of the garage and ride all over the neighborhood, by yourself and with others, until you can fly like the wind and jump hills like a pro and come back, often dirty and sometimes bloody, but always with a smile on your face and a story of adventure to tell.

When you receive them with delight, and in dependence on Jesus, **your rest, your work, and your play all move you into deeper relationship with God**, your Creator, Redeemer, and Sustainer. And that makes God rejoice with playful delight!

Jesus Near You And Formed In You

Even good gifts make terrible gods. When the people of God were wandering in the wilderness, their commitment to rebellion brought judgment. (Talk about intentionally playing in the traffic!) So God had to set things right in their relationship. That often involved the people experiencing the consequences of their broken relationship with God in ways that drove them back into relationship with the God who delights when sinners turn back and come home.

One case in point: the bronze snake on a pole. Venomous snakes infested the camp of God's wandering people. These "fiery serpents" manifested God's judgment on persistent and unrepentant sin. People were getting bit. People were suffering. People were dying.

When they turned back to the God of covenant faithfulness, God had Moses fashion a snake out of bronze and hang it on a pole where all the people could see it. People were still getting bit, but anyone who looked on the promise of God suspended on that crude tree, saw and lived. (See *Numbers 21:4–9* for the details.)

God gave a good gift. The people received the good gift. The good gift even saved. Years later, however, the people took that good gift and made it a god. Literally. The bronze snake became like any other idol. King Hezekiah, a king of Israel known for his thorough reform, had to destroy not only high places of Baal and the Asherah poles; the king had to get rid of the bronze snake on a pole (*2 Kings 18:4*). The good gift had been turned into a fake god to rival the Giver.

Before we shake our heads too smugly at the stubbornness and stupidity of these ancient people of God, recognize that we, too, readily take God's good gifts and turn them into idols. We can take God's good gift of *rest* and use it to avoid serving God and loving our neighbor. We can turn God's good gift of *work* into the thing that receives all of our attention and effort, an idol that promises us fulfillment and hope for the future. We can make God's good gift of *play* a competition to see who can gratify the sinful nature in the most spectacular ways (and post evidence on social media).

We are good at turning good gifts into idols. And good gifts make terrible gods. They always take and never give. They always expect more and more of you until you are exhausted in their service. Good gifts turned into gods always tear down your relationships, destroy your self-esteem, burden you beyond what you can bear, and maximize despair, self-centeredness, and burden in your life. Why do we do that to ourselves?

Thankfully, you have a God who delights to welcome sinners home. You have a God who continues to give you good gifts like rest, and work, and play because you can receive them even now in Jesus as good gifts that glorify the giver. You have a God who will perfect the gifts of rest, work, and play in the resurrection of the dead and the life of the world to come. What a relief!

Here's the thing, though: just as we can put rest, work, and play up on a pedestal and turn them into idols, we can actually take Jesus and turn him into a false god. I know that sounds odd. Jesus is good and holy and somehow *religious*. Jesus saves. How can we take something good and holy and religious that saves, and turn that good gift into an idol? It almost doesn't make sense.

Except that's exactly what God's people did with that bronze snake on a pole: it was good and holy and it saved, and people took it and put it on a pedestal and made a false god out of it. Jesus said that sign of death hanging above the earth that took away God's judgment was somehow a picture of his own life and ministry and sacrificial death.

> Just as Moses lifted up the snake in the wilderness,
>   so the Son of Man must be lifted up,
>   that everyone who believes
>   may have eternal life in him.
> For God so loved the world
>   that he gave his one and only Son,
>   that whoever believes in him shall not perish
>   but have eternal life.
>
> *John 3:14–16* NIV

Did you know John 3 verses 14–15 came right before John 3:16? No matter how often I see those verses back to back, I still get a little jolt of surprise! Like the bronze snake in the wilderness, Jesus is lifted up on a pole, and those who look on him in faith are saved. And, just like the bronze snake, we can take the good gift of Jesus and turn that gift into an idol. I know that sounds weird. Here's how it works.

We turn Jesus into an idol when we set him up on a pedestal, as an ideal to aspire to, way out there somewhere. We have some vague sense that we are supposed to be "like Jesus," and so we set the bar at *Jesus* and try our hardest to meet the standard of his love and life and work. Of course, we don't expect to do it perfectly, but the more we try to act like Jesus and love like Jesus and reach that ideal of Jesus way up on a pedestal, the more we despair of ever doing anything right. We get stuck between an unattainable goal and the sinking feeling that it would be better to throw in the towel. Just as we can take the mythical caricatures of an independent woman and a self-made man and set them up on a pedestal as an ideal to strive for, we can make Jesus a caricature of ideal ethical and moral behavior that we have to strive for.

I take charge of my discipleship, set Jesus as my goal, and end up having to work hard to make my life look more like Jesus, which doesn't really seem fair to me, since Jesus is God and therefore by definition already holy and perfect and loving in a way I could never be. And the more I struggle to bridge that gap between my life and the ideal Jesus, the more discouraged I get.

As soon as I get discouraged by seeing Jesus as an ideal to aspire to, way up there on a pedestal, I almost immediately start harboring the thought that Jesus must be cheating. I know that doesn't seem very pious, but even if I don't usually put it that crassly, it certainly seems to me that Jesus as an ideal is just not fair.

I mean, Jesus is God for crying out loud! Of course Jesus is going to resist temptation, and love the unlovable, and lay down his life for his friends. Jesus must be sneaking in a little divine power to resist the devil; pulling off a second-person-of-the-Trinity magic trick to point to the Kingdom; playing his God-in-the-flesh card whenever the going gets too tough for his flesh.

And as long as it seems to me that Jesus must be cheating, I can let myself off the hook. When I am called on to resist temptation or love my enemies or even delight in the work of the Kingdom, I have a fallback position: of course Jesus can do all those things; he's God! And I am not. So why even try?

Putting Jesus on a pedestal as the model of my own self-realized individualism makes *being like Jesus* a burden I have to carry. That burden sucks the joy out of my faith.

I can let myself off the hook by separating myself even more from Jesus (that perfect Jesus on a pedestal is God and I am not, so why even try being like him?). Or I can try harder and harder to reach that ideal, even though I am exhausted by the effort and secretly know I will never bridge the gap between my life and Jesus. Or maybe I can hope God is grading on a curve, and look at people around me to notice that no matter how much of a failure I am, I can always find someone worse.

That way of treating Jesus as a moral example tears down my relationships, destroys my self-esteem, burdens me beyond what I can bear, and maximizes despair, self-centeredness, and burden in my life. Just like an idol.

Thankfully, you have a God who delights to welcome sinners home. You have a God who continues to give you Jesus. You have a God who will perfect Jesus in you in the resurrection of the dead and the life of the world to come. What a relief!

You are not wrong if you think Jesus left you an example to follow. In fact, Jesus says he is intentionally leaving an example for his followers. What's wrong is taking Jesus as an example and *setting him up on a pedestal, outside of you*, outside of your reach, as a gold standard to aspire to. That puts Jesus far away from you and makes it *your work* to get closer to him. That makes Jesus an ideal or an idol, a relentless taskmaster that drives you to complacency or despair.

When Jesus talks about you being like Jesus, he reverses the direction: **Jesus bridges the gap from his side**. The actions and attitudes of Jesus are not a pattern you are supposed to aspire to in your attitudes and actions; rather, they are the pattern the Potter uses as the model for shaping and molding you. The Spirit shapes *the humble service of Jesus* in your life. The Spirit shapes *the dependence on the Father of Jesus* in your life. The Spirit shapes *the prayers of Jesus* in your life. Your job is not to make your service, dependence, prayers, and life look a little more like Jesus. No; **the Spirit is shaping the service, dependence, prayers, and life**

of Jesus in you. Jesus is not far off, up on a pedestal, for you to aspire to; Jesus is near you and being shaped in you by the loving hands of the Potter.

> For those God foreknew
> he also predestined
> **to be conformed**
> **to the image of his Son.**
>
> *Romans 8:29*, NIV

Jesus is the design the Potter has in mind as God shapes you and molds you and makes you beautiful and unique and useful. Becoming more like Jesus is not supposed to burden you or make you despair; Jesus explicitly says that the purpose and result of following his example is *joy*: not joy you are supposed to aspire to; the joy of Jesus shaped in you by the Spirit.

We looked at John 15:11 way back in Chapter 1: Joyful Delight. Do you remember? Here it is again:

> "I have told you this so that **my joy** may be in you
> and that your **joy** may be complete."
>
> *John 15:11*, ESV

You now know that "joy" word is *chara* (like caress with an ah!), the Joyful Delight word related to "grace." You remember that this is the Upper Room on Maundy Thursday, one of the places Jesus is most specific about the example he is leaving and about what it means to follow that example.

While teaching on the same night he washed his disciples' feet, Jesus makes his attitude and his work the exemplar of all those who follow him.

> If I then, your Lord and Teacher,
> have washed your feet,
> you also ought to wash one another's feet.
> For **I have given you an example,**
> that **you also should do**
> **just as I have done** to you...

A new command I give you: Love one another.
> **As I have loved** you,
> **so you must love** one another…

Very truly I tell you, whoever believes in me
> will **do the works I have been doing**,
> and they will do **even greater things** than these.

John 13:14–15, 34; 14:12 NIV

Jesus clearly thinks you are supposed to follow his example. And if these were the only things Jesus had said on that Command Thursday, it would be reasonable to set his life up on a pedestal as an ideal you are supposed to work hard to emulate.

Thankfully, as we saw in Chapter 1, that's not *all* Jesus said on Maundy/*Chara* Thursday. Jesus points to the way we are supposed to experience and engage his example, a way that completely reverses the direction of our idolatry, a way that brings *joy*.

The words I say to you
> I do not speak on my own authority.

Rather, it is **the Father, living in me**,
> who is **doing his work**…

I will ask the Father, and he will give you
> another advocate to **help you and be with you** forever—
> **the Spirit** of truth…

[The Spirit] lives **with you** and will be **in you**.
> I will not leave you as orphans;
> **I will come to you**…

I am in my Father,
> and **you are in me**,
> and I **am in you**…

Remain in me,
> as **I also remain in you**…

I have told you this
> so that my **joy** [*chara*] may be in you
> and that your **joy** [*chara*] may be complete.

John 14:10, 16, 18, 20; 15:4, 11, ESV

Jesus uses a logic we are familiar with: as I, so you. But we tend to think that means, *as Jesus* does all this awesome stuff, *so I* have to work really, really hard to do awesome stuff like that, too. We put Jesus way out there somewhere as an ideal and then crush ourselves trying to reach that ideal.

Notice how Jesus actually uses the logic of "as I, so you." (Spoiler alert: it's not how you think.) Jesus says:

> *As I* live in dependence on the Father,
>   and the Father works in me
>   through the power of the Spirit, who fills me,
> *so you* live in my dependence on the Father, shaped in you,
>   and I will be in you and work in you
>   through the power of that same Spirit,
>   who now fills you, and shapes me in you.

Jesus doesn't set himself up as an ideal outside of you, far away from you, that you are trying to climb up to reach. No! The exact opposite is true! **Jesus comes down to you and makes his home in you and pours out his Spirit on you**. The power of the Spirit working in you shapes your Desirable Delight to reflect the Desirable Delight of the Father, empowers your work to bring Thoughtful Delight to the Father, and in the process makes both Jesus' Joyful Delight and your Joyful Delight full to the point of overflowing.

God delights to shape your life and your heart to reflect the life and the heart of Jesus. As soon as you make it *your* work to shape your life to be more like Jesus, you set Jesus up as an ideal, as an idol, and you will kill yourself (and likely others) with the burden of running your own discipleship life.

But in his grace, and with great joy, Jesus steps off of the pedestal you have put him on. Jesus abandons the false throne of your ideal and instead sets up shop in your heart.

You don't have to work hard to climb up to the ideal of Jesus. **Jesus comes all the way down to meet you right where you are**. Jesus pours out his Spirit, the Spirit that enables Jesus to be with you and comfort you and forgive you and shape you. By the power of that Spirit at work in you every day, you begin to look more and more like Jesus, every day.

And as you look more and more like Jesus, you become more and more uniquely the person God created you to be. You aren't on an assembly line where one size fits all when it comes to following Jesus; you are being lovingly handcrafted by the skillful hands of a Master Potter whose ultimate design is Jesus and whose individual works are all unique masterpieces, as different from each other as they are like Jesus.

Discipleship not your work. You aren't in charge. And the result is not only a life that looks more and more like the Jesus who lives and works in you; the result is joy, real joy, full joy that flows out of your life into the lives of others.

Be at peace. Your job is not to rise up to the standard of Jesus. Jesus is near you. Jesus is being formed in you. And you get to enjoy the ride.

Yes, you will do the works Jesus did. Jesus seems to think you will do even greater things than these. But those works flow from the active presence of the Spirit in your life. Jesus himself is working in you both to will and to do that which is pleasing in his sight.

Set down the burden of trying to be like Jesus so you can receive the delight of Jesus being shaped in you by the power of the Spirit and to the immense delight of the Father.

Don't let the fear of failure suck the joy out of discipleship.

It's not your job to make yourself more like Jesus.

Your job is to keep needing Jesus, every day.

The Spirit will take care of the rest.

The Prayer of Examen

God's work shapes your adventure of discipleship. Your emotions, good or bad, often give you a glimpse of something the Spirit is up to in your heart or mind. Sometimes you can notice God's work through emotions of joy or delight; sometimes as clay your emotions are closer to confusion or anger or grief.

Your emotions are a part of who you are. And you have a God who delights in shaping and molding who you are for beautiful and useful purposes in the Kingdom. Paying attention to your emotions will often help you see where Jesus is inviting you to take a small next step in your relationship with him.

The prayer tool below designed to help you be more aware of your emotions. This particular prayer experiment is a modified version of a self-examination prayer from St. Ignatius of Loyola, called "The Prayer of Examen." Thoughtfully pray through these five topics at the end of the day several days this week.

Use your own thoughts and words; the prayers provided are just a starting place. See if this new pattern helps you delight in God's shaping activity in your life and Jesus' presence in you and with you by the power of his Spirit.

1. Become aware of God's Presence.

Jesus, I know you are with me always; I know your Spirit dwells within me. I acknowledge your accompanying presence even now. I entrust my faith, my life, and my future to your keeping. God, you are the potter; I am the clay. Do not forsake the work of your hands.

2. Recall your day in God's Presence with delight.

Thank you for the gift of today, Lord, especially for...

3. Notice your emotions in the presence of Jesus.

Jesus, I responded to my day in all kinds of ways; sometimes good and sometimes not. I don't know what all of these emotions mean, but I would like to notice before you the moments I responded in anger, love, thanksgiving, fear, shame, or ...

4. Prayerfully consider your life and God's Word.

Father, those emotions help me see places where you are working in my life. As I consider your Word of promise, I ask you specifically to...

5. Look forward to tomorrow.

I rest in your presence, Lord, knowing I am forgiven and loved. Give me the gift of sleep and teach me to rely on you. I can't wait to see what you are up to tomorrow! Amen.

GROUP DISCUSSION FOR CHAPTER 10

God's Work Shapes Your Adventure

Pick one or two of the following questions to help you get to know a friend, family member, or small group better.

1. When was the last time you did something creative? How did it turn out?

2. What was your first job? What was your favorite job? Who was your favorite boss, and why?

3. Did you play a musical instrument growing up? Were you in any clubs or interest groups? Did you play a sport?

4. What do you do nowadays for fun?

Go a little deeper with someone you trust to point you back to Jesus. You don't have to reflect on all of the following, but spend some time on the ones that catch your spiritual attention.

1. Rest, work, and play: do you have too much or not enough of any of those in your life?

2. How did you respond to the conversation about setting Jesus up on a pedestal, "way out there" somewhere?

3. What challenged you the most in this chapter? What gave you the most hope?

   Are you more likely to fly down the hill into traffic without a helmet, or wear so much protective gear that you can hardly pedal around the cul-de-sac?

   How do your habitual patterns of risk management affect your adventure of discipleship?

CHAPTER 11

God's Word Propels Your Adventure

Reading Plan

Day 1
God's Powerful and Delightful Word

Day 2
Savoring God's Word
(A Delicious Delight)

Day 3
Exploring God's Word
(A Playful Delight)

Day 4
Clinging to God's Word
(A Lamp to My Feet)

Day 5
Jesus and God's Word

Day 6
Meditating on the Word
&
Group Discussion

God's Powerful And Delightful Word

Every journey needs fuel; something to propel you forward. Your faith adventure is no different. And the fuel that God gives to propel your adventure of following Jesus is like no other. From the very beginning of the story, when God *speaks* creation into existence, God's Word is active and powerful. God's Word accomplishes God's will. God's Word is given to God's people as a way of making God's presence available to them. And God's Word is a delight. Every journey needs fuel, and your faith adventure is propelled forward by the very presence of the Almighty active in, with, and under the words of Scripture, the powerful, dynamic, and delightful Word of God.

God makes this promise in Isaiah 55:

> As the rain and the snow come down from heaven,
>   and do not return to it without watering the earth
>   and making it bud and flourish, so that it yields
>   seed for the sower and bread for the eater,
>
> so is my word that goes out from my mouth:
>   It will not return to me empty,
>   but will accomplish what I desire [*Yes, Please!!*]
>   and achieve the purpose for which I sent it.
>
> *Isaiah 55:10–11*, NIV

God's Word accomplishes God's *chephets*; God's Desirable Delight—the result God desires because it brings such joy.

God's Word gets stuff done. And that powerful, delightful Word has been given as a gift, *to you*.

> "The word of the Lord endures forever."
>   And this is the word that was *preached to you*.
>
> *1 Peter 1:25*, NIV

> "The word is *near you*,
>   in your mouth and in your heart"
>   (that is, the word of faith that we proclaim).
>
> *Romans 10:8*, ESV

When you received the word of God,
> which you heard from us,
> you accepted it not as a human word,
> but as it actually is,
> the word of God,
> which is indeed *at work in you* who believe.

1 Thessalonians 2:13, NIV

Let the word of Christ *dwell in you* richly.

Colossians 3:16, ESV

You have the Word of God at work (and at play!) in you, doing stuff, getting stuff done. God's Word is not some sort of magical incantation that lets you harness divine power; God's Word doesn't come under your control like that. In fact, we might say it the other way around: you come under the power of God's Word.

While that might sound a little scary to people who value being in control (I'm looking at you), coming under the power of God's Word may be the single best thing that ever happened to you. And the most fun. The river rapids can be dangerous; the biggest waves come with the most undertow. But for the whitewater kayaker or the surfing buff, riding the power that propels you is a delight!

God's Word is active and powerful in your life—God's Word propels you forward on your journey of faith—because of what God's Word delivers. **God's Word delivers Jesus**. Jesus is powerful. Jesus gets stuff done. Jesus is always loving and gracious and forgiving and patient and active and delightful. Jesus is always up to something in your life. Discipleship is the art, the adventure, and the delight of discovering what Jesus is up to in your day, today. That adventure is fueled by God's Word.

Savoring God's Word:
A Delicious Delight (Yum!)

How did you start your day today? Chances are, in the midst of your routine, you both *read something* and *ate something*. Maybe you checked the messages on your phone. Maybe you scrolled through the news online, or picked up a newspaper (do people still do that?). Maybe you read some of this book on your phone or on your tablet (or on your toilet). And at some point, you probably went to the kitchen and poured yourself some coffee, grabbed some cereal or a piece of toast, or maybe a granola bar for the road, and got on with the rest of your day. Sound familiar? Or at least, familiar enough to recognize, even if the details of your particular morning today happened to all be different from mine?

Reading and *eating* are so basic to your daily life, you hardly think about them. When I read, I read the words in my head; I actually sound out the words, which makes me a pretty slow reader. Not everyone does that. But everyone I know reads silently; they don't actually vocalize the words out loud unless they are children or reading to children.

But think about it for a moment: reading silently is *not* how most people in most places for almost all of human history have experienced words! You probably have some general knowledge that the times and cultures of the Bible were primarily oral (mouth) and aural (ear) cultures: all communication happened with your mouth and your ear. Most people didn't read. And if you did happen to read, you *always* read out loud. Even by yourself.

"Reading God's Word" probably meant reciting Scripture from memory, and even if you could actually *read* a copy of the scroll of Isaiah or Jeremiah at your local synagogue or one of the letters from Paul making the rounds to the estates that hosted churches, you would have read those words (even to yourself) *out loud*.

The "Reader" was an important position in the local congregations of the Early Church (though some historical evidence suggests not even all of the Readers were literate...) If you read God's Word, by yourself or with others, you read the Word *out loud*. And you probably read it out loud repeatedly.

And you probably memorized it by saying it repeatedly, out loud. That's quite a different experience from how I live out the activity of *reading* in my day-to-day life.

The differences with *eating* are no less stark. You can imagine the diversity in diet, eating positions, spices, utensils, and customs around meals in different biblical times and cultures and how strange any Bible character would find our experience of food and eating today. I want to focus on just one difference: the daily, ongoing question of what you are going to eat.

Of course, we wonder what's for dinner all the time in my house. But for us, the question is never if we have enough grain to grind into flour so we can bake our own bread. It's more like, whose turn it is to run to the store? (Or would we rather get takeout?)

Maybe you bake your own bread. But I'm guessing you don't have to; in a pinch, you could always stop at the local gas station and pick up a loaf. But I suspect you don't usually get Wonder Bread at Sunoco; you probably find a much wider selection at a finer food supplier than that. And if you have never wondered if you are going to have a next meal, let alone *where* that next meal might come from—if you have never visited a food bank or a homeless shelter as a way of making ends meet instead of as a volunteer—then maybe you don't understand the connection between *bread* and *food*, or between *bread* and *life* in the same visceral way that most of the people throughout the library of books we call the Bible would have.

The questions, "What will we eat?" and "What will we wear?" are not about making choices between multiple restaurants or choosing the right dinner dress. "What will we eat, and what will we wear?" are daily questions of survival. Life needs food. Food means bread. Bread means life.

You probably *read something* and *ate something* today—you are doing it right now! And I would bet dollars to donuts that you aren't reading this out loud to yourself, and you didn't make that donut from scratch. (Though you may be listening to an audiobook, as someone else reads this to you *out loud*. Our present post-literate communications culture sometimes works more like a pre-literate culture. But that's a different topic for a different time...)

You probably know stories of the people of God wandering in the wilderness and being fed daily with manna from heaven, but you don't feel that daily need in your belly in quite the same way they did. You know stories like the people who returned from Exile gathering to hear the books of Moses *read to them, out loud* by Ezra, the Priest, but you don't hold the physicality of those words in your mouth and in your eardrums and in your communal hearing.

As we talk about the Delicious Delight of God's Word, I want you to feel the physical sensation of chewing those words in your mouth as you say them out loud. I want you to have your daily need for daily bread in the forefront of your mind. I want you to hold onto that experience of mouth and belly and daily dependence as we talk about how the Word of God empowers your adventure of following Jesus. Because your daily experience of *reading* and *eating* can lead you to miss some of the most delightful aspects of our daily dependence on God's Word. (Try reading the following out loud, slowly chewing your way through each verse more than once...)

> Remember how the LORD your God led you
>   all the way in the wilderness these forty years,
> to humble and test you
>   in order to know what was in your heart,
>   whether or not you would keep his commands.
> He humbled you, causing you to hunger
>   and then feeding you with manna,
>   which neither you nor your ancestors had known,
> to teach you that
>   man does not **live on bread** alone
>   but **on every word** that comes
>   **from the mouth of the LORD.**

Deuteronomy 8:2–3, NIV

Manna, bread from heaven, kept these people alive on a daily basis during 40 years of wilderness wandering. Daily survival depended on eating that bread; and God's people learned, you need God's Word in your mouth and belly for daily survival even more than you need bread or food.

As God's people, you keep the Word *on your lips*, and *meditate* on it day and night (*Joshua 1:8*). That invitation to rumination is echoed at the very beginning of the Book of Psalms:

> Blessed is the one...
>> whose **delight** [*chephets*] is in the law of the LORD,
>> and who **meditates** on his law day and night.
>
> *Psalm 1:1–2*, NIV

The Torah of Yahweh—both commands and promises—is not a bland gruel you have to choke down just to stay alive. No, God's Word brings Desirable Delight (*chephets*) to the one who *meditates*. That meditation word is all about chewing and vocalization— like a wild animal growling over a gnawed bone—and involves the lips, teeth, tongue, and vocal cords. (I "meditated" over my breakfast cereal like that as a kid; drove my sister crazy...)

When you *chew* on God's Word, you release the flavor and the power of the food; you keep at it until you have sucked out the last of the marrow. That kind of ongoing eating is like crushing a fresh herb (think chocolate mint or lemon basil) so that the herb fills your personal space with its pungent aroma. The power and flavor was already there, in the food, in the herb, before you chewed and crushed and *meditated* it; but the chewing and crushing and lingering and savoring releases that power and flavor into your experience, for your benefit. Savoring God's Word is like that.

> When your words came, I **ate them**;
>> they were my **joy** [*sus*]
>> and my heart's **delight** [*simchah*].
>
> *Jeremiah 15:16*, NIV

שׂוּשׂ (Sus): exult, rejoice, take delight in, make mirth, be glad

The prophet Jeremiah used his mouth and lips and teeth to interact with God's Word. The result was both sustenance and delight: Joyful Delight in the form of *sus* (like "Dr. Seuss") and *simchah* (like "sim card," but with a backwards Ach!)—joy that makes you jump up and spin around and shout, *Woohoo!*

שִׂמְחָה (Simchah): joy, gladness, mirth, delight

> Why do you spend money
>   for what is not bread,
> And your wages
>   for what does not satisfy?
> Listen carefully to Me,
>   and eat what is good,
>   And let your soul **delight** itself [*ōneg*]
>   in abundance.
> Incline your ear, and come to Me.
>   Hear, and your soul shall live.
>
> *Isaiah 55:2–3*, NKJV

The prophet Isaiah knows you need daily bread to survive, and keeping God's Word in your mouth and in your ears is like eating the most delicious feast. God's Word is nourishment, yes; nourishment that you hold in your mouth and chew on and *meditate* on and savor. God's Word brings *ōneg* (rhymes with "no leg"), a Delicious Delight that gives pleasure as well as nourishment.

עֹנֶג (Ōneg): daintiness, tender or delectable, an exquisite delight

God's Word in your mouth, on your lips, as you growl over it and savor the food that sustains your life again today—that image of both **dependence and delight** is at the heart of what God's Word says about God's Word.

Psalm 119 is the longest of the Psalms—the longest chapter in the Bible, in fact—and Psalm 119 counts as a hymn of praise to

God for the Word. We've already seen how the word "Law" can sometimes mean *all of God's promises and commands together*. But page through Psalm 119 and you will find a variety of vocabulary words used in a parallel construction that indicates they are all roughly synonymous for the great Story of Scripture, both Law and Gospel given for the sake of people God dearly loves. "Your word"; "your faithfulness"; "your law"; "your precepts"; "your statutes"; "your testimonies"; "your words"; "your promise"; "your steadfast love"; "your justice"; "your commandments"; "your mercy"; "your rules"; all of these refer to God's Word and all of them are "my *delight*."

These synonyms for God's Word are always active, always doing something. In Psalm 119, God's Word "saves me"; "answers me"; "brings God near"; is "fixed in the heavens"; "endures to all generations"; and, again and again, God's Word "gives me life; gives me life; gives me life!" No wonder Psalm 119:103 says,

> How sweet are your words to my taste,
> sweeter than honey to my mouth!
>
> *Psalm 119:103*, NIV

God's Word is food you need; but it's also food that tastes amazing! So think of reading God's Word not as a silent activity in a moment of quiet holiness; rather, imagine chewing on God's Word like a hungry lion gnawing on a bone, trying to get the last wonderful deliciousness out of every bite, desperately needing that sustenance to make it through another day.

Deep need and Delicious Delight both belong to your relationship with God's Word.

Exploring God's Word: A Playful Delight (Whee!)

God's Word meets your deep and daily need with Delicious Delight. Don't get me wrong: reading, understanding, holding onto, and living out God's Word in your life can be really difficult. Sometimes God's Word is confusing. Sometimes the Bible seems closed; or worse, contradictory. Sometimes translating what was going on there and then to the here and now leaves you scratching your head and wondering what in the world that Word could possibly have to say about your day, your week, your job, or your family. Sometimes Scripture takes work to understand.

I bet you already knew God's Word takes work to understand. But I hope that you are beginning to imagine another truth: **God's Word also takes *play* to understand.** Based on our conversation in the last chapter, I wonder if God also intends your encounter with Scripture to bring you *rest* right along with *work* and *play*. But work for sure. And play; definitely play. Maybe God designed the *rest* and peace we get from Scripture to be the result of our full engagement; and maybe God designed the *work* of that full engagement to be, quite simply, *fun*. Rest, work, and play all come together to deliver God's good gifts to the people God loves.

Yep; that sounds like something God would do.

It also sounds like Psalm 119. Look at Psalm 119 in your Bible and you will see this love song is divided up into 22 different sections, one for each of the letters of the Hebrew alphabet. Your translation probably even lists the Hebrew letters in alphabetical order as headers for each of the 22 sections. That's because each section includes eight lines of Hebrew poetry *that all begin with the same letter*, each section advancing in *alphabetical order*, from beginning to end, one letter at a time. God's Word has got you covered from A to Z! (Or, rather, from *Aleph* to *Tav*!)

That delight with language is only one aspect of the poetry of Psalm 119, but it's enough for you to see that a skilled author crafted these lines carefully and with intention. The intentional interplay between letters, words, stanzas, and meaning is supposed to capture your fancy as well as your attention. Whoever wrote Psalm 119, they *had fun* writing it; and you are supposed to *have fun* reading it. Having fun is part of what it means to engage in the work it takes to rest in God's Word.

In the Waw (or V) section of Psalm 119, the poet writes:

Let **your steadfast love** come to me, O Lᴏʀᴅ,
    your salvation according to **your promise**;
then shall I have **an answer** for him who taunts me,
    for I trust in **your word**.
And take not **the word** of truth utterly out of **my mouth**,
    for my hope is in **your rules**.
I will keep **your law** continually,
    forever and ever,
and I shall walk in a wide place,
    for I have sought **your precepts**.
I will also speak of **your testimonies** before kings
    and shall not be put to shame,
for I find **my delight** [*sha'a'*] in **your commandments**,
    which I love.
I will lift up my hands toward **your commandments**,
    which I love,
    and I will **meditate** on **your statutes**.

    Psalm 119:41–48, ESV

You can't see it in translation, but the Hebrew words that begin each of these eight stanzas all begin with the Hebrew letter Waw. (You can pronounce *Waw* as "vau" if you like; when I first learned Hebrew, I was taught a soft consonant, which means I have always thought of this part of Psalm 119 as the "Wow" section…)

Look at how God's Word is associated with *the mouth* or with *speaking*, speaking in public (like before kings) or speaking out loud to yourself, as in the "meditate" verb in the last line.

Notice also all the *synonyms* for God's Word. In this one section alone we have "your promise"; "your word"; "the word of truth"; "your rules"; "your law"; "your precepts"; "your testimonies"; "your commands"; and "your statutes." And look at all the *outcomes* that result from the Psalmist encountering God's Word: "your salvation"; "an answer"; "trust"; "hope"; "walking in a wide place"; "not being put to shame"; "delight"; "lifting my hands"; "meditating" on the Word.

The sheer volume of variety in vocabulary leads us to imagine more than a narrow legalism when it comes to keeping God's "law," or even "hoping" in God's "rules." *Hoping in God's rules??* That hardly makes sense, unless we take a holistic approach to all of these ways of referring to God's Word: "God's Word" in the broadest sense includes both commands and promises, in the same way "obeying" God's Word can include both *receiving promises in faith* and *working out that faith in real life*, as the Spirit of Jesus works in you. The person described in this Waw section knows God's Word, and trusts God's Word, and lives under the grace of God's promise, and delights in God's will and walks in God's ways to the glory of God's holy name.

The delight word used in these verses is *sha'a'*, Playful Delight. You can use that verb to describe a child at play. Here I think it reflects engagement with the Word that is just plain fun. Of course, that engagement is work, too; but the type of work that enhances your delight and makes you lose track of time and lay down your burden. To *sha'a'* in God's Word is to ride your bike downhill at full speed, pedaling hard and having the time of your life. Wheeee!

שָׁעַע (Sha'a'): sport, take delight in, play

We have so many examples from both Old and New Testament of the playfulness involved in taking a high dive into the Word and splashing around and getting soaking wet and riding those powerful swells to discover the beauty and the humor and the care with which these Scriptures were written. Can we do just one more? Please??

Let's stick with some verses we've already looked at briefly in this chapter. Isaiah 55 is talking about God's Word. Take a dive into the playful structure and progression in verses 6–11 and splash around a little with me.

> Seek the LORD while he may be found;
> call on him while he is near.
>> Let the wicked forsake their ways
>> and the unrighteous their thoughts.

Let them turn to the Lord, and he will have mercy on
them, and to our God, for he will freely pardon.

"For my thoughts are not your thoughts,
neither are your ways my ways," declares the Lord.
"As the heavens are higher than the earth,
so are my ways higher than your ways
and my thoughts than your thoughts.

"As the rain and the snow come down from heaven,
and do not return to it without watering the earth
and making it bud and flourish, so that it yields
seed for the sower and bread for the eater,
so is my word that goes out from my mouth:
It will not return to me empty,
but will accomplish what I desire
and achieve the purpose for which I sent it."

Isaiah 55:6–11, NIV

This gushing torrent of ideas draws on three different kinds
of thought structures to develop one central theme, how the
unrighteous can come back to God by the power of God's Word.
Surf the waves of this text—ride those white-water rapids—and
the mastery of language is really quite breathtaking.

You can't see how the Hebrew lines rhyme in this complex
poem, which is just as well, *since they don't*. At least, the words
don't necessarily share similar sounds like we typically think of
rhyming. (*Ōneg* rhymes with "no leg.") Like we said way back
in the first chapter, Hebrew poetry likes to rhyme *meaning*, not
just sounds.

You can see this play with words in the first stanza: "Seek the
Lord" rhymes in meaning with "call on him," like "while he
may be found" balances with "while he is near." Such parallelism
highlights what's important by saying the same thing again, but
in a different way. You could call that first thought "Idea A," and
the second thought is really just a rephrasing of the first, so you
might call it "Idea A[1]."

The next line, however, gives us some new ideas: "the wicked" parallels "the unrighteous" and "forsaking their ways" is roughly the same thing as forsaking "their thoughts." So we again have meanings that rhyme, but with a new thought: Idea B and B¹.

But hold onto your hats, because the next line returns to Idea A from the opening verse, but this time expands the thought to give us the result of the action called for in Idea A. When the wicked or unrighteous "turn to the LORD," or "to our God," in stanza 3, that's the same as "seeking the LORD" or "calling on the LORD," in stanza 1, but now the result is clear: "he will have mercy on them," or, to put it another way, "he will freely pardon." It's the first thought, expanded; so maybe, Idea A+ and Idea A+¹.

All this poetic algebra is just trying to highlight the delightful interplay between the stanzas. The idea itself is beautiful, and the prophet is presenting the idea beautifully. Look at this first stanza again with the structure in mind: (A, A¹); (B, B¹); (A+, A+¹).

(A)   Seek the LORD while he may be found;
(A¹) call on him while he is near.
  (B) Let the wicked forsake their ways
  (B¹) and the unrighteous their thoughts.
(A+) Let them turn to the LORD, and he will
       have mercy on them,
(A+¹) and to our God, for he will freely pardon.

Pretty cool, right? But wait! There's more! (Stick with me on this; it will pay off when you read all of these verses together after you have looked at them separately in depth. You know those 3D pictures of a sunken ship where you have to keep looking at it and looking at it and suddenly it comes to life and you find the treasure that was hiding in plain sight all along? Working/ *playing* with the biblical text can be something like that...)

When you have a central idea "framed" like Idea B is framed with Ideas A and A+, it usually means the thought *inside* the frame is most important. That might seem odd to the Western mind; like me, you are probably less circular and more linear in your thinking. We tend to put the most important thought *at the end of a logic string*; it's the final destination to which the journey of our argument leads. And when everything we read or hear works like that, it's easy to see why we think the most important thing *always comes at the end.*

In contrast, some Eastern thinkers, including many Hebrew poets and prophets, tend to put the most important thought in the center of the argument.

I once had a seminary professor from India, and I could never follow his lectures or track with class discussion until it occurred to me that he was using this style of Eastern thought structure. Once I noticed it, I could see how he would put out a central premise and then circle around it four or five times, looking at it from different angles. His thinking was quite beautiful once you got used to it. Until then, you felt like he never gave a straight answer; which of course he *didn't*, because *straight* answers don't fit in that style of logical structure.

The logic of Isaiah 55 says Idea B/B¹ is the main thought, because B/B¹ is *inside the frame*. Isaiah's main focus is calling for repentance.

Look what happens next: the *central* idea from the first stanza gets picked up in the second stanza. Idea B is about the "ways" of the wicked, and B¹ is about their "thoughts." Ways and thoughts from the center of the logic of stanza 1 become the outside of the logical "sandwich" in stanza 2:

> (B¹) "For my thoughts are not your thoughts,
>> (B) neither are your ways my ways," declares the LORD.
>>> (C) "As the heavens are higher than the earth,
>> (B) so are my ways higher than your ways
> (B¹) and my thoughts than your thoughts."

Look at how that logical flow works! It's like climbing up one side of a mountain and down the other! Here the flow goes Thoughts/Ways/Distance Between/Ways/Thoughts. Do you see the movement toward and away from the central idea? (And how cool that these "stairs" are built out of the central thought of the previous stanza!)

We now have a new thought structure and a new central thought, a thought that builds on material from what came right before, but also presents a big problem: the wicked/unrighteous are supposed to seek/call on/turn to the LORD our God while he is near and may be found, so that the LORD will have mercy and freely pardon. That seeking, calling, and turning consists of forsaking wicked ways and unrighteous thoughts. Those thoughts and ways are far from this God of mercy and pardon, *and that's the problem.* How do you seek and call on and turn to a God who is *so far away,* indeed, *as far as the heavens are above the earth?* How are you supposed to bridge the gap in Idea C, the central thought of stanza 2? Well… that's why we have stanza 3… (Are you beginning to see that sunken ship yet? Or are you just getting a little dizzy? Hang in there!)

Once again using a *different* thought pattern, and once again building on material from the previous stanza, Isaiah the poet/prophet lays out the solution to the distance between God and those who would turn back to God for mercy and free pardon.

(C) "As the rain and the snow come down from heaven,
  (D) and do not return to it without watering the earth
    (D+) and making it bud and flourish, so that it yields
      seed for the sower and bread for the eater,
  (C¹) so is my word that goes out from my mouth:
    (D¹) It will not return to me empty,
      (D+¹) but will accomplish what I desire
      and achieve the purpose for which I sent it."

Here is the answer to the problem of distance between a holy God and sinful people. Here is how that gap gets bridged. Here is why the wicked can turn back to God to receive free pardon. Rain and snow bridge the distance between heaven and earth *from heaven's side.* When rain and snow bridge the distance, they have a job to do, and the result is abundant life. That progression of precipitation from heavenly origin to earthly harvest is parallel to the progression of God's Word: God's Word bridges the distance to sinners from heaven's side. When God's Word bridges the distance, it has a job to do; and the result is abundant life. Isn't that a beautiful solution to our problem?

Now consider how Jesus is called the Word, how Jesus came down and bridged the distance between God and a sinful humanity from heaven's side; how Jesus had a job to do, and the result is abundant life, and all of a sudden I am a little breathless and have tears in my eyes. Isn't God's Word *wonderful*? Isn't this *fun*?

I know we are all hardwired a little differently, and this may be more delightful for me than it is for you, but look at just these six verses and tell me if you don't at least see why I think this is so cool. Maybe try vocalizing these verses to yourself a few times, like a lion intently gnawing a bone while growling, deep and satisfied.

(A)　Seek the LORD while he may be found;
(A¹)　call on him while he is near.
　　　(B)　Let the wicked forsake their ways
　　　(B¹)　and the unrighteous their thoughts.
(A+)　Let them turn to the LORD, and he will have
　　　mercy on them,
(A+¹)　and to our God, for he will freely pardon.

(B¹)　"For my thoughts are not your thoughts,
　　　(B)　neither are your ways my ways," declares the LORD.
　　　　(C)　"As the heavens are higher than the earth,
　　　(B)　so are my ways higher than your ways
(B¹)　and my thoughts than your thoughts.

(C)　"As the rain and the snow come down from heaven,
　　　(D)　and do not return to it without watering the earth
　　　　(D+)　and making it bud and flourish, so that it yields
　　　　　seed for the sower and bread for the eater,
(C¹)　so is my word that goes out from my mouth:
　　　(D¹)　It will not return to me empty,
　　　　(D+1)　but will accomplish what I desire
　　　　　and achieve the purpose for which I sent it."

Isaiah 55:6–11, NIV

Did you see the sunken treasure ship in 3D? Did you notice that one shark swimming right at you? Isn't that cool?!

Of course, I didn't come up with this analysis all by myself. And you aren't supposed to either. But it is fun to play! In this case, I saw something similar in a book by Kenneth Bailey on how Paul shapes his argument in 1 Corinthians based on Hebrew thought structures. Bailey used Isaiah 55:6–11 as an example, and I modified his work, played with it some, and made it my own. That's how it works: you read, and study, and pray, and discuss, and *play*, and suddenly, the Word becomes planted deep in your own heart. The Word bridges the gap from heaven's side. The Word invites you to turn, and seek the Lord, and to find mercy and free pardon because Jesus creates abundant life in you.

These are just two examples from Psalm 119 and Isaiah 55. I would love to do more. I would love to show you the humor in Genesis 11, when God says, "What are they doing *way down there*? Let's go *all the way down there* so we can take a closer look..." when the people thought they were building a tower *all the way up to heaven*. I would love to show you the heartbreaking irony of Matthew's passion account, as the bystanders mock Jesus as king, when Matthew has gone out of his way to portray Jesus as the true King of Israel, but they don't have eyes to see. I'd love to sit with you and talk about the abrupt ending to the Gospel of Mark, because I am convinced it actually ends with the women leaving the tomb in fear and not saying anything to anyone, because they were terrified; and I think Mark ends it that way on purpose, for good reason, and it's absolutely brilliant. Oh, I'd love to go on and on about the seven signs in the Gospel of John, or the way Jesus gently reinstates Peter, or the tight and overlapping metaphors at the heart of Paul's letters, or the beauty and delight of the characters and events in the book of Luke and its sequel, Acts. But not now.

For now, let me content myself with saying, *God's Word is awesome!* And God gives us this Word to explore with Playful Delight. If you have never experienced God's Word that way, don't give up, and don't despair. Studying God's Word is difficult and complicated and can be frustrating and confusing.

And sometimes, studying God's Word is just plain fun. Trying to see a hidden 3D picture can give you a headache, but there is a knack to it, and you can get better at it. What's at stake here is so much more wonderful that an illusion of depth and movement. God's Word gives you access to the actual thoughts and intentions and heart of God.

When you engage Scripture, you begin to see your life with God in 3D—the movement of the Spirit and the treasures of your faith and the presence of Jesus, who is the Word, all of a sudden take on new depth and perspective. When God's Word and your life unexpectedly come together in a new way and your perspective shifts, it can take your breath away!

And, just as suddenly, that 3D image can collapse back into a random-seeming hodgepodge of geometric shapes with no decipherable pattern. So, like everything else in this book, **the Playful Delight of God's Word is not intended as a burden**; you don't have to have more fun, or else… Playful Delight is an **invitation to you from Jesus**.

Jesus bridges the gap from heaven's side and promises to meet you *as* the Word, *in* the Word. Trust that Jesus will show up by the power of the Spirit; find another follower of Jesus to walk this journey with you; and sit with even the difficult passages long enough to wonder what Jesus is up to in the text, and in your life. Studying the Bible won't be all sunshine and rainbows (or sharks and treasure chests). But, *Waw!* This powerful, engaging, poetic, challenging Word of God sure is *fun!*

Clinging To God's Word: A Lamp To My Feet

We have been talking about following Jesus as a kind of journey, or adventure, where you can make progress or get disoriented; take a detour or take the scenic route; or even engage completely in the activity of the journey while God remains in control of the direction and final destination. Discipleship is a journey—the adventure of following Jesus.

The Bible uses that language for discipleship, as well. A disciple is nothing less than a "follower," and following, by definition, requires progress across distance over time. When Jesus said to the first disciples, "Follow me," or even, "Come and see," he meant it literally and physically, but also as an invitation to be a traveling companion on the road of faith and life; to learn from Jesus by observation and imitation; to see Jesus interact with Scripture, and to hear Jesus pray, and to listen in on the conversations Jesus had with all kinds of people, from religious experts to scandalous sinners, from foreign women to desperate fathers, from people as far left on the political scale as you can get, to people farther right than you can imagine. And all that time, day by day, as they walked and rowed and crisscrossed the Judean countryside, the disciples were *following Jesus* in the fullest sense of the word.

You often experience your life as a journey where you do literally travel from time to time, but where you can also *make progress* at work, or *reach a dead end* in a relationship, or face a *crossroads* that will determine the *direction* of your life for years to come. You live your life as a kind of journey. People in both Old and New Testaments often shared that way of experiencing life and faith. Sticking with Psalm 119 for a moment, you can see that experience of life as a journey right from Section A.

> Blessed are those whose **way** is blameless,
>   who **walk** in the law of the LORD!
> Blessed are those who keep his testimonies,
>   who seek him with their whole heart,
> who also do no wrong,
>   but **walk in his ways!**
> Oh that **my ways** may be steadfast
>   in keeping your statutes!
>
> *Psalm 119:1–3, 5,* ESV

The Torah of Yahweh is a kind of path, or way. You can walk in that direction, toward that destination, or not. The Psalmist knows which way is better, and pronounces blessings on those who follow the Torah path. The Psalmist also expresses a personal desire to follow that same path, and by extension, to travel the route and reach the destination laid out by this path, the way of the statutes/testimonies/law/Word of God.

This journey can sometime be described as "seeking God," a type of movement with focused intention, while separation from God is experienced as "losing your path," "getting lost," or "wandering." Overall, the experience of this sort of faith adventure is described in terms of delight. From the B section of Psalm 119 we get:

> With my whole heart **I seek** you;
>> let me not **wander** from your commandments!
> With **my lips** I declare
>> all the rules of **your mouth**.
> In **the way** of your testimonies I **delight** [*sus*]
>> as much as in all riches.
> I will **meditate** on your precepts
>> and **fix my eyes on your ways**.
> I will **delight** [*sha'a'*] in your statutes;
>> I will not forget your word.
>
> *Psalm 119:10, 13-16*, ESV

Some of the rhythms of this Psalm may be familiar by now. Notice how the story of God's self-revelation in human history gets a long list of rough equivalents: in these few, short verses we get "your commandments"; "the rules of your mouth"; "your testimonies"; "your precepts"; "your statutes"; and "your word." If you were asked, "Do these words refer to God's *commands*? Or to God's *saving promises*?" I hope you would answer, "Why, yes; yes they do."

You can also see the connection between the mouth as the organ of the word, and meditation as keeping the word in your mouth: "With *my lips* I declare all the rules of *your mouth*." I don't think that's telling *other people* how to follow God's rules; I think that's the Psalmist chewing on and repeating and ingesting God's Word—the equivalent of "meditating on" or *repeating out loud to yourself* God's precepts a few verses later.

And of course you noticed two *delight* words: Joyful Delight (*sus*, Dr. Seuss, jump for joy) and Playful Delight (*sha'a*, Wheee!). But you probably also noticed the journey language: seeking, wandering, or fixing your eyes on and delighting in God's ways. So far we've only looked at sections A and B of this alphabetical tour de force, and we've already seen that faith is a journey, an adventure of delight, and God's Word points you the right way. You could explore God's Word and find some other places where delight and journey overlap. (In fact, you should! That would be *fun*.) Here are a few more I found in Psalm 119 alone.

I am a **sojourner** on the earth;
    hide not your commandments from me!
Your testimonies are my **delight** [*sha'a'*, Whee!];
    they are my counselors.

Psalm 119:19, 24, ESV

Lead me in the **path** of your commandments,
    for I **delight** [*chephets*, Yes, please!!] in it.

Psalm 119:35, ESV

Let your mercy **come to me**, that I may live;
    for your law is my **delight** [*sha'a'*, Whee!].

Psalm 119:77, ESV

The wicked have **laid a snare** for me,
    but I do not **stray** from your precepts.
Your testimonies are my heritage forever,
    for they are the **joy** [*sus*, Woohoo!] of my heart.

Psalm 119:110–11, ESV

I long for your salvation, O LORD,
    and your law is my **delight** [*sha'a'*, Whee!].
Let my soul live and praise you,
    and let your rules help me.
I have **gone astray** like a **lost** sheep; **seek** your servant,
    for I do not forget your commandments.

Psalm 119:174–76, ESV

From the very first verse to the very last verse of Psalm 119—
from *Aleph* to *Tav*—and everywhere in between, you find
delight in God's Word on the journey of faith.

There is one journey or adventure verse in Psalm 119 I've
avoided on purpose so far. Of all 176 verses of the Psalm, it's
the verse you know best. Maybe because Psalm 119:105 is so
familiar, it's also easy to gloss over quickly. So I want to slow
down and meditate on verse 105 a little bit; growl over it like
a lion gnawing a bone; rub it in my hands like lemon basil or
chocolate mint until the aroma fills my experience. I want to dig
in and get my hands dirty and see where this Word from God
takes me next.

You know Psalm 119:105; now let's chew on it together.

> Your word is a lamp to my feet
> and a light to my path.
>
> *Psalm 119:105,* ESV

(I told you, you knew it!) You usually see this verse out of context—
and hey! With 175 other verses in Psalm 119, I get it! Even out
of context, you can recognize the Hebrew parallelism we've seen
in other places: "lamp" is parallel to "light" and "my feet" parallel
"my path." You know life is a kind of journey, and this faithful
follower is using the lamp of God's Word to light the path they
are walking. A beautiful image, and one worth pondering.

Have you ever seen an oil lamp in real life? I mean, an ancient
oil lamp, a Bible-times oil lamp; the kind of lamp the psalmist
says the Word of God is like? I have, and it was pretty much
by accident.

I was down in the basement of a seminary library when I
opened the door to some back room and there it was: in a glass
display case, lit up all nice, was a real, bona fide, oil lamp from
Bible times. It looked something like your grandma's china
creamer or that miniature gravy boat that comes out only once
a year at Thanksgiving. That ancient artifact was roughly tear-
shaped with a small spout for the wick and some sort of opening
on the top for the olive oil. This oil lamp, like most from that era,

was small enough to be held in one hand, and it was fashioned carefully out of baked clay; you could see decorative tool marks all around the top rim.

It was pretty cool to think that here was something used by real people who lived at the time of Jesus or King David! No wonder the seminary kept it under lock and key, to keep it safe. No wonder they kept it under glass, to protect it from dust. No wonder they lit that clay oil lamp up so nicely, so you could see every detail of the design.

Now keep that picture in mind, of an artifact under glass, and then I want you to imagine how the psalmist would have used that same oil lamp in real life. You see, the psalmist isn't writing for people who see that small, clay lamp as an historical artifact to be lit up and put on display. No, the psalmist is writing for people who know from daily experience that the dark can be dangerous and scary. You can get hurt in the dark. You can become disoriented in the dark. You can lose your way in the dark. Without a lamp, the dark can be dangerous indeed.

"Your word is a lamp to my feet and a light to my path," the psalmist says—a path that is rocky and treacherous in the dark and full of sharp curves and steep hills. The psalmist understands the grave danger. What does the near context say?

> **I hold my life in my hand** continually,
>   but I do not forget your law.
> The wicked have **laid a snare** for me,
>   but **I do not stray** from your precepts.
> *Psalm 119:109–110*, ESV

This is risky business, this traveling at night. To travel at night is to take your life in your hands. You could get hurt. You could become disoriented. You could lose your way. And to lose your way is to fall into the traps set by the enemy. To lose your way is to be swallowed by the darkness. To lose your way is death. So you have to clutch that clay lamp tightly in your hand and watch your step because so much is at stake—because the dark all around you is dangerous indeed.

Chew on those verses awhile and you begin to see that, for the psalmist, the dark is a dangerous place. That idea is so different from my day to day reality! Do you know what I mean?

In our culture, darkness is little more than a minor hindrance; a very brief inconvenience. We're not afraid of the dark, and why should we be? We have flashlights and floodlights and emergency lights. We have streetlights and headlights and nightlights, all of which turn on *automatically* when it gets dark (so it *never* gets *dark*). We have lights on motion detectors and on timers and on wireless networks. We have lights you can switch on and dial on and (my favorite) ask *Siri* or *Google* or *Alexa* to turn on for you.

We don't live in a world where the difference between life and death is a small, clay oil lamp. We live in a 24-hour-drive-through, florescent-bulb-with-a-ten-year-guarantee, we'll-leave-the-light-on-for-you kind of culture, a culture that says, "You're not in danger; you're in control."

In a culture like ours, it's easy to see your oil lamp as something that might have been good for people at the time of Jesus or King David, but as mostly irrelevant today. It's easy to take that small, clay artifact and put it under glass, light it up real nice, and leave it in the basement of a library at the seminary, where it belongs. Nowadays, a biblical oil lamp is treasured more for its history than for its function. After all, in this fluorescent bulb culture, who needs the light of an outdated oil lamp?

In direct opposition to the idea that Scripture is an interesting relic that belongs under lock and key, the psalmist says to God, "Your Word is a *lamp* to my feet." With those words, Psalm 119 puts you in the dark, in a very dangerous place, where losing the path means falling into deadly traps. The darkness is oppressive; try traveling through the rocky hill country around Jerusalem at night with nothing but a small wick fed by olive oil. The darkness surrounds you on all sides. And without your iPhone or your Global Positioning System or your night vision goggles, you only have one hope. Psalm 119 puts you in the dark and then invites you to grasp, with firm hand, the light.

That small, ordinary, common oil lamp has a job to do; a crucial function; a clear-cut job description. You aren't supposed to shine a spotlight on the lamp and put it on display. No, it's the lamp's job to shed light; the lamp's job to give direction; the lamp's job is to light the way, the only way home.

God's Word is like that. God's Word is a lamp to my feet and a light to my path when I need it most. God's Word keeps me on the path that leads me home.

Jesus And God's Word

Jesus, in his human flesh, depended on God's Word. After his own wandering in the wilderness for 40 days, Jesus, in his flesh, was hungry. But when the tempter offered an easy way out, the faithful Son held onto God's Word:

> "It is written: 'Man shall not **live** on **bread** alone,
>   but on every **word** that comes
>   from the **mouth** of God.'"
>
> *Matthew 4:4*, NIV

Jesus makes the words of Moses his own words, and holds onto God's Word in a dangerous place, where it would be easy to lose your way. Jesus would later use the relationship between *word*, *mouth*, *bread*, *food*, and *life* to describe his own purpose and mission:

> [Jesus answered,]
>
> "Do not work for **food** that spoils,
>   but for **food that endures to eternal life**,
>   which the Son of Man will give you.
>   [*Sounds like Isaiah 55, right??*]
>
> "For on him God the Father
>   has placed his seal of approval.
>
> "Very truly I tell you, it is not Moses
>   who has given you the **bread** from heaven,
>   but it is my Father
>   who gives you the **true bread from heaven**.

"For the **bread of God**
  is the bread that **comes down from heave**n
  and **gives life** to the world.

"**I am the bread of life**."

  John 6:27, 32–33, 35, NIV

In his flesh, Jesus relies on God's Word; as God's Word in the flesh, Jesus offers himself as life-giving bread. Jesus bridges the distance between heaven and earth in his own body and becomes seed for the sower and bread for the eater.

Peter can write:

We have **the prophetic word** more fully confirmed,
  to which you will do well to pay attention
  as to **a lamp shining in a dark place**."

  2 Peter 1:19, ESV

John can write:

In the beginning was **the Word**…
In him was **life**, and that life
  was the **light** of all mankind.
  The light shines in the darkness,
  and the darkness has not overcome it…
The Word became flesh
  and made his dwelling among us.

  John 1:1, 4–5, 14, NIV

But Peter and John are only echoing the teachings of the rabbi they followed on their journey of faith, interpreting Scripture the way their rabbi interpreted Scripture. Jesus said:

"You study **the Scriptures** diligently because you
  think that in them you have **eternal life**.
  [And you are right! Because…]
"These are the very Scriptures that **testify about me**…
"If you believed **Moses**, you would believe me,
  for he **wrote about me**."

  John 5:39, 46, NIV

Jesus seems to think that the Word of God which Psalm 119 calls "a lamp to my feet and a light to my path," actually points people clearly to *him*.

> [Jesus] said to them [the Emmaus Road disciples],
> "How foolish you are, and how slow to believe
>   **all that the prophets have spoken!**
> Did not the Messiah have to suffer these things
>   and then enter his glory?"
>
> And beginning with **Moses** and **all the Prophets**,
>   he explained to them what was said
>   **in all the Scriptures concerning himself...**
>
> [Jesus] said to them [those in the Upper Room],
> "This is what I told you while I was still with you:
>   Everything must be fulfilled
>   **that is written about me**
>   **in the Law of Moses,**
>   **the Prophets** and **the Psalms.**"
>
> Then he opened their minds
>   so they could understand **the Scriptures.**
>
> *Luke 24:25–27, 44–45*, NIV

"Your Word is a lamp to my feet and a light for my path," the psalmist writes. Your faith life is a journey, and there is danger and darkness all around. The enemy has laid snares and set traps for you. The journey can be treacherous and confusing.

On that treacherous journey, you have a clear path, a way to get home, and the lamp points you to the way: the Way, the Truth, and the Life.

Your Bible is not intended to function like an ancient artifact that you put on display and dust off every now and then. You are supposed to need the Word, and desire the Word, and cling to this Word as if your life depended on it. Because it does. God's Word points us to Jesus, the Way; and even in the dark, Jesus can get you safely home.

I hate to sound like a squeaky bicycle wheel, but that sense of danger brings me back to the difference between *burden* and *delight*. You need to know, this journey you are on can be dangerous. There's even an enemy who has laid traps for you. Jesus doesn't want you to put your family Bible on display under glass and treat it like an artifact from a bygone age.

At the same time, *fear* is not the motivating factor for dusting off your Bible. While Psalm 119 does acknowledge difficulty and trial and danger, the overwhelming sense of Psalm 119 is a party with God's Word as the guest of honor. The psalmist absolutely loves God's Word. God's Word makes you go *Woohoo!*, and *Yum!*, and *Whee!*, and *Yes, Please!!*

In Psalm 119, God's Word brings Joyful Delight, and Delicious Delight, and Playful Delight, and Desirable Delight. Yes, the journey of faith can be dangerous; but then, all real adventures have some element of danger. It's true, you will even end up walking in the valley of the shadow of death. And holding firmly to God's Word as you follow God's path, even there you will know the light of life!

Like we said in the last chapter, **the fear of failure sucks joy**. Reading God's Word can be like that, too. If you are so hung up on getting every detail of every interpretation exactly right, you will die of exhaustion before you can take two steps following Jesus.

Eating an exquisite feast is not about how carefully you chew.

Releasing the aroma from a fresh sprig of chocolate mint is not about the skill or method of your rubbing fingers.

Walking a dangerous and adventurous road at night is not about how correctly you hold your lamp.

Yes, some ways of chewing or rubbing or lamp-holding produce unintended effects and could even defeat the purpose. If you don't pay attention and the oil spills everywhere, or your wick gets too long, or the fire goes out, that's *bad*. You are *supposed* to keep your wicks trimmed and burning.

But if you *carry the burden* of chewing or rubbing or holding the lamp *exactly right* every time, you will lose the joy of the feast, the aroma of the herb, the adventure in the journey. Fear sucks joy.

Of course, you want to interpret Scripture in *good* ways and not in *bad* ways. And of course, you will get better at handling the Word with practice. But it's never *merely about how well you handle the Word*. Your hermeneutics grade doesn't get you into heaven.

The technique, the method, the *how* of your interaction is not as important as *what* you are interacting with. The aroma is the focus, not your herb rubbing technique. The flavor and sustenance and delight of the feast is primary; your chewing method, less so. The light of the lamp you cling to is what will get you home; *how* you hold the lamp matters, but *only because the lamp matters more*.

The power is in the Word; the Word delivers Jesus. And you don't have to carry the burden of perfect interpretation: Jesus has got you covered. Jesus loves showing up to bridge the distance between you and God, between heaven and earth. Jesus loves being on this adventure with you. Jesus loves being your feast, your power, your light in the dark. Even when your biblical scholarship or interpretive technique is less than perfect, Jesus shows up.

Because Jesus absolutely loves meeting you in the Word.

What a delight!

Meditating on the Word

In *Meditating on the Word*, Pastor Dietrich Bonhoeffer shares a method for personal, daily meditation. First, **choose about ten to fifteen verses of Scripture** to sit with every day for a week. You'll find the text speaks in different ways depending on what's going on in your life in on a particular day. Based on this chapter, you might want to begin in John 1, or maybe Luke 24. Psalm 119 would be another obvious choice; just don't bite off more than you can *chew*; don't choose more verses than you can meditate on, gnaw, explore, rub together, and digest.

Next, **invite the Holy Spirit** to be present in your meditation. Bonhoeffer believed that the same Spirit who inspired the Scripture to be written in the first place is still present and active every time you seek to understand and live by God's Word. Pray for the Spirit's work on you through the text and pray for the Spirit's work in everyone who is meditating with you today. Even in solitude or personal meditation, we follow Jesus better when we follow him together, so Bonhoeffer suggest you find a friend or two who will commit to meditating on the same verses with you this week.

Once you have your chosen text and your traveling partners, set aside some time to **read the text slowly**, and more than once. Bonhoeffer even suggests reading it out loud. Speaking the words out loud might feel a little awkward at first, but remember that the vast majority of people who have ever read the Bible would have thought it strange to read it silently, inside your own head. The physical and acoustic is part of the experience.

Don't get hung up on something you don't understand. Don't give up easily, either (sometimes struggling to understand brings the most delightful insights); but mostly, Bonhoeffer doesn't want you to get stuck. Give God the glory and move on.

Once you have read and reread the selected verses, pray based on the words and message of the text. **Speak back to God the very words God inspired for you to read**. Let the text shape not only your thoughts, but the language you use as you pray.

Bonhoeffer knew that distractions are a regular part of the experience of prayer and meditation. I love his solution! He said to **use any distraction as a kind of prayer request** in your conversation with God; instead of trying to block out the distractions, bring them to God and, on the basis of the text, turn your list of distractions into a list of prayers.

Close your time of meditation with a simple prayer of thanks and take the words of the text with you into your day. That's it! Try this meditation process for a few weeks and **you will almost immediately have trouble**. That's OK. Bonhoeffer suggests you cut yourself some slack and just keep at it. Jesus is up to something in your life. And meeting Jesus in his Word is a delightful habit to get into again and again (and again and again and again). Jesus is patient; and Jesus can't wait to spend more time with you.

If you choose to begin with Psalm 119, know that Bonhoeffer connected the Psalms first and foremost to Jesus. Look for the way Jesus could pray whatever Psalm is in front of you, and then **join your prayer to his**. That might sound a little weird, but seeing Jesus through the lens of the Psalms and praying your prayer through the filter of the prayers of Jesus is actually really cool.

In all of this, don't forget that **Jesus himself is interceding** in prayer for you (*Hebrews 7:25*) and **the Holy Spirit is praying** even when you don't know what or how to pray (*Romans 8:24–25*).

Prayer and meditation are not burdens for the "good Christian" to carry; prayer and meditation are a delight Jesus intends for you, even in your weakest and most vulnerable moments. Prayer and meditation don't depend on you; they depend on Jesus, and on his Word, and on his Spirit. What a relief!

- Invite the Holy Spirit to be present

- Read the same 10-15 verses out loud daily for a week

- Pray based on the verses and in light of your day

- Use distractions as prayer requests

- Take the Word with you into your day

- Be patient with yourself, and keep at it

- Remember, Jesus is praying for you!

GROUP DISCUSSION FOR CHAPTER 11

God's Word Propels Your Adventure

Pick one or two of the following questions to help you get to know a friend, family member, or small group better.

1. Name a really chewy candy that takes a long time to eat.

   Do you have a favorite candy like that?

2. What was Halloween like in your family when you were a kid?

3. What were some of your favorite toys growing up?

   Why did you like to play with them? In what situations have you experienced a sense of playful curiosity?

4. When was the last time you were out in the dark with only a small light? Share more about that situation and experience.

Go a little deeper with someone you trust to point you back to Jesus. You don't have to reflect on all of the following, but spend some time on the ones that catch your spiritual attention.

1. When have you found God's Word most confusing? Most delightful or engaging? What made the difference?

2. What patterns for encountering God's Word have been most helpful for you? When you are being consistent in Bible reading and prayer, what does that look like? What have you tried?

3. If you experimented with the Prayer of Examen from the last chapter, talk about how it went. If you didn't try it at least once, talk about why you chose not to.

   How do emotions play a role in your adventure of following Jesus?

4. Discuss as a group if you would like to try Bonhoeffer's approach for meditating on the Word this week. Choose a text to mediate on together. Take some notes on how it went, and be ready to share next week. We follow Jesus better when we follow him together.

CHAPTER 12

Living With Delight

Reading Plan

Day 1
Review Section 1
The Architecture of Delight

Day 2
Vulnerability and Delight
&
Leaning into Vulnerable Discipleship

Day 3
A Small Step in the Right Direction
&
An Image of Mutual Delight

Day 4
Review Section 2
God Delights in You

Day 5
Review Section 3
Your Adventure of Delight

Day 6
Group Discussion

Vulnerability And Delight

Whew! It feels like we've been through a lot together! We've searched the Scriptures for evidence of a biblical word cloud of delight. We've made friends with some Greek and Hebrew words that kept popping in to see how we were getting along. We've dealt with some pretty deep theology and had a few laughs along the way.

As a result of this book, I want you to **see delight as an essential part of what it means to follow Jesus.** I want you to notice the areas of your life—even your religious life—where you carry obligations or expectations that rob you of joy and **lay those burdens down.** I want you to experience following Jesus as **an adventure** where you never know quite what's going to happen next, and you never know what new direction the plot is going to take. I want you to be **free** from the fear of failure. And I want you to know **mutual delight** in your relationship with God—Father, Son, and Holy Spirit.

Or perhaps better said: I want you to **take a small step** forward in all of those areas. Little by little the Spirit is shaping you as you grow more and more into a relationship of mutual delight with your God and Savior. That shaping will take time; in fact, that shaping will only come to complete fulfillment in the life of the world to come. So don't stress about how far you have to go; you've got all the time in the world.

Just as Jesus will bring that Life on the Last Day, so Jesus already now brings you that same Life. In your ordinary, everyday, complex and confusing journey of faith, Jesus brings you the Life of the world to come, ahead of time. I want more of that delight. And I want more of that delight for you.

My natural inclination is to want only delightful things in my life, and to protect myself and people I love from as many negative experiences as possible. But avoiding difficulty is not the key to delight. I have learned that walking with Jesus in a relationship of delight *transforms* the difficult and painful things in my life; but it certainly doesn't avoid difficulty or pain.

In fact, if I could make myself impervious to suffering or failure or doubt or shame—and honestly, part of me wants that protection, for myself and for people I love—if I could make myself immune to vulnerability I would also be making myself immune to delight.

In this present, broken world, **vulnerability is a prerequisite of delight**. I don't mean you can't have any fun on your bike unless you play in traffic. You shouldn't go looking for pain or challenge, and you really shouldn't take unreasonable risks that have huge consequences. At the same time, to experience delight you have to take some risks. You have to actually *get on the bike.*

The joy of flying down that hill at top speed comes at the risk of skinning your knee. And yes, you should wear a helmet. But get on that bike and fly, baby, fly!

I remember when our first child was a toddler, I was in full-protection mode. I wouldn't say I was a helicopter parent, but I did tend to hover around Naomi, *just in case.* If she wanted to climb up a big rock or go up the ladder to a slide, I was there.

As some point, she got big enough to do more adventurous things than I could keep up with, and as a young dad, I had to figure out the balance between her freedom and her safety. I finally came up with what I called The Broken Arm Rule: if the worst that could happen was breaking an arm, the answer was yes! Go play! If you could *die* from doing that, then No! Off limits.

Naomi never broke her arm. But I experienced way more freedom in saying yes to more fun and adventurous things because I was willing to deal with a broken arm. No, you can't go play in the street. But get out of bed and go play on the swings, and climb the monkey bars, and ride your bike down that hill at top speed. Go have fun! (And wear your helmet!)

At least in this present, broken world, vulnerability is a prerequisite of delight. (I think that might be true of the New Creation, too; only without the chance of pain or disappointment or failure. Can you imagine? Perfect vulnerability that only ever leads to perfect delight? Come, Lord Jesus.)

Brené Brown studies people for a living. As a world-renowned author and research professor, Brown has put in thousands and thousands of hours digging into the dynamics of human relationships and our experience with things like fear and shame. One observation from her research shows up again and again in her books: delight comes not in the absence of difficulty, but in, with, and under experiences we often see as uncomfortable or even painful. Brené writes:

> **Vulnerability** is the birthplace
> of love, belonging, and joy.
> **Brené Brown,** *Dare to Lead*

If love, belonging, and Joyful Delight come from vulnerability, then I imagine vulnerability (made complete and full and perfect) will be part of the New Creation, since the New Creation is defined by love, belonging, and delight.

Already now, on this side of eternity, you can't create an experience of true joy without the risk of personal exposure. A feeling of vulnerability is the threshold of the door that opens into the garden and playground of delight. And an experience of delight brings its own variety of dangers:

> **Joy is the most vulnerable emotion we feel**.
> And that's saying something,
>   given that I study fear and shame.

> When we feel joy,
>   it is a place of incredible vulnerability—
>   it's beauty and fragility and deep gratitude and
>   impermanence all wrapped up in one experience.
> **Brené Brown,** *Dare to Lead*

That doesn't seem fair! Vulnerability is the birthplace of joy; and joy is the most vulnerable emotion we feel. So if you do set your foot on a path of delight in following Jesus, you need to know that vulnerability will be your traveling companion. But it's going to be OK; first, because vulnerability isn't exactly what you think it is, and second, because Jesus walks with you, too.

Jesus knows vulnerability. Jesus knows delight. Jesus knows how to navigate the path of the Father's delight in ways that bring you joy. And he is more than happy to show you the way.

Leaning Into Vulnerable Discipleship

Vulnerability isn't being a wimp or bleeding all over the carpet all the time. In fact, choosing vulnerability takes both strength and courage. Vulnerability isn't living in constant pain; but it is having the guts to open yourself up again, even after you have been hurt. Vulnerability isn't something to be ashamed of; in fact, vulnerability is a requirement of actually dealing with shame.

Vulnerability is the act of being open with someone else, even when the situation makes you uncomfortable. I don't like to be uncomfortable, and I *really* hate it when someone else is uncomfortable. Vulnerability is being OK with being uncomfortable and leaning in to discover what's really going on instead of shutting down a moment of connection because your awkward alarm is going off.

You know that alarm, right? "Warning! Warning! Some *emotions* are likely to happen! And they might get messy! Run! Hide! Duck and cover! Danger! Danger! Feelings ahead!"

This study of delight has taught me more concretely that we are complex creations: we were designed to experience Joyful Delight, Thoughtful Delight, Playful Delight, Delicious Delight, and Desirable Delight in our relationship with creation and with the Creator. In the same way, we can experience vulnerability in our emotions, our minds, our senses, and our will. Delight and vulnerability intertwine in wonderful and complex ways.

Of all of those experiences, our emotions appear to function as a kind of dashboard, a clear indicator light that something is going on under the hood. An intellectual experience of Thoughtful Delight will often come with a corresponding emotion (even if you only jump and spin around and shout, "Woohoo!" quietly, inside your head). In the same way, if you feel vulnerable in your mind or your body or your will, you will likely experience corresponding emotions; fight or flight would be typical responses.

Because your emotions function as a kind of dashboard for delight, paying attention to them can help you see what the Spirit is up to in your life. But when emotions seem too complex, or get too unpredictable, or hit too close to home, we get uncomfortable because strong, personal emotions tend to make us feel, well... *vulnerable.* Brené Brown's research suggests that we try to numb emotions that cause discomfort or pain. The problem is, no matter what numbing method you use—and we invent more every day—**you can't selectively numb your emotions**. In order to never feel uncomfortable or vulnerable again, you have to give up ever feeling joy or love or belonging or delight.

It doesn't have to be that way. But unless you pay attention to your emotions, you will likely end up there.

So how do we avoid numbing our emotions? How do we stay open to vulnerability, and therefore to delight? How do we follow Jesus in our emotions just as we do in every other area of our lives? It's not easy, but Dr. Brown has at least the beginnings of an answer.

> The cure for numbing
> is developing tools and practices that allow you to
> **lean into discomfort** and renew your spirit...
>
> Instead of asking,
> "What's the quickest way to
> make these feelings go away?" ask,
> "What are these feelings and
> where did they come from?"
>
> **Brené Brown,** *Dare to Lead*

Pay attention to your emotions: they are a clue to what the Spirit is shaping in your life. But don't do it alone. Lean into discomfort *in the presence of Jesus.* Renew your spirit *in repentance and prayer and conversation with your Heavenly Father.* Instead of asking, "What's the quickest way to get rid of these uncomfortable feelings?" *ask Jesus,* "Lord, what are these feelings and where did they come from? What do they tell me about what You are doing in my life? Jesus, help!"

As you lean into what Jesus is doing in your life of faith, **stay curious.** Notice what's going on and wonder what it means. If you are having a really difficult time getting motivated to delight in God's Word, don't hide that feeling or the corresponding sense of failure: take it to Jesus and wonder what that feeling might mean. If you are feeling really close to God and the Spirit seems clearly present and active in your life, don't run away from that feeling or numb the experience (so you won't feel let down when it passes); first, say thank you. Then, wonder with Jesus what that feeling means, what that experience is shaping in your life, what gift or benefit Jesus intends for you or for those around you.

Do you feel guilty? Take it to Jesus. Do you feel shame? Wonder with Jesus what that's all about. Do you feel a sense of pride or accomplishment? Ask Jesus what he wants to do with that. Do you feel weak, or lonely, or tired, or excited, or hopeful, or invincible? Set aside the time and space to invite the Spirit of Jesus into your experience. Ask how being open and vulnerable to that emotion might lead you to more dependence on Jesus or into a deeper understanding of delight.

Treat God's Word the same way. Read, mark, learn, and inwardly digest the Word: God's Word brings Joyful, Thoughtful, Playful, Delicious, and Desirable Delight! Stay curious. Does a Scripture passage make you confused or excited or angry or sad? Wonder with Jesus about it. Invite the Spirit to be present and to work in you. Ask your Father to give you what you need just as a loving parent provides for dearly loved children.

And don't do it alone.

Being vulnerable is no solo quest.

Following Jesus is a team sport.

On Easter evening, the Emmaus Road disciples were walking and talking *together* about everything that had happened on Palm Sunday, and Maundy (*Chara*) Thursday, and Good (*Charis*) Friday, and even the crazy report from that very morning saying the tomb was empty. In their mutual confusion and mutual discussion and mutual struggle, Jesus shows up and *walks with them* (see *Luke 24*).

That's the way it works. We follow Jesus better when we follow him together. Discipleship loves company. Jesus shows up in the mutual conversation of confused and weary followers, and walks with them on the road, and opens the Scriptures to them, so that their minds understand and their hearts burn. And when these traveling companions finally do recognize Jesus (in the breaking of the bread, no less), their first instinct is to high tail it back to a locked and fear-filled Upper Room in Jerusalem to share with other followers and traveling companions what they had seen and heard.

And get this: *while they were still speaking*, Jesus shows up and offers his peace, real peace, peace that comes from knowing a crucified and risen Savior. Jesus shows up when people walk together and talk together on the road.

So **don't do this alone.** It is way more dangerous and scary and vulnerable to try and follow Jesus with another sinful human being. You will, without fail, suffer pain and confusion and loss because you choose discipleship in relationship. But that vulnerability is also the only way you will be open to true delight. You can't follow Jesus all by yourself.

You can go on a spiritual retreat and find a time of solitude refreshing and invigorating and even formative. And taking what you experienced in solitude and *sharing it with someone else* is the awesome sauce that makes the journey worthwhile.

Being open and vulnerable, by definition, means you will experience emotions that make *you* feel uncomfortable. Following Jesus with someone else, by definition, means watching them run into experiences where *they* feel uncomfortable. Your natural tendency is to avoid that uncomfortable feeling, in yourself and in others, at all costs.

Don't do it.

A safe life is a numb life.

That's too high a price to pay.

And it's not the way of the cross and open tomb.

Lean into moments of discomfort. Invoke the Spirit. Stay open and curious about what Jesus is up to in your life. Embrace vulnerability as a dangerous and powerful tool for experiencing God's delight.

Then buckle up! People who live like that are in for the adventure of their lives!

A Small Step In The Right Direction

If you grew up in a culture anything like the one I grew up in, then **your sense of identity is probably performance-based** (whether you like it or not; whether you are aware of it or not).

Think back to your formative years. One of the first mirrors that gave you a sense of who you are as an individual in a larger community of individuals was probably some sort of *report card*.

It doesn't matter whether you looked forward to or dreaded seeing your grades. It doesn't matter whether you lived and died on the difference between an A and an A- or you were just hoping to avoid an F. It doesn't matter whether you ignored your report card entirely or your parents tied financial incentives to your grades, you learned to evaluate your performance—and, in a sense, your *identity*—in terms of a GPA.

That Grade Point Average mentality becomes a tool you use to evaluate yourself and your life long after your last class. Think about it: you have a sense of your performance right now (1) in relationship to your performance in the past as well as (2) in comparison to the current performance of your peer group. You intuitively know (3) what average, and below average, and above average looks like for what you are doing right now; and you (4) have a general sense of how well you are doing whatever it is you do.

At work or at play, you could grade yourself. You could be a B worker and a B- softball player; you could be an A+ accountant with a D average in relationships; you could be acing your weekends and struggling to pass in your career. You could feel like a B student in an A crowd. You could even feel like a C+ Christian.

How you think and what you do about feeling like a C+ Christian is shaped by what you already know about how a GPA works. You have options. You could look around and feel shamed by the real A++ Christians in your life. (Of course, you only have your external evaluation to go by; their internal report card might look very different than you think.) Or you can find as many D and D- Christians as you can: hanging out with short people always makes you feel tall. You might feel real grief if your Religion grade came back a C, and you might therefore do everything you can to avoid anything that feels like a way of evaluating your Christian life, because you are afraid of that sense of failure. Or maybe you find yourself parsing the difference between an A and A- and stressing over whether or not you have done enough, and maybe you should do a little more to make the grade, just in case...

Can you see how a GPA mentality can work its way into your heart and affect how you experience the people around you as well as your own sense of value and identity?

GPAs are not inherently evil. But they are a hell of a way to evaluate your Christian life. That might sound flippant, but I mean it almost literally: constantly evaluating your performance and the performance of those around you and shaping your sense of personal value based on your performance—that is the definition of living under the burden of the Law. Carrying that weight can crush you. Living in constant fear and shame with a constant pull to do more or to just give up—that's an experience of separation from God's grace that belongs to hell. And putting your confidence in the quality your own performance, or at least banking that the Divine Examiner is grading on a curve—living consistently like that is the opposite of ongoing dependence on Jesus, and will eventually, eventually, eventually, lead you down a path that ends with Jesus giving you what you have been demanding all along: an eternity without him.

So I mean it when I say the GPA mentality is a hell of a way to evaluate your Christian life. That way of thinking is so ingrained in our experience that it might be impossible to root it out entirely.

You know what? That's OK.

How good or bad you are at avoiding a GPA mentality is not what makes you a good or bad Christian. Your performance in avoiding a performance mentality is not what you are being graded on. Jesus is not concerned at all that you are still struggling with this.

My sense is, Jesus would laugh and wipe the grass off your

knee and kiss your boo-boo and tell you to get back in the game, and have fun, and for heaven's sake, *try and kick the ball this time.*

I've discovered something that helps me kick the ball a little more regularly, and fall down a little less frequently. I've found it has helped some of my teammates have more fun playing discipleship, too. (Remember, following Jesus is difficult; and it's also supposed to be fun. *Sha'a'!*)

This change of mindset is not a magic trick and it hasn't made me or any of my friends the lead goal-scorer on our team; nor are any of us ready for the World Cup. But it does help relieve the burden of performing well as a Christian and replaces that burden with a kind of delight in being a follower.

The important shift is this: **replace your GPA with a GPS.**

You are on an adventure of discipleship that includes learning but is so much more than a classroom. You do need a way of evaluating, of checking in, of wondering with Jesus about where you have been and where you are headed. But a report card doesn't do much good on a journey. A GPS tells you where you are.

A GPS doesn't *grade* where you are, or *shame you* because of where you are, or even *evaluate* your past performance on how you got there. A GPS just says: You are here. (And if you experience *"recalculating"* as reproach, I'm pretty sure you are projecting your emotions onto your car's persona. *You* might care that you took a wrong turn, *again*; your *spouse* might care that you are late and getting later; but your GPS is fine recalculating your route as often as you need it. *You're an idiot; no problem; I'll just recalculate…*)

Replace your GPA with a GPS and you can stop judging your value based on your performance or on the performance of others around you. Both vulnerability and delight stem from simply accepting this fact: *You are here.*

As you begin to adopt a GPS attitude to your life of faith, your sense of burden and anxiety will likely begin to shrink. I guess you might still feel some anxiety about where you are (as opposed to where you wanted to be, or where you think others are), but simply accepting where you are can be freeing. You don't need to be someone else, or be anywhere else, or be any better or different than you are at this present moment: Jesus meets you right where you are.

When your burden begins to shrink, room for curiosity begins to grow. If you don't feel as much fear or shame or pride or complacency about where you are, you can begin to wonder where Jesus will lead you next.

That **focus on Jesus** is what prevents your GPS from becoming a GPA in disguise. We are so hardwired for performance (and therefore, for the Law) that we even judge our accomplishments in terms of *how far we have traveled* in life, or the *distance we have covered* as we progress, or *how close we are* to our life goals.

As the "master of my fate" and the "captain of my soul," I set my course and can evaluate my self-worth and identity in terms of how well I can steer my life around obstacles to reach the goals or destinations I have set for myself. And even if I rate a C- at achieving life goals, as long as I am in control of my direction, I can look back at the end of my journey and say, "At least *I did it my way*."

Enter Frank Sinatra; exit the Holy Spirit.

That's turning your GPS back into a GPA; the grading scale is in *distance covered* and *proximity to goals*, but it is a grading scale nonetheless. If you measure your value based on the grading scale of the progress you make toward the goals you choose, that evaluation will constantly drive you back to fear, shame, avoidance, complacency, anxiety, and doubt. That's no way to live.

I take that back. That's the way most of us live, most of the time. But there is a more excellent way.

When you replace your GPA with a GPS, the GPS will tell you where you are, without judgment. If the map you are holding and the journey you are on is of your own design, knowing where you are will automatically bring with it all kinds of judgments and evaluations. But notice, that judgment comes from the map and the destination, not from the GPS itself.

What if, instead of having your own life goals primarily in mind, you focus on Jesus? What if you asked Jesus to choose your next destination on the journey? What if, instead of having your own ideal for Christian living in mind, you asked the Spirit to shape you in ways that made you more like Jesus? What if you accepted the GPS as a neutral statement of where you are, and asked God the Father to show you where Jesus is, and where Jesus is heading?

A focus on Jesus—seeking where Jesus is and where Jesus is heading—is at the heart of the adventure of discipleship; that's why we call discipleship *following Jesus*.

As long as I set the course and the destinations for my own life (and for my life of faith), I will have little sense of adventure and all kinds of performance anxiety. As soon as I look for what Jesus is up to in my life and **what small next step Jesus is inviting me to take**, I am vulnerable to confusion and doubt and even looking or feeling foolish; but I also become open to adventure and risk and new experiences of delight.

You end up with the same command as Abraham, the father of all who believe: "Go … and I'll tell you when you get there!" (see Genesis 12). You end up with the same promise as those first followers of Jesus: "Go … and I will be with you!" (see Matthew 28). You have to live with the tension of not knowing clearly where you are going next; and you get the comfort of knowing the One who walks with you every step of the way.

Every step.

Every small, seemingly insignificant step.

Every step you take in confidence; every step you take in doubt. Every time you take a small next step following Jesus, you are on the adventure of your life.

Not every step will feel like an adventure, of course; but practice engaging God's Word, and seeking God's delight/will in prayer, and walking with a fellow traveler on the road, and discussing what has been happening in your own *Chara* Thursdays and *Charis* Fridays and confusing Easter Sundays, and you will begin to see, little by little, over time, that this adventure has very little if anything to do with how good you are at walking, and everything to do with the One who walks with you and opens your mind and makes your heart burn so you can't wait to get back to scared friends behind locked doors with a message that has changed your life. And in that moment, while you are still talking, don't be surprised if Jesus shows up and offers you all peace; his peace; the peace of knowing the crucified and risen Savior.

You are not in control of your journey of faith. You need to know where you are. (Where you are is just fine with Jesus.) And then you get to look for one small step you can take today, or this week, or this month that seems to follow where Jesus leads.

Don't let fear of taking a wrong step paralyze you. You might take a wrong step or head in the wrong direction for awhile; but then again, maybe a "*wrong* step" in the "*wrong* direction" is back to GPA thinking.

Movement is the key. Take one small step. Run one low risk experiment. Practice moving forward in faith and you will find steady movement with small next steps allows you to turn or even change direction in a way standing still never can.

You are on the adventure of a lifetime. Your job is not to own the path or even the destination. You get to engage fully without the burden of being graded, or even the burden of being in control. You can have the time of your life on this journey without fear of failure, because the Guide who walks with you knows the destination; and he himself is the Way.

What small step is Jesus is inviting you to take next? Who are you walking with on your Emmaus road? What adventure do you sense just around the bend? I bet it's going to be awesome!!

An Image Of Mutual Delight

That talk of active engagement as you move forward on a journey that is out of your control brings us full circle, back to *mutual delight*. God loves it when you depend on Jesus to set your course; God loves it when you take a small step in the power of the Holy Spirit; God loves it when you hear, "Go... and I will tell you when we get there," and respond with a "Sign me up!!" God intends the adventure of following Jesus to bring you peace and confidence and excitement and tons and tons and tons of *joy*.

As you stay curious and open to what the Spirit is shaping in you, as you lean into vulnerability in order live more fully, I want to leave you with the image I shared way back in the Introduction. We've come a long way since then. We've looked at all kinds of vocabulary words and Bible verses. We've explored some pretty deep theology in ways I hope open up the possibility of delight in your life of faith. And we have fought to hold onto God's heart and God's delight in the midst of our own wrestling with the biblical text and struggling with our own sins and failures.

If I have been something of a tour guide on this journey of delight, I have constantly been aware of Who is really guiding this conversation. Imagine one more time a parent—is it a mom or a dad in your mind's eye? Imagine the open arms, the beaming eyes, the smile of encouragement that makes the toddler begin to laugh as tiny feet take awkward steps more and more quickly toward that loving embrace.

And if the toddler weaves back and forth a little; if the toddler falls down and has to get back up; if the toddler gets turned around and even runs in the wrong direction for a bit, who cares? That mom or dad is there, delighting in those awkward steps. Mom or Dad will keep encouraging and smiling and reaching out with loving arms, not just because the toddler needs it, but because loving that child is an absolute joy.

If that toddler begins to run off, how quickly, how faithfully that loving parent playfully accommodates the "wrong" direction! Somehow the ultimate destination is still a loving embrace. Somehow that child is still captured by love, and thrown up in the air. And the giggles and smiles and belly laughs that come from that young child bring such smiles and laughter from their mom or dad that the kid can't help squealing with delight; which makes Mom guffaw; which makes the toddler chortle; which makes Mom weep for joy; and those two sillies end up rolling around in the grass and the sun and the summer breeze with no concept of time and no concern at all for propriety.

That.

That's God's heart for you.

That's what following Jesus is all about.

That's what the Spirit is up to in your life.

Mutual delight.

It's not the only experience you'll have following Jesus. (Believe me, I know.) But delight is one of the most fundamental and important experiences in the lives of those who have been claimed by a God who loves them in emotional, thoughtful, and visceral ways, and who intends the feeling to be mutual.

To follow Jesus is to have playful confidence in God's unconditional delight. To follow Jesus is to be caught up in a love story beyond your wildest dreams. To follow Jesus is to put your foot on a path of adventure, marked by vulnerability and challenge and sorrow and failure, but **marked** *most fundamentally* **by delight**.

To follow Jesus is to know Joyful Delight, and Thoughtful Delight, and Playful Delight, and Delicious Delight, and Desirable Delight in God, because that's exactly what God feels about you.

Discipleship is the adventure of loving and being loved.

GROUP DISCUSSION FOR CHAPTER 12

Living With Delight

Pick one or two of the following questions to help you get to know a friend, family member, or small group better.

1. How do you experience vulnerability in your life?

   How is vulnerability tied to delight?

2. As you look back over the different chapters in this book, what's one thing you want to remember or live out?

3. What one small step is Jesus inviting you to take this week?

   What promise from Jesus gives you confidence as you take that step? Who in your life will be your cheerleader and confidant for that step?

4. Did you try Meditating on the Word from last week?

   If you did, how did it go? If you didn't, what got in the way?

5. So, what do we want to do next?

If you don't have a clear idea of a study or book you want to tackle together, consider choosing

A Simple Way to Pray (from chapter 9); or
The Prayer of Examen (from chapter 10); or
Meditating on the Word (from chapter 11).

Commit to practicing whichever one you choose separately during the week. Then discuss how it went when you get together.

Revisit question 3 above each time you meet. Be on the lookout for one small step Jesus is inviting you to take. As you practice that awareness together over time, you will find your sense of anticipation and adventure actually grows. Trying to actively follow Jesus is really hard! But it is so much fun!

6. Let us know how it went.

As a group or individual, share your experience with *Delight!* or your story of discipleship adventure with us by emailing Curator@findmynextstep.org

We'd love to hear what Jesus is up to in your life!

More About

Justin Rossow

Rev. Dr. Justin Rossow preaches, teaches, presents, and writes at the intersection of Scripture, culture, and metaphor theory.

With 20 years of ministry experience focused especially on discipleship, Justin brings a refreshing and encouraging voice to the adventure of helping people delight in taking a next step.

Justin is known for his insight and energy, and writes like he talks: with humor, humility, and profound dependence on Jesus. Justin and his wife Miriam live in Michigan with their four children.

Justin is the founder of Next Step Press and The Next Step Community and host of The Next Step Podcast. Season 3 of The Next Step Podcast focuses on this *Delight!* book. Find listening options online at https://anchor.fm/mynextstep

Also from Justin Rossow and Next Step Press:

You, Follow Me:
A Daily Discipleship Travel Log for Advent/Christmas

When from Death I'm Free:
A Hymn Journal for Holy Week

Preaching Metaphor:
How to Shape Sermons that Shape People

Ponder Anew:
A Hymn Journal of Trust and Confidence

Light in the Darkness:
A Hymn Journal for Advent/Christmas

More About
NEXT STEP PRESS ▶

You're trying to follow Jesus; that's awesome!

We want to help.

Next Step Press is a ministry devoted to cultivating intentional discipleship in individuals and self-sustaining communities that infuse innovation, collaboration, and delight into the adventure of following Jesus. As part of our mission, we regularly produce engaging resources that help you delight in taking a next step.

When you need to find your path forward, either as an individual or in a small group, we're there for you. One size does not fit all when it comes to discipleship; find something that works for you.

When the task of leading a group feels overwhelming, we can help with that, too. Everything we design for congregations and leaders will support your effort to build and sustain a culture of next step discipleship, no matter the size of your community. From books, to sermon series, to staff training, to weekend retreats, we've got your back.

We know it's not easy to follow Jesus, and the Next Step Press team wants to alleviate the burden of being a Christian with the joy of being a follower.

What's your next step?

Join the Next Step Community at

community.FindMyNextStep.org

Become a Next Step Patron at

www.patreon.com/findmynextstep

Made in the USA
Monee, IL
20 June 2021